QUEER THEATRE AND
THE LEGACY OF CAL YEOMANS

ALSO BY ROBERT A. SCHANKE

Angels in the American Theatre: Patrons, Patronage, and Philanthropy
The Gay and Lesbian Theatrical Legacy, coedited by Billy J. Harbin and Kim Marra
That Furious Lesbian: The Story of Mercedes de Acosta
Women in Turmoil: Six Plays by Mercedes de Acosta
Staging Desire: Queer Readings of American Theater History, coedited by Kim Marra
Passing Performances: Queer Readings of Leading Players in American Theater History, coedited by Kim Marra
Shattered Applause: The Lives of Eva Le Gallienne
Eva Le Gallienne: A Bio-Bibliography
Ibsen in America: A Century of Change

QUEER THEATRE AND
THE LEGACY OF CAL YEOMANS

Robert A. Schanke

First published in hardcover in 2011 by PALGRAVE MACMILLAN® in the
United States— a division of St. Martin's Press LLC, 175 Fifth Avenue,
New York, NY 10010.

Where this book is distributed in the UK, Europe and the rest of the world,
this is by Palgrave Macmillan, a division of Macmillan Publishers Limited,
registered in England, company number 785998, of Houndmills,
Basingstoke, Hampshire RG21 6XS.

Palgrave Macmillan is the global academic imprint of the above companies
and has companies and representatives throughout the world.

Palgrave® and Macmillan® are registered trademarks in the United States,
the United Kingdom, Europe and other countries.

ISBN: 978–1–137–34942–2

The Library of Congress has cataloged the hardcover edition as follows:

Schanke, Robert A., 1940–
    Queer theatre and the legacy of Cal Yeomans / Robert A. Schanke.
      p. cm.
    ISBN 978–0–230–11575–0 (hardback)
      1. Gay theater—United States. 2. Homosexuality and theater. 3. Sex
in the theater. 4. Yeomans, Cal, 1938–2001 I. Title.

PN2270.G39S33 2011
812'.54—dc22   2011002900
[B]

A catalogue record of the book is available from the British Library.

Design by Newgen Imaging Systems (P) Ltd., Chennai, India.

First PALGRAVE MACMILLAN paperback edition: August 2013

10 9 8 7 6 5 4 3 2 1

In the fall of 2010, we learned of nine teenagers who ended their lives rather than face their bullies. And, of course, there were more.

This book is dedicated to all LGBT students who are trying to survive.

CONTENTS

ILLUSTRATIONS

ACKNOWLEDGMENTS

Since Cal Yeomans so methodically saved over forty years of his personal journals, as well as thousands of letters he had received and copies of letters he had written, he must have hoped that one day someone would use the gold mine of documents he donated to the University of Florida library and write his biography. I am sure that he would agree that I need to thank and acknowledge all of the people who helped to make this book possible.

Jack Barnhart, for his love and his use of the red pen as he examined every word of the manuscript. His constant encouragement that my manuscript would find a publisher kept me going.

I am extremely grateful to the following, who helped bring this book to fruition:

Samantha Hasey, Associate Editor at Palgrave Macmillan, who saw the potential in the original draft of the manuscript and shepherded it to publication.

Kim Marra and Meredith Alexander, for suggesting I write the book.

Patrick Phillips, for commenting on early drafts of each chapter.

Rich Joens, for helping me understand Cal's bipolar disorder.

Scott Smith, Rob Dillard, Karen Wendt, Fred and Sandie Nelson, for reading and responding to the Preface.

Florence Babb, the Vada Yeomans Professor at the University of Florida, and her partner, Vicki Rovine, who were the first ones to recognize the value of the Cal Yeomans Collection.

Emily Armstrong, Tim and Martha Hoggard, for sharing their memories of living near Cal.

Donald Arrington, Fred Chappell, Fergus Currie, Patrika Darbo, Richard Fallon, Grainger Hines, Ellen Stewart, and Jeff Weiss, for sharing memories of Cal and of working with him on theatre projects.

Victor Bumbalo, for expressing his appreciation of Robert Chesley and Cal.

Gary Bukovnik, Mary Will Burton nee Woodard, Mark I. Chester, Mark Cowan, Bruce Emerton, Michael Haykin, Joe Hendrix, Jonah Hendrix, Dana Ivey, Diamond Lil, Bruce McCoy, Martin Palmer, Michael Parker, Robert Patrick, Frank Regan, Zacq Reid, Troy Sanders, Chris Trohimchuk, David Williams, Chuck Woods, and Peter Zettler, for sharing their memories of Cal.

Jacques-Pierre Caussin, Bruce Emerton, Vern Gransden, and Jon Wesley Porch, for sharing recollections of their relationship with Cal.

The Robert Chesley Foundation, for granting permission to quote from Chesley's letters and writings.

Bud Coleman, Alan Sikes, and Lionel Walsh, for presenting a staged reading of *Richmond Jim* at the 2008 national convention of the Association for Theatre in Higher Education in Denver, and Bud Coleman for presenting a staged reading of *The Line Forms to the Rear* at the 2009 national convention in New York City.

Billy Cunningham, John Glines, Larry Hough, John Karr, Evan Senreich, Tom Starace, Kenneth Talberth, and Doric Wilson, for sharing their memories of *Richmond Jim* and *Sunsets: A Beach Trilogy*.

Dr. Phillip Cushman, for sharing his notes about his thirty years of counseling Cal.

Ruth Drier, for sharing her memories of Cal when he lived in Amsterdam.

Roger Carol Dumas and Byron Nichols, for sharing their memories of childhood friendships with Cal in Crystal River.

Joan Engelhaupt and Thomas Kuhner, Robert Chesley's sister and brother, for supplying information about her brother and his plays.

Norma Ferdon Eder, for sharing her memories of her brother and Cal's good friend, Johnny Ferdon.

Cal's cousins John Grannan, Sid Kennedy, and Bobby Wilder, for sharing their memories of Cal and of his family.

Kelly Hill, for providing information about the plays of Robert Chesley.

James F. Hudson, for sharing his memories of Cal in high school while he was the principal.

Bill Kaiser, founder of The Purple Circuit, for providing information about Cal's readings and exhibits in California.

Michael Kearns, for sharing his memories of the impact of AIDS on gay theatre and his memories of Cal.

Anne Levins, for sharing her memories of Cal's mother, Vada Yeomans.

John McGorty, Peter Ware, and Jeff Wentzel, for sharing their memories of Cal during his last few years in New York.

Andy Mangels, Susie Shepherd, and Kaite Chase, for providing information about a production of Cal's *Sunsets* in Portland, OR, in 1990.

Marlene Oberst, for sharing her stories of Cal's art collecting.

Jerry Sitton, Karen Sitton, and Eglé Gatins Weiland, for sharing their memories of the tragic murder of Cal's friend, Jim Sitton.

Rev. L.B. Thomason, for sharing his memories of Cal and his mother, Miss Vada.

Mark Thompson, former editor of *The Advocate*, for sharing his memories of Cal's plays.

John H. Williams, for sharing information about the family finances.

Very special thanks to Eric Garber and Grady McClendon. This book could not have been written without their help.

I also wish to acknowledge the assistance I received from many others: Kathy Turner Thompson, Museum Services Director, Citrus County (FL) Historical Society; James Cusick, Curator of the P.K. Yonge Library of Florida History; Roger Goettleman, director of Crystal River Redevelopment Agency, and his wife Lois; Ozzie Rodriquez, archivist for Café La MaMa; Lucky Lewis, librarian of the Crystal River High School; Edith Meeks, Executive Director of the HB Studio; Joanna Norman, Archives Supervisor, State Library & Archives of Florida; Bonnie Bonsall, Crystal River librarian; Deborah Mekeel, State Library of Florida; Nick Conroy, Program and Residency Manager, Atlantic Center for the Arts; Rebekah Kim, director of the GLBT Historical Society in San Francisco; Naomi Rose-Mock, Acting Executive Director of the Tallahassee Little Theatre; Rick Storer, Executive Director of Leather Archives & Museum; David Holbrook, Manager of the Seagle Building in Gainesville, Florida.

Very special thanks to James Liversidge, Curator of the Popular Culture Collections, and Carl Van Ness, Curator of Manuscripts and Archives; Florence M. Turcotte, and Mil Willis—all of the George A. Smathers Library at the University of Florida. Their assistance has been exceptional!

Every effort has been made to trace all copyright holders, but if any have been inadvertently overlooked, the publisher will be pleased to make the necessary arrangements at the first opportunity.

Finally, I am very grateful to the American Society for Theatre Research for awarding me a Research Fellowship to help defray some of my research expenses.

PREFACE

Am I vain and stupid to think that someone one day far away in the future beyond the year 2000 will read with interest and joy these tales I write of my ecstatic wanderings lost in the miracles of the night?[1]

Cal Yeomans, 1977

Perhaps in years to come some young queen will find [my writings] in an old trunk bought at an auction, will read [them] and say, "My God! Was that the way it was? Times sure have changed." Let us pray for that anyway.[2]

Cal Yeomans, 1979

Wonder what will become of it all [my papers at the University] one day after I'm gone.[3]

Cal Yeomans, 1987

The year is 2006. Hidden away in fifty scruffy cardboard boxes under worktables in a back room at the University of Florida Smathers Library is the vast collection of papers Cal Yeomans began donating to the library twenty years earlier. Five years had passed since he died, and the boxes were still unopened. No attempt had been made to catalog the material. In his will, he requested "that such items be made available for research as soon as possible."[4] His request had been forgotten. He had been forgotten. It appeared as if no one would ever read his tales of "ecstatic wanderings." No young queen would realize that "times sure have changed." Nothing would become of his legacy. He had come, and gone.

I learned about the collection quite by accident in late 2006. Kim Marra, with whom I had collaborated on three earlier books, got a call from a former colleague of hers at the University of Iowa, who was then teaching at the University of Florida as the Vada Yeomans professor in Women's Studies. She had learned that Vada's son, Cal, had been a playwright, had donated over half a million dollars to set up this professorship, and had also contributed a truckload of his papers to the university library. More than curious, Kim and her partner, Meredith Alexander, flew to Gainesville and spent two days looking over the collection, and were the first to open these boxes. When they returned to Iowa, Kim telephoned me: "Bob, you have to look at this stuff. It's a gold mine. It must be your next book."

"If it is so great, why don't you want to do it?" I asked.

"Well," she paused, "I really don't want to look at men's dicks for the next two years!" Truth be told, she was already up to her neck in writing another book and felt she did not want to be interrupted by this new project. Besides, she believed that my being gay and a contemporary of Cal's—we were born two years apart—might give me an advantage. Being a gay man growing up in a conservative city in Iowa, I might better understand his very complicated journey.

Upon her urging, I traveled to Gainesville the next spring and spent an intensive week, scanning through boxes stuffed with memorabilia. The library policy is to complete all cataloging of materials before researchers can begin digging, but, luckily, they bent their rules and granted me permission to scan the entire collection and to photocopy hundreds of items.

As I plowed through the mountain of boxes, I discovered an absolute bonanza. Knowing there was a sea of material to explore and no indexing or cataloging to guide me, I decided that I did not have time to inspect anything very closely. I uncovered stacks of letters—from authors (May Sarton, Ernie Mickler, Boyd McDonald, and Eric Garber aka Andrew Holleran), from playwrights (Robert Chesley and Robert Patrick), from actors (Dana Ivey, Michael Kearns, Pat Bond, John Ponyman, Grainger Hines, and Jeff Weiss), from directors (Allan Estes, Guy Bishop, Fred Chappell, and Evan Senreich), from psychiatrist Tom Smith, from photographer Mark I. Chester, from artists (Gary Bukovnik, Michael Haykin, Joe Hendrix, Zacq Reid, and Peter Zettler), from Off-Broadway impresario Ellen Stewart—thousands of letters, most still preserved in their original envelopes.

Whenever I noticed a return address being repeated, I jotted it down, gambling that some of the addresses might still be correct and lead me to his friends, maybe even to his enemies. I also uncovered original theatre programs and posters, family photographs, forty years of journals, original poetry, more than forty typewritten scripts, audio tapes of theatre productions, photographs of male nudes, bank statements, tax records, passports, doctors' reports, psychiatric evaluations, and lecture notes. Needless to say, by the end of the week I agreed with Kim; this was a gold mine. I decided that my next few years would belong to Cal.

I learned during my busy week that Cal Yeomans had critically acclaimed plays produced in Chicago and on both coasts in the late 1970s and early 1980s. Two of his plays, *Richmond Jim* and *Sunsets: A Beach Trilogy* (sometimes subtitled *Three Acts on a Beach*), were chosen to play at National Gay Arts Festivals in New York and Chicago alongside the works of Doric Wilson and Robert Patrick. But Cal's plays, unlike those of other gay playwrights at the time, explored sex and sexuality directly and unapologetically. He found it challenging to get his work produced—even in the gay community. When *Richmond Jim* was being rehearsed for its run in New York, for example, the producers threatened to censor the script.

Intrigued by what I learned about Cal and his plays, I was suddenly faced with road blocks. The staff at the library decided that they needed to begin the cataloging and would close the collection for over a year. Once they began, issues of privacy surfaced. If Cal described in his journal an actor having a "big old dangling dick," could the actor sue the library for allowing me to read about it? Could the actor sue me as well? If such statements were found just in letters, the library could simply photocopy them and black out the names or other identifying information. But as Carl Van Ness, curator of manuscripts and archives explained, "The mechanics of doing this with a spiral bound notebook [is] difficult. How do we prevent you or another researcher from accessing a specific page in a journal with 100 pages, 99 of which are OK to view? There are some journals that have only one or two sensitive references while others have many. Needless to say, it's the latter that's giving us fits."[5]

By the time they completed their cataloging in October 2008, they had designated several journal entries "restricted until the year 2060." Many of those entries, however, they simply covered with yellow legal paper that they paper clipped to the pages and instructed me not to look at those pages. I agreed, but what a temptation! How I wished I had X-ray vision. Some of the correspondence from Mark Cowan, Bruce Emerton, Eric Garber aka Andrew Holleran, Michael Haykin, Joe Hendrix, and Jeff Wentzel was also marked as restricted. Joe Hendrix was kind enough to tell the library that he granted me permission to read his letters, which I did. Unfortunately, even if the other five had granted permission, the library concluded that many of their letters must remain restricted, since certain people are mentioned in their letters, some in salacious description, who could claim an invasion of privacy, and sue. Even though all five of those people had granted me extensive interviews, their letters still remained restricted. Although frustrated by this, I could certainly understand the rationale and the challenges confronting the library and their lawyers.

But while they cataloged, I kept busy. My brainstorm to record return addresses on envelopes proved to be brilliant. Soon after I returned home, I tracked down many of them. One source led to twenty more. In the end, I had compiled a list of nearly seventy people and proceeded to interview them all, some by telephone, some by email, and some in person, as I traveled to New York City, Washington DC, Denver, New Orleans, and various places in Florida where Cal had been born and raised.

Since Cal was openly gay and championed a radical kind of theatre replete with sexual activity, scheduling and conducting interviews presented special challenges. Would people be willing to talk about him and his writing? How should I approach them and get them to confide? Would his former lovers (many) come clean and discuss their relationship—how they met, how they loved, how they broke up? Would former roommates be honest? How personal might I get with them before they threw up a wall?

An accomplished actress who had known Cal for forty years refused to cooperate in any way, as did the woman who jilted him in the 1960s. They both seemed intent on protecting their images. Another woman, who sent me a lengthy, hand-written letter and several emails, suddenly stopped all communication when I asked her if she and Cal had ever been romantically involved. Apparently, this hit a nerve. I had gone too far with my questions. A man who had worked with Cal in Atlanta instructed me to destroy the taped interview I had with him after he consulted with his lawyer. The man had told me about the drugs he and Cal had used in the past, and his lawyer thought this might cause problems if that information were made public. One man refused to divulge how and where they had met. Another would not grant permission for his name to be used in any way until he saw the final manuscript. Two men who had accompanied Cal to AIDS support groups in New York refused to see me a second time. It seems they were angry when they learned that Cal had bequeathed money in his will to some people, but not to them.

A further complication was how to deal with Cal's having a bipolar disorder. During his frequent periods of deep depression, Cal could not endure any kind of criticism, whether it be about him personally or about his writing. His dread of rejection was so discouraging that he continued writing plays, but only for himself, and never for production. Since he had such dramatic manic / depressive mood swings, how credible and reliable were the entries in his journals? Was he always interpreting other people's behavior accurately? Then again, how credible/reliable are anyone's journals? I must agree with Georges Gusdorf, who writes in his classic essay, "Conditions and Limits of Autobiography," that "the biographer remains uncertain of his hero's intentions; he must be content to decipher signs, and his work is in certain ways always related to the detective story."[6] In spite of Cal's being bipolar, I concluded that his journals are no less credible than anyone's and must be seen as reliable.

Eager to share my discoveries, I sponsored a staged reading of Cal's first major success, *Richmond Jim*, at the 2008 annual convention of the Association for Theatre in Higher Education. Briefly, the one-act play is the account of a young man from Richmond, Virginia, who goes home with an older gay man that he has met at a bar in New York and within his first night is transformed from an innocent boy into a leather man. The curtain comes down as Jim's host for the night kneels in front of Jim, who is naked, and, in full view of the audience, slides a silver ring around Jim's cock, hands him handcuffs and bullwhip, and pleads, "The rest is up to you." Thanks to my friends Bud Coleman, Alan Sikes, and Lionel Walsh, who volunteered to perform, the reading, minus certain visuals, was a rouser, to say the least.

In the talk back afterwards, enthusiastic audience members remarked:

"It's wonderful; very current."

"It's the basic plot of a lot of gay porn of that time period, but the dialogue allows us to think about the meaning of self-imaging and making choices."

"It's a play about our gay lives that we should know about. It puts a historical perspective on gay relationships. I'm so glad I saw it."

"It's *A* gay play for *A* gay audience."

"The play works especially well for today by showing a motive for speaking about sex and a kind of exchanging repartee of sex, particularly as sexual hookups today have moved into the realm of the internet where a lot of that kind of information happens beforehand and the exchange is very quick. It's a play showing how those conversations can occur."

Needless to say, the responses convinced me to charge ahead with my project. Several audience members even asked me to stage a reading of another of Cal's plays at the next convention. I complied. Bud Coleman, who a year earlier had been in the cast of *Richmond Jim*, gave a stunning performance of Cal's *The Line Forms to the Rear*, the first act of his *Sunsets*. In this play, set outside a glory hole along a remote Florida beach, Henry, a former drag queen, explains that he frequents the glory hole in order to administer "mercy sex to any and all comers." It is "fee-lay-shee-oh on the masses." As the play ends and a leather queen walks into the glory hole, Henry winks to the audience, "The line forms to the rear" and walks in behind him. The house went up for grabs!

As luck would have it, I had previously interviewed the producer, director, and three cast members of the 1981 premiere production of *Sunsets* at New York's Stonewall Repertory Theater and convinced all of them to lead the postshow discussion. They clearly recalled their enthusiasm when they first received the script. The dialogue, male nudity, and simulation of fucking in the last play of the trilogy made it different from other gay plays being done at the time.

By the early 1980s, Cal had received outstanding reviews and awards; his plays were sought after; theatre producers were hounding him for more scripts. But his fame was not to last. Just two months prior to the premiere of *Sunsets*, the *New York Times* published the first article on the "Gay Cancer," the first public news of what was to become AIDS. Almost overnight, Cal's style of play was out of favor, and he faced threats of censorship. Writing poetry and photography soon became his creative outlets.

Even though I became personally captivated by his story and was determined to continue with my research, important questions kept needling me. To be sure, he had written more than forty plays and had seen nine of them produced. In addition, seven of his scripts are listed in Terry Helbing's 1980 landmark book, *Gay Theatre Alliance Directory of Gay Plays*, and two of them, *Richmond Jim* and *Sunsets*, clearly pioneered the subject matter for gay theatre. None of them, however, had been seen in major houses before large audiences, and none had been produced after 1990. Did this person, then, who had a successful yet very brief career as a playwright merit a full-length book? Would readers find that his story had merit?

I began to pose questions that I must address: What were the attitudes in Florida in the 1940s, in the 1950s, and in the 1960s toward gay men? How did Cal Yeomans suffer from discrimination and oppression, growing up as he did in a conservative town in Florida? What was unique and revolutionary in his plays? Why was it so pressing for him to present such explicit sexuality on stage in that particular historical moment in the late 1970s and in the early 1980s? How were his plays, poetry, and photography related to his own personal experiences and to other gay men of the era? Most important, how did he contribute to the development and evolution of queer theatre?

Most of his creative work appeared in about a fifteen-year period, between the bookends of Gay Liberation that exploded with the Stonewall riots in 1969 and the onslaught of AIDS in the early 1980s. What was it about Stonewall that fueled his writing? How did the AIDS epidemic silence him? If biography is "the prism of history," as Pulitzer Prize-winning historian Barbara Tuchman has argued, then a study of the life of Cal Yeomans, along with his plays, diaries, poetry, photography, and patronage, will provide new perceptions of this pivotal moment of gay American history and illuminate the lost legacy of this neglected pioneer.

At one time, Cal noted that if he were to write his autobiography he would title it "Cooked Down to Nothing." He had suffered such sorrow in his sixty-three years that he felt there was no soul left, no substance to show for his life. It had all been reduced to nothing. Hopefully, this book will prove he was wrong, and that Mark Thompson, the former editor of *The Advocate*, was correct when he reported it is an "important documentation of a gifted man and his era cut short by AIDS."[7]

ROBERT A. SCHANKE

CHAPTER 1

"HORRIBLE MISFIT"

Front page headlines on June 16, 1938, of the weekly *Citrus County* (FL) *Chronicle* announced the "Methodist Church Gets New Pastor to Succeed Cook," the sheriff was "Restrained from Confiscating Amusement Devices," and the fraternal organization "Eastern Star Will Present Minstrel Here Next Tuesday." The Valerie Theatre at nearby Inverness, Florida, advertised Judy Garland in *Everybody Sing* the previous week, and now was showing a double feature with John Wayne in *Born to the West* and Robert Taylor, Lionel Barrymore, and Maureen O'Sullivan in *A Yank at Oxford*. Just three days earlier, on June 13, Calvin Lee Yeomans was born in nearby Ocala, Florida, location of the closest hospital to where his parents lived in Crystal River. Although the *Citrus County Chronicle* was one of the main newspapers covering Ocala and Crystal River, it made no mention of his birth. Thus begins Calvin Yeomans's lifelong struggle with dismissal and rejection.

His mother was born in Lecanto, Florida, on October 3, 1896, the eighth child out of fourteen. Although raised in Lecanto, her grandparents had founded the town of Crystal River on the Gulf Coast, when they homesteaded there in the 1850s. When Vada's grandfather died of malaria in 1872, the Allens moved ten miles inland to Lecanto to escape from the deadly mosquitoes.

In one of her diaries, Calvin's mother noted that "Pop always had the earliest best garden in the neighborhood—there was enough to feed us beautifully and to divide with the neighbors, and for Pop to peddle on Saturdays." Sometimes, Calvin's mother would accompany her father as he peddled. "We would be up and ready to go, long before daylight, with our wagon loaded down...and we always sold everything we had by dinner time."

Vada's parents were not wealthy, by any means. In contrast with her diary entry, she admitted to Calvin, "[We] went hungry sometimes. Ate lard on bread. Didn't have no meat. Oranges. What vegetables we could grow here on the place. Milk from the cow. Eggs from the chickens and guineas." She also told him of a childhood tragedy that plagued her throughout her life.

> There was a fire in papa's fireplace. He'd built it that morning before we children had got up. Mama had gone back to the kitchen and had told me to tend to Arliss—our baby sister [who was two years old.] It'd been alright if papa hadn't come by driving the cows back into the orange grove. I wanted to go with him. I forgot that I was supposed to be watching Arliss. I ran out to help him run the cows. The baby got to playing with the paper things that papa kept by his chair to light his pipe. She put it in the fire like he does & lit it but somehow she caught her clothes on fire and she screamed and screamed and.... Momma came running from back in the kitchen—rolled her in a quilt, but already she was burned too bad. She lived a day or so—in horrible suffering. They wasn't no doctors. I was too young to be blamed, but I was. It hurt momma so bad. She didn't never get over it. She didn't never love me again after that. She tried to but she said always she heard the screams. It was her baby girl, the last one. I still here [sic] her scream, "mama." I hear her helpless suffering. She cried and moaned for days. Papa put her in the wagon to try to take her to Inverness to [the] doctor. But she died before he got to the gate. Mama never got over it. She died herself just a few years later. It still with me. It hurt my momma bad. I became my daddy's boy. That's what he called me. He took me up for her.[1]

Vada's father was so disturbed and angry to have lost a child that he obliterated all visual signs of having an eleven-year-old daughter named Vada. For the next many years, he insisted that she shave her head so she would look like a boy and forced her to wear boy's clothes.[2] When Vada assisted him on his peddling trips, he treated her as a hired hand. Such a response by her parents just as she was about to enter puberty surely affected the young girl's sexual identity, her concepts of family and parenting, and, eventually, her role as a wife and mother.

Vada's nephew, John Grannan, "never heard anything nice about Vada's father." Vada's mother was warned by her brother not to marry the man in the first place, since he was known to be a mean man with an ugly temper. He was stingy, treated her badly, and kept her pregnant most of the time. Ultimately, upon learning that Vada's father beat her mother, his brother-in-law swore, "If you ever hit my sister again, I will personally come over here and wring your neck and kill you." The two men never spoke to each other again. Still, when somebody asked Vada's mother if she would ever leave her husband, she answered, "No. I made my bed hard, and I'm going to lie in it."[3]

At an early age, Calvin's mother yearned for a very different kind of life. She wanted so many things—pretty clothes, a house in the city, better food, and above all, her own car. In 1915, when she was almost nineteen, she earned a teaching certificate. Her first job, however, was not in a big city, but rather for a six-month term at a new school called Magnolia in an isolated rural settlement near what is now Floral City, Florida. Her monthly salary—$35. In 1917, she received a four-year certificate, qualifying her to teach second grade in Crystal River.

No one seems to know how and when Vada met Calvin's father, Lee Columbus Yeomans, but Calvin remarked in a draft of a short story that he wrote in 1993 that "On the day she married L.C. Yeomans [April 24, 1921]...she never again wanted, really, for anything money could buy." He remembered her telling one of his friends, "Best day's work I ever did when I married L.C. Yeomans!" Calvin continues in his short story, "Vada was the first generation of her line to step out of the backwoods of Florida and into the disneyworld-like world of the Twentieth Century."[4] She wanted finer things in life, and L.C., she reckoned, was her ticket.

L.C. was born in Glennville, Georgia, on November 26, 1892. He attended public schools in Tattnall County, Georgia, through the eighth grade. When he was seventeen years of age, he left home and moved to Macon where he became a collector for the Western Loan and Investment Company. In 1911, he moved to Birmingham where he worked briefly with the Rhodes-Carroll Furniture Company, but upon the death of his father he returned to Glennville to run the family farm. Three years later, he was back in Macon where he became a salesman and shipping clerk for the National Fish Company.

On August 26, 1918, just two-and-a-half months before armistice was declared, he enlisted in the army. After he was discharged, L.C. returned to Macon and to the National Fish Company, but later that year, he set off to make his fortune in Crystal River, Florida. The location was ideal. As early as 1888 the railroad had reached the city. New highways were now being completed in the state, leading to a surge in the local population. Electricity appeared in 1917; the telephone two years later. The boom town atmosphere was certainly appealing. The small but active business district boasted all the big-city attractions—gas stations, drugstores, meat markets, bakeries, a furniture store, a barbershop, and hardware stores. On Saturdays, everyone from the nearby area came to town to buy the next week's supplies and to socialize. Those who lived on the various nearby islands came by boat. "By late afternoon," writes historian Evelyn C. Bash, "there was hardly a place to park."[5]

Upon his arrival in Crystal River, L.C. purchased half interest in the Miller Point Fish Company and, in 1925, became sole owner, paying the owner a mere $30 for the business and the property.[6] Because owner Henry Miller was usually drunk, Calvin's father was able to pull off the deal with no problems; some people would argue that he managed to steal the place. That same year, he founded the Citrus County Ice Company. Fishermen brought in fish they had stored in ice boats loaded with L.C. ice, and the fish were then transported out of Crystal River by train and L.C.'s trucks, again loaded with his ice. As Calvin later remarked, "The ice company was a natural tie-in."[7] The business was so profitable that in no time at all Calvin's father had established fish houses from Cedar Key all the way south to Hudson, a distance of about a hundred miles along the Gulf Coast. Encouraged by his success in the fishing industry, L.C. built up his vast land holdings. During the Great Depression, when so many people in the area had to sell their property for whatever cash they could get, L.C. could easily step in and purchase the property. Eventually, he owned dozens of rental houses in addition to over half of the buildings downtown.

He also began a career in politics, serving three terms as a member of the County Commission, from 1925 to 1931, and was a city councilman for Crystal River from 1924 to 1939. In the boom year of 1926, he purchased the Regent Theatre. It was basically a babysitting service where, for twelve cents, parents could park their children for however long it took the movie to play twice. Calvin's father "had his own padded chair and that's where he went at night. Nobody sat in Mr. Yeomans' chair."[8] Calvin's mother was usually in charge of selling tickets. It was hardly a movie palace. There was only one restroom "for the sole use of white women." Everyone else went out behind the theatre to an old pecan tree that grew up on the edge of a swamp.[9]

The boom was not to last. When the Bank of Crystal River failed to open for business on June 10, 1929, it was a tragic blow for Vada, since her uncle Charlie was president of the bank and a major stockholder. He wound up losing everything he had at the time—cattle, land, and home. There is no evidence that L.C. helped him out in any way. And when another of Vada's uncles eventually tried to buy back some land that he had been forced to sell to L.C. during the Depression, Calvin's father refused to sell, arguing that it was "not good to do business with family."[10]

Calvin's parents were fortunate during these rough years, since their livelihood depended on the fishing industry. Everyone ate his $0.05 a pound mullet. His boxcars filled with oysters, red fish, mullet, and trout were shipped to points north, mainly to Georgia. Fishermen had to continue working in order to feed their families, and they had no choice but to sell their catches to L.C.. Before they went out on their ships they would ask L.C. what price he would give them for their catch that day, but when they returned he would quote a lower price. When challenged about the lower price, he would say, "Well, the price dropped. You catch the fish, and I'll sell them." He was shrewd. The story goes that during the Depression, Calvin's father claimed he was so concerned that every family would have food on their table that he would only buy a certain amount of fish from each fisherman. He supposedly did not want to give any fisherman an advantage, but the real reason for his practice was quite different. None of the fishermen had much money, so L.C. wanted to make sure that he got his take first. He gained the reputation of being a miserly tightwad. Because everyone knew he would choke the last nickel out of you, he earned the nickname "Choke 'em Yeomans."

In early 1933, two young boys entered the lives of Vada and L.C.. When Vada's sister, Jessie, died that year at the age of thirty-eight, she left her husband to care for nine children. When Vada visited the family in Lakeland, Florida, a few months after the funeral and saw how skinny and weak the seven-year-old Van looked, she begged her brother-in-law to let her take Van and his older brother James, nicknamed "Bunna," back to Crystal River for a few weeks. James returned home after a short time, but Van stayed for several months. By the time his father came to get him for school in August, the boy had gained six pounds. Vada and L.C. begged for Van to stay and be allowed to go to school in Crystal River. "That's exactly what we did for years, begged for him to stay awhile longer. We loved him so. We would have loved to adopt him, but didn't dare ask about that, so afraid we would loose [sic] him.... Such joy and pleasure he was to us."[11] Van remained with them until he was seventeen.

Miss Vada, as she came to be called, believed she could not bear children—until she unexpectedly became pregnant at the age of forty-three. Calvin often referred to his birth as a "menopause miracle" and felt guilty that he had been born. By the time of his birth in 1938, the Yeomans were clearly an established and prominent family in Crystal River. His father, who was almost forty-six at the time, was known as a shrewd businessman, an able politician, and a community leader. Calvin's mother was from one of the town's founding families. They owned a great deal of property, were active in the Baptist church, and were acting as foster parents to their nephew.

Until he was about eight years old, Calvin slept in the same double bed with his mother, on her left. His father slept in a single bed that was pushed up next to Calvin in the double bed. In the middle of the night, his father often woke up, walked around to the other side of the bed, cuddled up to his wife, thrust until he reached a climax, and then returned to his side of the bed.[12] What must have been going on in Calvin's mind at the time, seeing and hearing his parents doing this right in his own bed? As Vada moaned or sighed, did he think his father was hurting her? Did he want to protect her? Since Calvin never felt much affection from his father, was he envious? Did he wish he could have that kind of attention from his daddy? Did he wonder why his mother received attention and he did not? Even after his father died when Calvin was only thirteen, he continued to sleep in his mother's bedroom until he graduated from high school. Calvin has recorded that she wanted him to sleep in her room because she was "afraid," but he never offers a more detailed explanation of what she feared. Exactly how this strange sleeping arrangement must have affected Calvin is unclear. What is certain, however, is that Calvin's attitude about sexuality was certainly confused. He could not have been serious when he remarked to a friend many years later, "Oh, yeah! I had a very normal childhood."[13]

Adding to his discomfort was the presence of his cousin Van, who lived with the family until Calvin was five. The jealousy and resentment between them was evident. Calvin did not have his own bedroom; Van did. Calvin felt neglected and overlooked and wondered why his parents showed more affection toward Van than toward him. Van, however, felt that his place of honor in the household had somehow been usurped by Calvin's birth. He had been "rejected" before when his real mother had died and his father could not care for him, and now, with the birth of their "real" son, he felt rejected again by Vada and L.C. The strained relationship between the two boys came to a head one day while they were playing on the front porch. In the midst of their horseplay, Van began his unmerciful kidding and tormenting until Calvin could take no more. He reached up and slapped Van hard on the face. Calvin recalls in his journal the hurt in Van's eyes—the surprise. The child's play ended, and, as Calvin lamented, "Brothers ceased to be."[14] Soon after, Van signed up to join in the war effort and left Crystal River.

In a note that she penned years later, Miss Vada confessed, "Having a son of our own didn't make us love Van less, but more if possible." She continues, remarking that when Van joined the army in 1943, "I couldn't talk him out of it. But to say Yeomans and I prayed, tells mildly what we did, we agonized over that boy."[15] Perhaps their young and impressionable son was justified for feeling unloved. Although his impressions changed in later years, when he was in his early thirties, Calvin remembered how he used to think of his mother in his youth as an "uptight,

Bible-spouting bitch."[16] She, like her husband, was incapable of showing much love—physically or emotionally.

Mr. Yeomans, physically large and masculine, continued to hustle his way through business and politics, not leaving much time for his son. Stern and businesslike, he was the provider, not the nurturer, and always with a cigar in his mouth. He undoubtedly disapproved when he found Calvin cutting paper dolls out of the Sears Roebuck catalog. Not wanting his son to be a sissy, one day when Calvin was only about eight years old, he took his son to visit relatives on their farm in Lecanto and insisted that Calvin castrate a pig. Calvin ran from the barn, screaming and crying. At one point, L.C. had planned to send Calvin away to the Georgia Military Academy, now known as the Woodward Academy—probably with the goal to toughen him up, and make a man out of him. Calvin had resisted, frightened with the prospect of "being with all those brutal males."[17] According to Calvin's lifelong friend, Grady McClendon, "Mr. Yeomans must have been rather intimidating to a young, introverted, effeminate boy.... Calvin never said it, but he must have THOUGHT that he was a disappointment to his father."[18] He perceived that Calvin was "scared to death of his father; terrified of him."[19]

A major issue in the household was his father's extramarital affair with his secretary, often prompting Vada to pack Calvin and their things into her car and drive off for weeks at a time to visit relatives in Georgia. On at least one occasion, Calvin's parents separated, and Miss Vada rented an apartment for her and Calvin in Ocala, Florida. This time, she packed many of her prized possessions in the trunk of her Buick—her fancy linens, hand-embroidered tablecloths, her quilting supplies—"because she could no longer tolerate their soured marriage."[20] Her intent was to find work and begin a new and independent life. But attitudes toward women in the mid-1940s were not encouraging; women were told that their most important role was domestic. The ideal woman did not work, but remained at home to create a happy nest for her husband and family. After several weeks of job hunting, Vada returned to Crystal River and L.C., perhaps reciting her mother's pledge: "I made my bed hard, and I'm going to lie in it."

Calvin's mother had married L.C., thinking it would lead to a better life. Bitter and feeling cheated, she used Calvin "as a tool" between herself and his father. When Calvin was nine or ten years old, she began taking him along in her car to shadow his father's car as he drove to where he was rendezvousing with his secretary. Calvin grew to despise his father, which undoubtedly was behind L.C.'s pleading with Vada, "Tell him how hard I worked for him to have almost anything he wants and to quit being so disrespectful to me."[21]

Calvin tried to understand why his parents had such dislike for each other. Perhaps his father's maleness and the power that implied was too much for her, he wondered. Perhaps it was his hearty vulgarity, perhaps his success. Perhaps it was her inability to free herself to go on her own, he thought. Perhaps it was some sexual failure. Certainly they took no joy in each other. Being seen out in public with his parents was a silent rite of endurance on his mother's part and a blustering bravado of genuine success on his father's part. It was a hazard to ride in the car with his father. He chewed Prince Albert tobacco and the ends of Tamp Nugget cigars, and as he drove, he'd lower his window and spit out his tobacco juice into the air. Generous drops would fly back into the car and spatter Calvin and his mother in the face. The inside roof of the car was streaked and stained from the spitting.

When Calvin was growing up, his very close friends—neighbors Charlie and Lynn Bowman, Byron Nichols, and sometimes his cousin Sid Kennedy, who was a bit younger—often went to the river to swim. The Legion Beach where they swam in town was segregated, blacks swam on one side of the concrete dock and high dive; whites on the other side. Calvin and his buddies "loved to go out and hike through the swamps, take picnics and hike." Calvin's mother often made them little, individual pecan pies. "Miss Vada was just an institution around here," Byron remarked. "She was a real nice lady." She frequently gave Calvin a stack of oatmeal cookies to share with his buddies. "She was always fattening me up," Byron smiled. "She was a wonderful lady." Byron's father let them use one of his boats, and with a 3 ½ horsepower motor Byron had gotten one Christmas they explored all the swamps and inlets. Ironically, even though Calvin's father was making his fortune through the fishing industry, Calvin did not like the sport and never accompanied his friends when they went fishing.[22]

Calvin grew up with an extremely conflicted self-image. He had been taught to dream higher than the heavens; he could do and accomplish anything he wanted. At times, his inner voice would whisper, "I'm special," "I'm not like the rest of them, I'm better." Occasionally, he would walk down the main street of town, holding his head up high, pretending he was a prince who was heir to the Yeomans fortune. Yet other times, that inner voice would whisper, "I'm different," "I deserve more," "Everyone is laughing at me." During those times, he felt like he was a complete misfit and that when people looked at him all they saw was an obese oaf—a fat, ugly body with glazed, lifeless eyes and drooping eyelids. He shifted often between the highs and lows, the optimism and pessimism, the positive and negative feelings—certainly early signs of a bipolar disorder. If his parents had been more educated, or if they had lived in a more cosmopolitan city, they may have questioned these mood swings with professionals and sought help for their son. As it was, they had no way of predicting what was in store for his future.

Literally all children in Crystal River, including Calvin, took music lessons from the renowned Miss Ada B. Twice weekly, she taught piano and voice classes for the local schoolchildren and conducted the youth choir at the Baptist church. "I dutifully trudged to Miss Ada B's parlor studio and was taught by her faithfully," Calvin wrote. "Probably I learned more about social graces and their ceremonies and etiquette than I did about music, but if nothing more, a deep appreciation for music was irrevocably instilled as well as a profound love and respect for it, its makers and its instruments."[23] Like all the other students, Calvin sang in duets, quartets, and performed at the annual recital. "Artistically, Miss Ada B was the kind of person that promoted you to do anything that you wanted to do....Never got mad at you...but would be very insistent," Byron stressed, "and if you got mad at her that was alright, she would still be insistent."[24] When Miss Ada B died in 1973, etched on her tombstone was the lesson from Psalm 100:2, "Come Before His Presence With Singing."

Church activities were an essential part of the Yeomans family. L.C. was a deacon of the church, and Miss Vada taught Sunday School as well as Vacation Bible School. At one time, she was also president of the Women's Missionary Union, an auxiliary to the Southern Baptist Convention. Annually, Miss Vada invited all of the women at her church to an oyster fry at the family cottage, a concrete blockhouse on nearby Ozello Island, for their monthly meeting. Besides the weekly church services, every Wednesday Calvin attended prayer meeting and choir rehearsal. When just a youngster, he told his mother that he wanted to be in the girls' Sunday School class, becoming very embarrassed when told that it was not proper. "Boys," his mother decreed, "should not be in girls' classes."[25]

Sometimes Calvin and his friends could be mischievous. Byron Nichols recalls several pranks they pulled. "We would take a big can from the ice house that Calvin's Dad owned and cover up a letter on the neon sign of a local motel. The name was Bass Galore and we would cover up the 'B' every Halloween. We thought that was so clever, so naughty," he laughed. Another time "we tied shut with ropes all the doors to the shops on Citrus Avenue one night, so the next morning nobody could get in without undoing all the knots. That might have been Calvin's idea."[26] They couldn't buy cigarettes because everybody in town knew them, so they had to steal them at home. Calvin sometimes stole his father's cigars. Roger Carol relayed one of their favorite pranks: "We kids would take a long string, tie one end of it to the clapper of the school bell up in the cupola, run it out to an oak tree on the street, and then pull the string to ring the bell. The sheriff would come running."[27]

School years provided unique memories for Calvin. All schools in the county were segregated. Even in 1954, when the U.S. Supreme Court ordered desegregation, the local superintendent of schools spoke with black leaders and convinced some of them to continue with their segregation. The Citrus County Board of Instruction announced they would put off desegregation "as long as possible."[28] One favorite teacher, Miss Rockefeller, was a math teacher who had a passion for history, often taking them to the Indian mounds where they would dig for Indian artifacts and arrow heads. Miss Haggerty, who taught English, was another favorite—"You could not pull the wool over her eyes."[29]

Everyone agreed that one of their teachers, Mrs. Allen, "was a witch, spelled with a capital 'B'! You did not move if she was in one of her moods; you froze in space. We just dreaded getting to the sixth grade," Byron recalled. "I had nightmares about going to school that sixth grade year."[30] Every year during the state fair in Tampa, a school bus would pick them up at dawn on a Saturday and not return until midnight. Calvin and his friends would explore the livestock exhibits, the carnival rides, and the sideshows.

When he was in the tenth grade, Calvin finished a biology exam in about fifteen minutes but was required to sit in the classroom for two hours while the other students were still working. To pass the time, he began to sketch women's dresses on the back of the test's pages while he waited. A day or so later, he was called into the principal's office and was told that even though he had received a grade of 90 in the exam his teacher had considered failing him because of the drawings. Calvin was absolutely mystified. "He was really furious at me," Calvin recalled. It only reinforced his belief that in Crystal River "anything new or changed was not good. One does not deviate from their pitiful, pitiful norm and achieve praise."[31]

In 1951, L.C. died. Calvin, who was thirteen years old, was somewhat relieved, since he always felt caught in the middle between his parents, literally, in terms of their sleeping arrangements. The previous year, L.C. had lost a reelection contest to the state legislature with Francis "Cowboy" Williams, the mayor of Inverness, losing by a vote of 1,580 to 828. It was a devastating blow to this proud and arrogant community leader; L.C.'s death certificate listed his cause of death as a cerebral hemorrhage due to hypertension. As Calvin explained to his good friend Ernie Mickler nearly forty years later, "When the city slickers started coming in [to Crystal River] they began to take advantage of him and that's when he had his stroke and everything began to fall apart."[32] Writing about his father's death years later, Calvin realized that his father had achieved "gigantic, legendary accomplishments with very little education or real preparation. Toward the end, his insecurities got the best of him & he could not trust anyone and believed everyone was out to destroy what he had so hard worked for. It was a living hell. Finally, one day in early Sept. his brain exploded from the anxiety."[33]

In the fifty boxes of Calvin's personal papers that he donated to the University of Florida, very little reference is made of Mr. Yeomans. In one letter that he had sent to a friend, he remembers how his father would threaten him if he complained at the supper table about the food they were eating. "Eat what's set before you," he'd shout, "and shut your mouth before I slap you away from the table."[34] Shortly before Calvin died, he wrote in his journal, **"I don't recall that my mother and I ever talked about my father after he was gone other than to be warned that 'You're going to turn-out like him if you're not careful.'"**[35]

The death of Calvin's father was extremely difficult for Miss Vada. Although she had always helped in operating the movie theatre and had run a concession stand at the icehouse, she now had the full responsibility of running their family businesses and overseeing all of the various rental properties. One of the first things she did was to build a new house for her and Calvin at Miller's Point and near their icehouse. The drive to the property was lined with huge oak trees, dripping with heavy Spanish moss. There was a spring behind the house and manatees in the river. Wild orchid trees and tall palms were everywhere. The interior boasted a brick fireplace and many walls lined with authentic pine paneling. Every room had a different bright color. A showpiece was the lovely brick-lined pond surrounded by graceful ferns. When it was completed, the house was considered one of the finest in Crystal River. But on May 1, 1953, when the fireplace was used the first time, the fire got out of hand and nearly destroyed the house. There was no insurance. Luckily, a good friend who sold insurance submitted a claim as if Cal's mother had signed the contract the day before the blaze. Vada proceeded to immediately restore what she called The House by the River at a cost of nearly $10,000.[36]

A few years later, when Calvin was in high school, he talked his mother into buying him a Lincoln. He and his friends would all pile into his car and head off to the Crystal Drive Inn or Jesse's Diner for a hamburger and fries or to the soda fountain at the Winn Drugstore for a ham salad sandwich and a chocolate coke. Some of them formed a little jazz band and played at the Community Center for dances almost every weekend. On hot summer evenings, they all flocked to the snowball stand, run by Anne Levins. And then there were the basketball games and football games.

Or the movies. Since Calvin's father owned the local cinema, he went to the movies nearly every weekend. Vada sold tickets, and Calvin ran the concession stand before the featured movies started. He often boasted that he was probably one of the few people in the world to have ever gone swimming in the auditorium of a motion picture theatre. During every hurricane and high tide when he was growing up, the theatre would fill-up with water and had to be pumped out—of great delight to Calvin but of considerable cost for his parents. For a brief period, he thought he would enjoy being a set decorator—a job title he saw flashed in the credits on the screen. He later admitted, however, that he dreamed of being Betty Grable so he could "sing and dance and wear pretty dresses and be beautiful and glamorous [but] it didn't seem a viable option for a male child stuck in the swamps of rural Florida in the '40s and '50s."[37]

Classmates remember him walking the halls of the high school quoting Shakespeare. He was class president in the ninth grade and was on the student council his junior year. The summer of 1955, he was chosen to participate in the prestigious Boys' State in Tallahassee, a leadership and citizenship program sponsored by the American Legion. The *Citrus County Chronicle* reported that during a school contest for subscription sales of magazines Calvin received the winning trophy as the outstanding salesman. A few weeks later, the newspaper ran a front-page story and headline, proclaiming Calvin Yeomans the valedictorian in his class, and subsequently reporting that he had achieved the highest four-year scholastic standing of anyone in his class.[38]

Ironically, the records also reveal that he was not a particularly good student, earning very few A's and several C's and D's. As he confessed in one of his journals, "I never learned the elements of English composition (or anything else for that matter)....I have the most half-assed education—partly because I was a brilliant child and found it easier to fake my way through school." His classmates probably agreed with his conclusion that it was "rather extraordinary that I graduated with the title of valedictorian not knowing what an adverb was...and just barely the difference between a verb and an adjective."[39] One of his classmates remarked that Calvin's low grades may have been overlooked by school authorities for political reasons—wanting to please Calvin's influential family. After all, academic achievements were not highly sought after by his peers. In fact, the twenty-four students in his junior class shrunk to only eighteen the next year. Many of the students didn't want to put up with school; they would rather drop out and go to work in the fishing industry.

Extracurricular activities were an important outlet for Calvin. Once the dramatics club was started in his senior year, he and his handsome cousin, Bobby Wilder, were among the first to join—the only two boys to do so—and both performed in the senior class play, Le Roma Greth's *Hillbilly Weddin'*. Bobby played Pa Belsnickle, a man with six unmarried daughters. In order to find them husbands, he took his shotgun off the wall and planned to "wing" the eligible bachelors, pick out the buckshot, and have the boys married to his girls before they figured out what happened. Unfortunately, Pa misses Ronald, played by Calvin. At one point, in order to escape Pa, Calvin threw on a dress to disguise himself as a girl. In the end, all of the boys and Pa are feuding over who will marry the most attractive daughter.

Even though they were cousins living only a few miles apart, Calvin and Bobby met only once before they were in high school together. The occasion was a big Halloween party that Bobby's mother organized at their home in Lecanto, Florida. Calvin came dressed like a gentleman from China. Bobby thought at the time that the Yeomans must have money to afford such a costume. "They were our rich relatives," he thought.[40] In 1952, Bobby enrolled in Crystal River High School, and the friendship between the two boys began. Calvin noted in his journal of January 29, 1953, that he had "made a new *close* friend Bobby Wilder from Lecanto I like him heaps." He realized that he was attracted to Bobby, even though he had no real understanding of his sexuality, nor of Bobby's. Rather than travel back to his home in Lecanto after school, Bobby often stayed overnight with the Yeomans in Crystal River.

Calvin played drums in the band in his sophomore, junior, and senior years. Bobby had convinced the band director to allow him to be the drum major, not a particularly popular role for a boy in those days. When the director overheard some of the other band members making off-color remarks and teasing Bobby for really strutting his stuff, he ordered them to stop or quit the band. They stopped. During another one of their band trips to a neighboring high school, Bobby and Calvin began a heated argument. But whenever Bobby tried to get a word in edgewise, Calvin would beat on his drum, prompting the band director to chide, "Alright now, ladies, quit your fighting." John Grannan, the band director's son and a gay cousin of Calvin's, overheard the comment and always wondered if his father was suspicious of the sexual orientation of the two boys.[41]

Highly talented and the best dancer in the class, Bobby was also quite flamboyant and managed to talk Calvin into appearing in a variety show. With Calvin in drag again, they presented their talents with several brawny football players also "*en transvesti*." Calvin walked onto the stage wearing a huge, pink, floor-length formal. The emcee for the night, Roger Carol, quipped, "As you can see it comes in extra large sizes" as Calvin then pirouetted off the stage. Bobby and Roger sang "Make Believe" from *Show Boat*. Bobby and Calvin played Schubert's "Military March," which they had learned from Miss Ada B. Calvin noted that the stunning show was received with "great acclaim and success [by] the local Methodist Church," even though for some unknown reason they were not enthusiastic about booking the show for additional performances.[42] The show was so popular, however, that several Crystal River organizations asked them to repeat it. Years later, Bobby laughed, "Calvin never passed up a chance to be in drag!"[43]

He first became aware of the sexes when he was about six or seven years old, sometime during World War II when he viewed nude bodies in a newsreel coverage of Nazi concentration camp atrocities—enormous mounds of male and female bodies piled in pits like garbage. It was the first time he had ever seen a naked man or woman. "My curiosity was electric," he wrote, "viewing all of that anatomical correctness—dead or alive."[44]

Calvin was introduced to homosexuality soon after that. Every afternoon after school, a sixteen-year-old neighbor boy invited Calvin to his bedroom and seduced him on a regular basis. He undressed and fondled him, held him in his arms, caressed and kissed him, and played with him "as his girlfriend." The older boy would whisper, "I wish you were a 14 year-old girl." Calvin wished he were, too, as he "watched in awestruck fascination," as the older boy masturbated and rubbed his big cock all over Calvin's body until he finally "shot his strange white stuff into a dirty old pair of BVD's." Fascinated perhaps, but the daily abuse left a lasting mark on him. He experienced enough gender confusion to realize that his life "might have been easier as a female. The dolls I enjoyed playing with and making clothes for would certainly have made more sense."[45] He looked on masturbating as something "dirty, ugly, and tawdry, beneath a good person." He had been raised with a strong religious background and felt God didn't approve of masturbating. And those few times through the years when he would have a relapse and pleasure himself, he continued to "scorn the solitary vices."[46]

By the time he was twelve or thirteen, he had become even more sexually aware and recalled one adolescent boy in the neighborhood masturbating and having anal intercourse with another older boy. Calvin's closest friend in high school, cousin Bobby Wilder, was gay, but Calvin didn't know it at the time. Calvin did not admit to himself that he was gay until he was in his mid-twenties.

Figure 1.1 For one variety show, Cal, standing far right, wore a 1920s flapper dress. Kneeling is Roger Carol Daniels. From left to right: Bobby Wilder, Ralph Walker, Cal Yeomans.

Source: Courtesy Cal Yeomans Collection, Special Area Studies, George A. Smathers Libraries, University of Florida.

In spite of his academic and extracurricular achievements, Calvin did not look favorably on his high school years and considered himself "a horrible misfit." By the time he reached high school, he felt totally alienated until the eleventh grade when he somehow joked himself into the students' graces. Then, in the twelfth grade, he again didn't care and became miserable and fat. His old friend Byron confirmed that Calvin was not really popular "because he always heard his own drumbeat." True or not, Calvin sensed that his classmates were leering and laughing at him. Sometimes he fantasized that he would go to Hollywood, make movies, become a matinee idol like Errol Flynn, and have them shown at his father's movie theatre so that "everybody could see that the silly fat sissy" was a success.[47] It would be his way of thumbing his nose at all of those people who made fun of him.

On April 27, 1956, a reluctant Calvin attended the junior-senior banquet and prom, dressed in a white dinner jacket and danced on the ballroom floor with his date until midnight. As he recounted the event to a friend many years later, "There's a photo of me as a tragically, homely fat boy and a tragically, homely girl after the worst night of their lives and their parents couldn't have been happier."[48] When the high school yearbook appeared, it included the customary Senior Class Prophecy: "Bankrupt Calvin Yeomans collects garbage for the city."[49] No one could begin to predict the colorful and complicated life that was about to begin.

CHAPTER 2

"WHAT A WONDROUS ONSLAUGHT"

Growing up in small, conservative Crystal River, Calvin's exposure to professional, live entertainment was extremely limited. He listened occasionally to music on the car radio, broadcast live from the Blue Room of the Roosevelt Hotel in New Orleans and sometimes from a station in Del Rio, Texas, which beamed its strong signals across the Gulf of Mexico. While they were in high school, his cousin, Bobby Wilder, listened weekly to the Metropolitan Opera broadcasts, but Calvin never did: "I would have been the laughing stock of the town if anyone had caught me tuning in to such stuff."[1] Bobby could get away with his interest in opera because he appeared to be quite the ladies' man.

Calvin went with his father one time to a touring performance of *Silas Green and His High Yellers*. Part minstrel show, part revue, the all African American troupe had been touring the South since 1904; African Americans in the audiences usually outnumbered whites about three to one. Featured sideshows included a retarded black girl who bit the head off a chicken. Also, while on a trip to North Carolina, he saw the third-oldest outdoor historical drama in the country, the Cherokee Indian pageant *Unto These Hills*. Even with such little contact with live theatre, something about those few experiences undoubtedly peaked his interest. As he looked back on the spring of 1956, he remarked, "My going away to college…was my first venture outside the boundaries of our little town and my goodness!: what a confusing but wondrous onslaught!"[2]

After he graduated from high school, Miss Vada, being a staunch Baptist, sent her son off to conservative Mars Hill College in North Carolina. Calvin, though not enthusiastic about his mother's decision, enrolled in ten hours of courses during the summer—a couple of English classes, a composition class, a course in stagecraft—and performed in their summer production of J. Hartley Manners's *Peg O' My Heart*. Ironically, the play is the story of a teenager, much like Calvin, who is forced to live in a society where she feels unwelcome and ostracized.

Even though Calvin was active on the campus that summer, when contacted about his attendance, college officials—alumni office, registrar's office, admissions office—insisted they had no record of his enrollment. Even when informed that in Calvin's papers at the University of Florida there was a photo of him in *Peg O' My Heart* and a booklet from their English department instructing students on how to write an essay, they still refused to acknowledge his attendance. Finally, after being told that the registrar's office at Florida State University had records revealing that he had transferred courses from Mars Hill, they finally came clean.

The reasons for their deception are murky. The year was 1956. The college was and still is affiliated with the Southern Baptists. As recently as June 2003, at their annual meeting in Phoenix, Arizona, the Southern Baptist Convention called on its 16 million members and 42,000 churches to mount a massive campaign to convert gays into ex-gays by convincing them that they could become heterosexual if they accepted Jesus Christ as their savior and rejected their "sinful, destructive lifestyle."[3] And in 2005, the college was threatened by the Baptist church that they would lose nearly $1 million in donations if it approved a club for gay, lesbian, and transgendered students. It is certainly understandable that fifty years ago Calvin felt uncomfortable at Mars Hill. It is even possible that his sexuality was discovered, and he was ushered out the door.

After all, this nearly happened to a friend of his who attended a public university. One night in 1960, Chuck Woods, who was a sophomore at the University of Florida, heard a knock on his dormitory room door. When he opened it, a policeman told him they had evidence that Chuck was a homosexual. The police said they had a "homo file," and that another student had snitched and had said Chuck was homosexual. They hauled him to the police station. Chuck was released only when he told them that he would report this to his father, and that they would sue the university. He knew that if he admitted it, he would be expelled.[4]

Curiously, Calvin never wrote about Mars Hill, nor did he ever talk about it. Whatever his reason for leaving, Cal transferred after that one summer to Florida State University in Tallahassee. Even at this large university in a large city he must have felt uneasy. From the mid-1950s to the mid-1960s the notorious "Johns Committee," named after a Florida governor, sought to discover all communists and homosexuals in Florida universities. By 1963, the committee had forced the dismissal or resignation of over a hundred professors and deans. One professor attempted suicide. Certainly making the situation even more uncomfortable for

Calvin was knowing that his father had been a good friend of Governor Charley E. Johns.[5]

Addressing an audience at the University of Florida a quarter of a century later, Calvin reminded his mainly gay audience,

> When I was in college if any one, any group had attempted a meeting such as this one tonight…each and every one of us would have risked—by coming here—being arrested, going to jail—surely being expelled from the university.…Our young lives would have been ruined—there would have been nothing left but disgrace and/or suicide. If we had gathered like this, we would have had lookouts posted and all of us would be sitting wondering which window we could jump out of when the police came— which closet we could hide in until they were gone. NO professor could have been here.[6]

From the first day he arrived at the Florida State campus, he felt ill at ease, driving up in his shiny, expensive, brand new Lincoln Capri convertible and two suitcases full of new shirts handmade by his mother. Even though very few students at that time owned cars, especially new ones, no one was impressed. "The incongruities of my appearance & behavior must have confounded the most careful analyzers," he mused. It was clearly "country come to town.… Throw in all my confused sexuality and gender identification and I must have been quite a sight."[7] Feeling self-conscious about being a rich kid from a little provincial town, Calvin decided the first thing to do was "learn to talk like something that you aren't. I mean the minute I got to college I learned how to talk in perfect radio speaking cause the last thing you want to do was let them know you were from the South."[8]

During his freshman year at Florida State, Calvin shared an apartment with his cousin, Bobby Wilder. To please his mother, he majored in business, but he enrolled in some theatre classes and served on several stage crews. He really wanted to study interior decoration, but knew that would signal him as a homosexual. Not wanting to live at home the summer of 1957, Calvin enrolled in Principles of Economics at Tulane University in New Orleans. Although he makes no mention in any of his journals of the class he took that summer, he did record what was probably one of the most significant experiences of his life up to that point. "I had my first homosex there," he confessed, "a handjob by the famous author of southern romance novels, Harnett T. Kane, in the slave quarters of the Pontalba Apartments on Jackson Square, summer, 1957. I was 19 and going to summer school at Tulane. I think I was very depressed somehow thru all of that; felt dirty, wrong, lost, depraved."[9] Afterwards, wracked with guilt and the terrible feeling of being irrevocably soiled, he rode the St. Charles streetcar back to campus and "took the longest hottest shower of any college jock that summer."[10] Apparently, the afternoons he spent with the neighbor boy when he was eight did not count as his inauguration.

When he returned to Florida State for the fall semester, Calvin began dating Carolyn Eastwood. Since he had not dated much in high school, he felt pleased that he was finally "doing what other guys were doing." He escorted her to the Military Ball, and, to his surprise, maintained a rewarding physical relationship with her most of the academic year. And yet, even though he may have blanched at his "first homosex" in New Orleans, at the same time he was dating her, he pursued more of it. He had learned that his cousin Bobby was gay, and they occasionally were "gay together."[11]

This complicated practice, leading two different sexual lives, was hardly uncommon for young college men back in the late 1950s who were questioning their sexual identity, and it was based on more than just the fear of being expelled. Information about gay sexuality was not prevalent, certainly not reported on the front pages of newspapers as it is today. About the only time it was mentioned was in terms of some horrific scandal. Homosexuals, labeled pansies or fairies back then, were considered sick. If caught performing a sex act, a homosexual could be thrown in jail. Young men who were sexually attracted to other men, especially those who had been raised in small, conservative, religious communities such as Crystal River, prayed that if they met the right woman and got married that their problems would be solved. They may have wondered about or questioned their sexuality but thought that marriage would solve their confusion. This did not mean, however, that they did not do a lot of backpedaling and pursue their same-sex desires... precisely what Calvin was doing.

During his third year at Florida State, Calvin became involved in productions sponsored by the School of Music. Thanks to his voice classes with Miss Ada B, he was selected for the chorus in the November 1958 production of *Rigoletto* and was cast as the Stage Doorman in their spring production of *Kiss Me, Kate*. One of the highlights of the year was a trip to Atlanta. A quarter century later, he remarked that "going to the moon would be no more strange for a 20 year old now." He and his friends from the music department purchased tickets to a professional touring show, piled into his Lincoln Capri, and took off for a weekend in the big city.[12]

Becoming more and more intrigued by his theatre experiences and the people he met, Calvin decided to join a summer theatre company once he had completed his final exams, and not just because he wanted more experience as an actor. He knew he could also engage in some hot gay times that he felt were acceptable there but not in the business world. He was thrilled when offered an invitation to become one of fifteen apprentices the summer of 1959 at the Flat Rock Playhouse in North Carolina. Each year there was a resident company, many performers returning year after year. Most of the apprentices were from the South, and it was their opportunity to work with an equity company and get experience. They all lived on the grounds in a huge, old house and took their meals in a communal dining room. It was at this point that Calvin became Cal. Tad Currie, the assistant manager, began using the abbreviation and it stuck. Everyone outside of Crystal River would now know him as Cal until the day he died.

None of the apprentices had auditioned in advance. In fact, in those days summer stock theatres actually charged the apprentices a fee for the opportunity to become slave labor. It was a rough schedule—ten shows in ten weeks. The only day off for actors was Sunday until about 6 P.M. But for the apprentices and techies, they worked around the clock, striking the previous set all day Sunday in order to mount the next production and be ready for the first dress rehearsal Sunday evening, followed by a tech rehearsal Monday afternoon, a final dress rehearsal Tuesday morning, and an opening performance Tuesday evening. Tad sighed, "I mean, you worked your ass off! Never a dull moment."[13]

The managing director, Robroy Farquhar, ran a very tight ship and was even tighter with money. Sometimes apprentices even pulled nails out of boards, flattened and reused, rather than throw them away. Apprentices did everything—run props, scrub and paint flats, work the light board, sell tickets, usher. One thing always assigned to Cal was directing the parking. Because he was so tall, he could always be seen. The apprenticeship program "was darn good training," Tad insisted. "If you can survive that, you could survive anything."[14] Equity rules prevented using apprentices in more than three productions in a ten-week season. Because of Cal's height (6'2") and deep voice, he was used in the maximum number, with small parts in *Room Service*, *The Happiest Millionaire*, and *Angel in the Pawn Shop*.

When the exhausting summer season finally came to a close in early September 1959, Cal returned to Florida State. Frustrated because he had not been cast in a single show of the university theatre during his first three years as a student, he turned his attention to the Tallahassee Little Theatre. The fall of 1959, Calvin played Waldo in their production of *Laura*. In January 1960, the Department of Speech chose him to play the title role in *The Sleeping King*. Later in the spring he was back at the Tallahassee Little Theatre, performing in *Kind Lady*. His cousin and roommate, Bobby Wilder, thought Cal's performance as Robert Browning in their production of *The Barretts of Wimpole Street* was superb. "Of all my theatregoing through the years," he claimed, "that one remains a definite highlight."[15]

Rather than return to Flat Rock for a second season the summer of 1960, Cal accepted a theatre position in Michigan. Earlier in the year, Tad Currie, who had been Cal's boss at the Flat Rock Playhouse the year before, learned that the owner of the Wingspread Summer Theatre in Colon, Michigan, did not plan to reopen the barn theatre, so he, his lover Richard Bennett, and their gay friend, Richard Beirne, rented it. Since Tad had been impressed with Cal's work ethic, artistic skills, and acting ability, he hired Cal as their designer/technical director, with the salary of $35 per week, including room and board.

This time he was not a lowly apprentice; in fact, the seven apprentices hired were under his supervision. The work was still grueling, another season of ten shows in ten weeks—"the same nightmare" as at Flat Rock.[16] A significant difference, however, was that the three men

Figure 2.1   Cal, fourth from the left, in a production meeting at Wingspread Summer Theatre.

Source: Courtesy Fergus Currie Private Collection.

running the theatre, had no money, "not a pot to piss in," Tad chuckled. "It was a shoestring operation." It was a theatre in the round with the seats slightly banked around a 20 x 30 foot playing area. Fortunately, Cal "was very imaginative, always very cognizant of furniture placement," Tad recalled.

"He did a lot of creative stuff like hanging a piece of a door from the rafters to suggest a door. He was very aware that the audience was right there and was very attentive to detail. He would go all over town to find things and barter." What Tad particularly liked about Cal was that he was "very laid back, almost unflappable. That's what you want," he stressed. "You don't want prima donnas."

Cal's artistic work was quickly noticed. A local critic commended his attractive set for F. Hugh Herbert's *The Moon is Blue*: "All three sets created by Mr. Yeoman [*sic*] have been imaginative and appropriate. This week the suggestion of the Observation Tower of the Empire State Building is cleverly and simply presented.... Then, in a flash, we find ourselves in a plush, modern, New York apartment. In that apartment you will find two hours of light-hearted fun."[17] Two weeks later, the same critic raved about the "side-splitting laughter and wacky fun" in *The Golden Fleecing* and singled out Cal's set design of a "rococo hideaway in one of Venice's plushiest hotels, in a room occupied by Eleonora Duse, all ornate gold and glass" that helped achieve a "screw-ball pace...leaving the opening night audience weak from laughter."[18]

Cal was not amused, however, when one critic who praised his work referred to him in print as Leola Yeomans. For a young man who wanted to appear straight, such an innocent mistake was embarrassing, especially since staff members began teasing him by calling him Leola.

Cal also found time to act in several of the shows, playing Pierre in *The Deadly Game*, Dr. John Buchanan, Sr., in *Summer and Smoke*, St. Clare in *Uncle Tom's Cabin*, Rev. Humphrey in *See How They Run*, Uncle Clam and Uncle Zed in *Salad Days*, and Taylor in *The Golden Fleecing*. In the latter, he was praised for "a show stopping bit, getting drunk in three minutes flat and carrying off the craziest curtain line yet...in this riotous, pun-propelled frolic."[19] The company seldom presented musicals, but when they offered Julian Slade and Dorothy Reynolds's *Salad Days*, Cal was recognized for displaying such "fine ability as an actor and singer."[20]

All of his experience at Wingspread clearly enhanced his acting and technical skills, for he was involved in three productions at Florida State during the 1960–1961 academic year, his fifth year at the university. He played Charles Bentham in the theatre department's fall production of *Juno and the Paycock*, served on the lighting crew for Richard Fallon's April production of *Inherit the Wind*, and guest director Eddie Dowling directed him in the premiere production of *Assignment in Judea*. Regardless of his development in the theatre department, Cal hated the university and wrote about "those awful years of school in Tallahassee, when so much I wanted to be a part of and knew I should and could be—was going on about me and I had not the guts and or the know how to even open the front door and let it in."[21]

The summer of 1961, he returned to Wingspread, again designing sets and acting in seven of the ten productions: Charley in *Death of a Salesman*, Sir Francis Chesney in *Charley's Aunt*, David McComber in *Ah! Wilderness*, Beauregard Jackson in *Auntie Mame*, Mr. Witherspoon in *Arsenic and Old Lace*, Willy Banbury in *Fallen Angels*, and Doc in *Mr. Roberts*.

Although Cal undoubtedly pursued his gay interests while at Wingspread, his boss, Tad Currie, was clueless. Since graduation from high school, Cal had managed to shed his pudgy, baby-fat look and had even become a good-looking Troy Donahue or Tab Hunter. Tad found him to be "extremely sexual but at the same time distant." Because they lived a communal lifestyle with all the staff sleeping in the loft of the barn and sharing a common shower, Tad could not help but notice that Cal was "hung like a stud." Even though Tad and his two partners were openly gay, he suspects that because they were heavily involved in the leather scene, Cal may have been reluctant to come out to them. He was not yet ready to embrace that lifestyle. "Something in his psyche," Currie suspected, "wouldn't let him be himself."[22]

While at Wingspread the second season, Cal met and fell in love with Diane Deckard, an actress in the company. A graduate of Bennington College, she had appeared Off-Broadway in *Sweeney Todd* and *A Child is Born*. During the previous Wingspread season, audiences had seen her in *Angel Street*, *The Moon is Blue,* and *Blue Denim*; in the 1961 season she performed in eight of the ten shows. She told Cal that she did not think premarital sex was proper, so he apparently complied and even suspended his gay pursuits—at least for awhile.

Rather than return to Florida State at the end of the summer where he did not feel accepted, Cal dropped all plans to complete his degree and chose instead to follow his newfound love to New York where he hoped to become a professional actor. Before going to New York, however, he first returned home to Crystal River for two weeks, during which time he received fifteen letters from Diane. When he got to New York, at first, he found a cheap room at the Hotel Columbus at 52 West 84th Street, but soon moved into a little, sixth-floor walk-up apartment in Hell's Kitchen, between Ninth and Tenth Avenues on West 50th Street, a neighborhood that had become the base of the Westies, a

Figure 2.2 Cal used this photo for theatre auditions.

Source: Courtesy Cal Yeomans Collection, Special Area Studies, George A. Smathers Libraries, University of Florida.

violent Irish-American gang aligned with the Gambino family of organized crime.

Once settled, he registered for acting classes taught by Bill Hickey at the HB Studio on Bank Street. Classes met once a week for two to four hours each session. Bill was a wonderful storyteller and would use the range of his own experiences and instincts to arrive at the truth of a moment and to help his students find themselves in their roles. It was a game of make-believe with some improvisations to get students freed of external approaches to the text. He was funny, intuitive, challenging, and very supportive. Cal remained in the class through the winter of 1962, taking only a few weeks off in the summer to appear in Saul Levitt's *The Andersonville Trial* at the Mt. Cathalia Playhouse in the Catskills. He also enrolled in private acting classes with Frank Cossaro.

His plans came to an abrupt halt in late fall 1962. He and Diane had continued seeing each other, and Cal thought there was hope for a future wedding. Cal told his psychiatrist twenty years later that one day Diane confessed to him that she had been seeing another man whom she had planned to marry, but that he had suddenly broken up with her. Cal, heartsick and angry at her deception, needed to get out of New York and totally away from Diane. Although he had often felt unaccepted by his peers, this was even more crucial; this time he felt jilted and took it as an assault on his sexuality. He explains in his journal, "We had quite a scene, it was so bad I didn't think I'd ever see her again. It was final. I walked out and left her with it all. I started running then and ran and ran and ran and ran running from her."[23]

He first ran home to Crystal River for a brief month but then, in April 1963, he ran off to Atlanta, Georgia. Still reeling from his breakup with Diane, he began what he called "my new life in the Jesus Christ of homosexuality.... Needless to say, I got fucked a lot.... Rarely did any of these people want to talk and certainly not learn anything about my soul or my mind or my talents. The length of my peter, yes."[24] Cal began to frequent the two main gay bars in Atlanta, Miss P's and the Piccolo Lounge, staying until closing, going home with anyone and everyone.

Dick Munroe, who had run the Tallahassee Little Theatre where Cal had acted a few years earlier, had moved with his partner to Atlanta where he had opened the Pocket Theatre, a small theatre in the round with two hundred seats and a resident company of fourteen players. Cal was hired to be part of the company, and by late September he was performing in *The Importance of Being Earnest*. Following a champagne preview to celebrate the opening, critic Hal Gulliver noted that "Cal Yeomans as Jack Worthing and C.B. Anderson as Algernon...were superb in their roles as leisurely gentlemen-about-London."[25] The plan was for Cal to occasionally direct contemporary one-act plays such as Edward Albee's *The Zoo Story* on Sunday matinees.

Unfortunately, Cal's association with the Pocket came to a crushing halt. When President Kennedy was assassinated on November 22, Munroe wanted to continue as scheduled with their nightly performance. Cal disagreed and argued: How could they perform when the president had been murdered? Who would want to go to a play that night? How could Munroe even consider a performance? Didn't he realize it would be considered an insult, and theatregoers would be outraged? Whatever Munroe said, Cal became infuriated, argued vehemently, and subsequently lost his job. Cal never forgave him.

Shortly thereafter, he returned to New York and moved in with Fred Chappell, whom Cal had known since their days at the Wingspread Summer Theatre. Fred had been hired in 1960 as an apprentice at Wingspread directly out of high school, and had returned to the theatre the next summer. He had worked closely with Cal, building sets, running props, designing posters. The second season, Cal had even tutored Fred as he designed the set for *Death of a Salesman*. During the school year, Fred occasionally spent weekends with Cal and Miss Vada in Crystal River, since he was attending nearby Rollins College, in Winter Park, Florida.

When he finally graduated in 1964, Fred moved to New York and found a tiny, three-room apartment in Little Italy, complete with a bathtub in the kitchen. Cal shared the apartment with Chappell and a third roommate, Freddie Walker. The summer of 1965 they all three moved to another small walk-up on Eighth Avenue, between 42nd and 43rd Streets, right in the center of all the gritty and busy porn shops. Although Fred remembers those days fondly, the hysterical laughs and great fun they had, he also witnessed another side to Cal's personality. He could be very moody, not budging out of bed, not wanting to do anything all day long, not giving a damn about anything.

Although he and Fred yearned for careers in the theatre, they both were becoming disillusioned. "We saw so much terrible theatre," Cal wrote. The big, blockbuster musicals were *Hello, Dolly!* and *Fiddler on the Roof*. Hit comedies included *Any Wednesday*, *Cactus Flower*, and *The Odd Couple*. Most of the serious dramas were revivals—*Hamlet*, *Medea*, *The Seagull*, *The Three Sisters*, *You Can't Take It with You*, and *The Glass Menagerie*. There was a dearth of hard-hitting, contemporary, serious drama. "And we asked ourselves why and we read other people's opinions and at times we despaired," Cal continued. "We loved theatre—the magic of the theatre as much as ever, but we had to admit that most of the theatre we saw bored us just as much as it bored the audience." They concluded that "the true fault of theatre today lay not in an outmoded art form, but rather in the general ineptitude of many of its practitioners to adjust theatre to our contemporary and infinitely 'new' society."[26]

In the summer of 1965, Cal ventured to Fire Island for his first visit. Already by that time many gays went there because it provided a safe haven. Men could hold hands, kiss publicly, and have sex on the dunes. Since no one could get there except by ferry from Sayville, the island was virtually isolated and protected from the snooping straight world. Beautiful tanned men with chiseled abs in gym shorts or jockstraps crowded the afternoon tea dances and chic dinner parties that often led to lavish orgies, sometimes hidden in the deserted parks. The oasis was a natural setting for Cal, who only recently had thrown himself into the gay scene and was searching for love.

Before the summer was over, Cal and Fred had decided to move to Atlanta where they landed jobs at Rich's Department Store. Founded in 1867, the six-story department store came to be known as a landmark Southern institution, famous all over the country with seven branches in Atlanta. Christmas celebrations were especially phenomenal. Every year, a seventy-foot live Christmas tree was placed on the roof of the downtown store and became an annual tradition when it was lit each Thanksgiving. Families would bring their children to ride Priscilla the Pink Pig, a children's train that ran through the toy department; and Percival, another train that ran on the rooftop around the Christmas tree.

Cal and Fred, who had both taken interior design courses at Parsons School of Design while they were in New York, were hired to design window displays. It was an exciting dream job with a huge budget; Rich's spent more money at that time on fashions and displays than any other store in the country. Cal eventually became head of the display department at the prestigious Lenox Square store, with a staff of twenty-eight men—all of them gay. Often they would take six months to plan a major promotional event. One extravaganza was the Hail Britannia promotion.

In 1964, the Beatles began their invasion of American culture with songs such as "I Want to Hold Your Hand," appearances on "The Ed Sullivan Show," and their trademark fashions—mop-top haircuts, Edwardian collarless suits interchanged with bright paisley suits, and what became known as the John Lennon sunglasses. Just three years later, Twiggy, known for her large eyes, long eyelashes, short hair, and androgynous build, took New York and the country by storm as the latest fashion sensation. Cal decided to exploit the craze for anything British. He and his crew built a replica of Warwick Castle on the roof of Rich's as well as replicas of dozens of shops that line the narrow street outside the castle walls. Using an expense account from Rich's, he flew to England and convinced the actual shopkeepers to travel to Atlanta to staff the shops. He and fashion director Mary Will Woodard traveled to New York to find the exact props, furniture, mannequins, and clothes. For several weeks, customers could stroll along what seemed to be an English lane and purchase English goods—jewelry, soaps, chocolate, china, clothes, crafts. There was even a small café to enjoy tea and scones.

His workload was grueling, though he clearly found time for hot sexual adventures. He wrote about one young man he had met: "Body of a young un-bruised boxer, so beautiful. He may rob me, he may kill me, but until then I drink of his young virility & sap his manhood. I steal all I can as I have none myself. I suck it from him & violate his body in total hatred." Cal ends the journal entry, "The funny part: 2 days ago, M.W. [Mary Will] & I were in each others arms. Once again normalcy was a warm pink dream. It was possible. Today it is shattered."[27]

He did not limit himself to duets. He describes Pete, who was the bottom for a group of men: "A face of a strange elf, a body of a young fawn, unconscious sexual appetites of a Marquis de Sade, tied to the bed, beaten, fucked.... He somehow managed to find love in it.... He was our toy, our object of amusement. We used him as surely and efficiently as you might flush the commode after filling it with your excrement." He ends the account of this sexual encounter with melancholy: "I grew bored, bored of contrived sensuality. I longed, somewhere in my deepest being, for a bit of a touch, of a gentle hand, a kiss."[28]

The fall of 1967, Cal decided to tour Europe, undoubtedly inspired by a dear friend whom he emulated, artist Jarvin Parks, who had recently died from the complications of a brain tumor. He was a thin, wiry, hawkish-looking guy with glasses, a dapper dresser who bought Brooks Brothers fashions, children size. A very clever, Toulouse Lautrec type, he had a whole coterie of "artsy" friends. His vast apartment/studio was lavishly furnished and decorated with expensive French antiques and objet d'arts—sphinxes, obelisks, statuary—some of which Cal inherited when Jarvin died. Cal scribbled in one of his diaries while in Europe, "I could not have come to Europe without Jarvin, had he lived." Cal credited his friend for teaching him elegance. "I was his pupil, one of the many, but there weren't so many who needed him as badly as did I."[29]

For two weeks, Cal traveled to Amsterdam, Copenhagen, Hamburg, Berlin, Munich, Rome, Cannes, Paris, and London. Aspiring to be a gentleman, when he arrived in Paris he bought expensive Brioni garments—a dark-blue crew neck knit sweater, blue blazer, tan trousers. He also splurged on some Pierre Cardin fashions and knew how thrilled

Jarvin would have been at the extravagance. As Cal moved about from city to city, he kept a journal of his experiences:

October 6, 1967: He stayed at one of the notorious gay hotels in Amsterdam. They had no rooms so they put him up in the basement. At breakfast he felt he was with "a stranded group of moral fugitives." When he returned from breakfast "there was a lovely pile of feline shit on the middle of his bed." He went to the baths at night and visited museums during the day. He bought a boy for the night for $14, called "a business boy," and notes that "he was magnificent. He kissed me many times. He was worth all the perfume of Arabia. He was all volcano, spewing over me. I selfishly needed the boy."

"I know now why I have always had a creative spirit. I will never be able to manifest my spirit in a physical way. If it is to come out it will be in an intellectual way."

October 13: "Is it possible I came all the way to Europe—subconsciously at least—just to find sexual fulfillment? Could I have been so stupid— Why did I come?"

"When I am attracted to someone I always feel it is because he looks like I would like to look. When I seduce this object, it is mine—for a few moments anyway—since I cannot look the way he does—I can at least possess his appearance for myself."

October 16: "I myself am nothing. I exist only as a reflection of others. I need mirrors, many mirrors to reflect my image."

October 24: "I have feelings of inferiority that just won't quit. Is it possibly due entirely to the sex rejection I have had to cope with?...I have always felt that I am a no-good, worthless disappointment not deserving of success of any kind....I don't think I will ever be able to succeed, to accomplish anything."

October 25: Cal rented another boy for $20—"a poem, a dream." After Cal discovered the boy had stolen some of his money, Cal recalled a line from his friend, Johnny Ferdon, "Thank you for last night. It was an oasis in a desert of lonely nights."

October 28: "It is so strange how closely I've come to Sebastian [a character in Tennessee Williams's *Suddenly Last Summer*]. I see the same behavior as the terrible children in the vultures that fly around me."

After two weeks of one-night stands, often with rent boys, Cal was exhausted as well as confused. Why was he being so promiscuous? Why did he still feel so lonely and unloved? Why did he have such low self-esteem? What was it going to be like returning to Atlanta and a job that was becoming more tedious by the day? Mary Will, his friend from

Rich's Department Store, had promised to meet Cal at the airport when he returned from his European adventure, but Cal feared the reunion and asked her not to meet him. Although she has denied they had a physical relationship, Cal includes her name in one of his diaries as a former lover. He did not know how he could resume his relationship with Mary. He had begun to learn about his emotional needs during his weeks abroad and had thrived on all of the sexual encounters, but he wrestled with his choices and discoveries.

Soon after he returned to Atlanta, Cal began seeing a psychiatrist. In his initial letter of introduction to Dr. L. Brannan, he reveals his turmoil:

> I am a homo—not by choice—no—but rather by accident. A simple accident that occurred somewhere between the time when I was only a gleam in my parents eyes until that hot summer day when for the first time I felt another man's hands on my body awakening it to suspected but long suppressed flames of sensual response.... Today I find myself capable only of sexual physical response to men instead of women.... I will never command total respect from anyone who knows my sexual choice—not even be allowed respect for having the courage to pursue one's natural desires.[30]

After their first session together, Cal was ecstatic. "I felt good about going to him," he wrote. "It was terribly nice to say, 'Help me' to someone. There are so terribly few whom one can utter those words to."[31]

By the end of the year, however, his attitude had changed. "I've emerged a ferocious tormented angel. After years of admiring [actress] Kim Stanley, I suddenly am she. A stupid session with the psy [sic] today.... I'll stick it out a while longer...then resign myself to my destiny of torment. I seemed better able to cope with it all before I turned the responsibility over to someone else—now I have a reason to act erratic & peculiar: 'I'm going to a psychiatrist.'"[32] There is no further mention of his seeing Dr. Brannan.

On April 4, 1968, Mary Will was at home getting ready to settle in for the evening when she received a frantic phone call from Cal. Martin Luther King had been assassinated in Memphis. "Get dressed," he cried. "We have got to work all night." He instructed Mary to meet him as soon as possible at Rich's where they proceeded to drape all of the store windows in black fabric. About sunrise when they finished, they went to an all-night coffee shop, dazed with the events—trying to imagine how the night would affect Atlanta, the South, the country. They feared riots and violence.[33] They had reason to fear. Riots were erupting in hundreds of cities across the country—Chicago, Washington DC, Kansas City,

Wilmington—that would lead to thirty-nine deaths and $50 million in damage. Federal troops and the National Guard were called in. King was a native of Atlanta; would there be rioting now in his hometown? But miraculously, the city was somehow spared, and Cal and Mary breathed a sigh of relief.

Cal was so successful at Rich's that in late fall of 1968 the Fashion Institute of Atlanta invited him to join their teaching faculty. He had certainly enjoyed his three years at Rich's—the limitless budgets, opportunities for designing, travel expenses, friendly colleagues—but he was the kind of person who would immerse himself totally into a new project, make it his full-time passion, and then become worn out, bored, and in need of a new challenge.

The Institute was part of Massey College, an academic business institution that had been operating under various names since 1949 and later merged with the Art Institute of Atlanta. In the mid-1960s, Massey began offering programs in fashion merchandising, modeling, and interior design. Hired to teach fashion design, Cal lectured his students on all the top figures of the day—Chanel, Schiaparelli, Dior, St. Laurent, Cardin, Valentino, Pucci—and he interviewed Bonnie Cashin, Bill Blass, and Roy Halston. Occasionally, he would take his top students to New York where they would meet with designers, and he would help introduce modeling students to the Ford and Wilhelmina agencies. Cal himself even did some modeling. Mary Will became the coordinator of the program and the two of them started working on a textbook for a course in fashion design. Although his essay on Bonnie Cashin, known as one of the mothers of American sportswear, still exists in his collected papers at the University of Florida, the book never materialized.

Soon after they were both hired at the Institute, Cal and Mary were faced with a monumental assignment. The Atlanta premiere of Franco Zeffirelli's *Romeo and Juliet* was slated for a December date, and they were asked to design costumes influenced by the movie and to promote them at a fashion show prior to the film's screening. They had practiced for days with their student models, Mary polishing her commentary, and Cal supervising the backstage cues and getting the models on stage. By the day of the event, two-thirds of the models had contracted the Hong Kong flu! Mary was up in a dark projection booth, reading her commentary with a flashlight—"Lisa feels very romantic in a soft pink, rose petal plumed skirt"—and Cal's voice would boom from the edge of the stage and say, "But Lisa is a shy creature; it is Cornelia who has arrived in her scandalous lilac." A narrator's nightmare, Mary was blinded from where she was sitting as to which models were alive and well that night and which ones were ready to go on stage next. Cal was having to jettison the models, and whoever got into their next costume first was pushed on stage. Mary would coo, "Deanna dreamed of the palest blue tulle," and Cal would say from offstage, "But Adrianna, Maria, and Olivia's mother made them stay at home and our surprise guest is wearing the peasant blouse, velvet vest and ribboned skirt from her village, leaving the other girls behind in her wake." The whole night was up for grabs. Mary laughed years later that it was something like the wacky play *Noises Off*. She and Cal decided to write a script of the chaotic scene, since the audience loved it, and they could not wait to relive it and act it out for their friends.[34]

That Christmas, Mary, along with six of Cal's gay friends, spent the holidays with him and Miss Vada in Crystal River. After their elegant feast, Cal and Mary had the group howling as they restaged the infamous fashion show. Then, they sang and danced, and with drinks in hand began to reenact the musical *Mame*, the current Broadway hit. Miss Vada was Mame and apparently did a fantastic job. They were certain they were better than Angela Lansbury and her cast.

Clearly, Cal and Mary had a special relationship. From the first day they worked together and had lunch, they were soul mates. Every time she moved, he was there to help. When she hosted parties, he was always there arranging flowers, preparing hors d'oeuvres, setting the table. They were in love, she conceded, but not physically. She knew that Cal had a tendency toward depression. She would listen, even cry with him, and then become furious when he refused to recognize his talents, his gifts. Mary concluded that at times he hated himself for being gay. However, because Cal always invited Mary to dinner when his mother visited him, Mary began to wonder if he was using her as some kind of cover, wanting his mother to think he was straight.

Mary was definitely aware of a strained relationship between Cal and his mother. Miss Vada was always warm and friendly toward her, but Mary noticed how she behaved differently with her own son. She would often make disparaging remarks about how he spent his money recklessly. Cal would then become absolutely livid with rage. Although his father's estate was divided equally between Miss Vada and Cal, L.C.'s will designated his wife to be in control. She always shared money with Cal, but kept him in constant abeyance, granting him only $500 per month. Mary remembers one time in particular when Cal was really strapped financially and lacked funds to have his air conditioner repaired, yet his mother set off on a Caribbean cruise. At times like that he would then cut off all communication with his mother for several weeks—no letters, no phone calls.

Though he aspired to be a gentleman, Cal's insatiable search for love meant that he was not above scrounging the lower depths in order to find sex. One of his romances for several months in 1969 was a young, down-and-out man whom he had picked up in a bar. Overpowered by his staggering physical beauty when they first met, Cal began to sense that the man had a need and desire for decency and a better life. He allowed him to live rent-free in an apartment he owned, bought him a color television, gave him keys to his car, signed checks for him, often paid his bills, and got him a job working in the photo department at Rich's. He even took him to Crystal River several weekends and introduced him to Vada. Ultimately, Cal came to realize that once again he'd played the fool, that the handsome hunk was interested only in Cal's wallet. "I'm always anxious to help people," he explained, "because you see, when I needed help, there was no one. I always had to do it myself. No one saw the good in me."[35]

Colleagues at Rich's, some sixty people, would have blowouts at Cal's house in Ansley Park. They often would drink so much that the booze would quickly disappear. Cal would then grab everyone's bottle, take them into the kitchen, pour all that remained into a communal bowl, and then return with a new drink concoction. Living directly across the street from Cal's house in the governor's mansion was the staunch segregationist Lester Maddox. One Sunday afternoon, Cal hosted a beer blast, and as his guests began to gather up all the empties, Cal bellowed out, "Take 'em and throw 'em on Lester Maddox's lawn." They all then lobbed dozens of empty cans over the iron fence onto the lawn of the mansion. Most of the parties were at Cal's, but sometimes they would go to Jim Sitton's apartment and after several drinks wind up swimming nude in his pool.

Sometimes, however, Peachtree Street turned ugly. After a party one night, Cal and some of his guests decided to walk to the nearby Piccolo Lounge for a nightcap. As they approached the gay bar, several teenagers jumped out at them and stabbed Troy Sanders several times. Cal rushed him to the hospital and called their boss at Rich's, Mr. Pope. Employees never dared phone him; he was a big shot in town and very powerful. But Cal did, and managed to convince him to arrange for a top-notch surgeon for his friend and colleague.

Mr. Pope had been so impressed with the film *Blow-Up* that he arranged a special showing of it for all Rich's employees, followed by a dinner. During the conversation, Cal, who could always be very dramatic with his deep voice, decided to make a weighty comment about the film and began, "I thought Blow-Job...!" His eyes bugged out, and for one of the very few times in his life his face turned beet red. On another occasion, Troy and Cal were invited to a party at a colleague's house in the country. Cal got so smashed that he asked Troy to drive them back to town, not realizing that Troy was also drunk. Troy agreed and somehow got them onto the freeway, and then suddenly slammed on the brakes. They both realized at the same time that they were in the middle of a cow pasture and had no idea how they had gotten there.[36]

During these years in Atlanta, Cal considered himself a bright young man on the way up with lots of friends, most of them gay. Grady McClendon, Fred Chappell, Jarvin Parks, Gordon Little, Jim Sitton, Zacq Reid, Don Tucker, Phillip Ferrato, Troy Sanders—they had great times together. They would dress fancy in Bill Blass suits and Halston scarves. They drank a lot, flirted with drugs, and were sexually wild. They would go to parties hosted by bank presidents, and then end the night by stopping off at one of the gay bars. As Cal looked back, he remembered "the carefree days of our youth in Atlanta when our only worries were what to wear to the next weekend's cocktail parties—and how to get a dick."[37] The last thirteen years since graduating from high school had certainly been "a wondrous onslaught," full of creative experiences—acting, directing, designing, teching, mentoring, teaching, writing, and a good deal of fucking. He seldom thought about returning to a career in the theatre—not until he got a tempting offer from his old friend, Fred Chappell.

CHAPTER 3

"GOT THE DREAM, YEAH, BUT NOT THE GUTS"

Cal had followed closely as his friend, Fred Chappell, made his theatrical comeback. In November 1968, Fred had performed *Red, White and Maddox* in Atlanta, a satire that imagines Governor Lester Maddox becoming president of the United States and starting a war with the Soviet Union. The show was a great hit locally and was scheduled for a short run on Broadway in February 1969. Since Fred had been teaching an acting class in Atlanta, he begged Cal to take over the class for the weeks he would be in New York.

What a dilemma! Cal loved the social life he was leading, but he was envious of Fred's success. After teaching the acting class for six weeks, would he be tempted to resume a theatre career? Could he return to the rigors and discipline required of the theatre? He could hear Mama Rose screaming in his ear, "Got the dream, yeah, but not the guts."[1] In the end, he accepted Fred's offer. Ironically, at that same time, Tad Currie, who had worked with Cal and Fred a decade earlier at the Wingspread Summer Theatre, had fallen on hard times financially and had come to Atlanta in hopes of resurrecting his career.

All three—Cal, Fred, and Tad—were hungry; Tad wanted to produce again, Fred needed a job after *Red, White and Maddox* closed, and Cal, soon after he began teaching the acting class, knew he wanted to get back into theatre. They managed to pull their slim resources together enough so as to rent part of the old D.A.R. building on Peachtree Circle where they established the Atlanta School of Acting and Workshop Theatre. This crumbling, storefront building served as their headquarters. In the basement, they created a little blackbox theatre where they held classes for their twenty students and produced workshop shows. Fred taught directing; Cal taught acting; and Tad assumed the role of producer.

Cal continued to work at the Fashion Institute but conducted acting classes in the evenings. They were structured rather loosely with some improvisations, some theatre games, and lots of scene work. He apparently had a good eye and sensitivity for critiquing a scene, but students were frustrated that he offered few specific suggestions, often shrugging, "Oh, hell, I don't know what to do with it; the hell with it."[2] He refused to show them or to tell them what to do. Instead, he would say, "Guys, the bottom line here is just do it. We can go through the plot and break it down and determine motivations and all that, but just do it. Economize; make it simple."[3]

Several of Cal's acting students went on to have successful careers. Patrika Darbo (née Davidson), who was twenty-one years old at the time, appeared in films such as *In the Line of Fire* and *Midnight in the Garden of Good and Evil*. She received an Emmy nomination for her role in the television series *Days of Our Lives,* and starred as Roseanne Barr in the 1994 NBC biopic *Roseanne and Tom: Behind the Scenes*. Grainger Hines was only nineteen when he joined the school. He later worked on several television series such as *CSI: Miami, Cold Case,* and *Star Trek: The Next Generation* and in the films *Protocol* and *Rocky II*. Mike Coolik taped dozens of television commercials and had a starring role in *Demented Death Farm Massacre* (also known as *Honey Britches*). Brad Blaisdell worked steadily on television, playing roles in *Three's Company, Happy Days, Murphy Brown, Judging Amy,* and *Star Trek*—as well as performing in feature films such as *The Negotiator* and *Letters from a Killer*.

Patrika insists that Cal played a major role in her successful career. Through high school and college, she had always been known as a natural comic with perfect timing. Being short and overweight, her book cover, as she calls it, was her size. She would always try to make people laugh before they would laugh at her. When something didn't go right in a performance, she would always go straight to comedy. It was a safety mechanism. One of the scenes Cal assigned for her was from Chekhov's *The Three Sisters*. As the women performed the scene in front of the class, everything seemed to be going wrong. To save the situation, Patrika turned it into a farcical scene and had the class screaming with laughter. Cal really let her have it. For the next several months, he would not allow her to play anything comic. She recognizes now that she is a better actress for it because "he made me use that side of myself that I was afraid of." She had to stretch. It was a superb lesson that she never forgot. Toward the end of the course, Cal coached her in a scene from Shelagh Delaney's *A Taste of Honey*. She took a one-minute monologue from the scene to auditions at the Southeast Theatre Conference and subsequently received scholarship offers from Northwestern University and Florida

State University. Although her family could not afford to send her, "it was an incredible ego boost. I could never have done that dramatic piece if it had not been for Cal. He gave me some of the best advice I ever got!" She was convinced that she could make a career of acting and was thankful that Cal had taken the time to help her.[4]

Sporting a panama hat with a Halston scarf flipped casually around his neck, Cal directed students Grainger Hines and Mike Coolik in a production of Edward Albee's *The Zoo Story*. Grainger had been performing in a successful Atlanta band but simply on a whim decided to audition for the play when he saw a casting call in the *Atlanta Journal*. It was the first time he had ever acted and found memorizing his lines for the character of Jerry extremely difficult, especially the one four-page monologue. Using a kind of reverse psychology, Cal would say to him, "If you can't do it or if you don't want to do it, tell me now. I'll get somebody else." Cal kept pushing him, encouraging him. Cal told him, "You've got talent. Don't let this go to waste; do something with it." Grainger, who likened himself as another handsome and sexy James Dean, tended to swagger around the stage. Cal objected and advised him to simply read the lines—"Don't act; just do it!" At one point during rehearsals, Cal told Grainger he needed to read Tennessee Williams's *Sweet Bird of Youth* and especially study the role of Chance Wayne, a character Cal felt was very similar to Albee's Jerry. What assisted his performance then, was his imagining that Chance Wayne had returned to New York and was now Jerry, walking to Central Park where he meets Peter. Grainger was so taken by Cal and theatre that on New Year's Eve of that year he quit the band and became an actor.[5]

Cal also directed students in Jean-Claude Van Itallie's *The Serpent*. A contemporary, improvisational tour de force that had just opened in New York a few months earlier, it progresses from scenes of the assassinations of John F. Kennedy and Martin Luther King to the temptations of Adam and Eve in the Garden of Eden. Most of the action was choreographed movement and pantomime with actors beating out sounds on their bodies along with music from bells, horns, whistles, and tambourines. In the end, the cast reenacts the discovery of sexual love.

The production, which included nudity, "was quite sensual," Tad remarked. "Cal had a very smooth way about him. He could find sex in a table. It was languid, very soft. Everything hinted at, nothing spoken. We were all stunned. None of us expected anything of it."[6] Grainger Hines acknowledged that the cast "let it all hang out.... It was way out there. We were all over each other. It was like a big orgy on stage."[7] They even presented one performance on a Sunday afternoon, outdoors in Piedmont Park. Theatre in Atlanta at the time was not very exciting, and suddenly there was this little pip-squeak company that nobody had heard of, doing exceedingly well-directed shows, and selling out every performance.

One evening, Cal created with his students a play without words. A strange, young hippy happened to appear at the entrance to the building, nearly starving. They fed him and asked him to stand in a corner and play some music that they had hooked up to an amplifier. When the actors entered through doorways that were draped in white plastic, they slowly moved to the center of the space, allowing the music to inspire their movements while they engaged in some dazzling, truth-searching theatre games. Many, if not all of them, were a bit high on pot. At intervals, Cal was supposed to turn on a strobe light, but he could barely function, since he was floating somewhere near the ceiling, swaggering about in whirling circles, his body completely detached from earth and reality. He looked around the room and saw his friend, Johnny Ferdon, also caught up in the beauty of the music, the bodies, the youth, and the energy. Johnny was holding onto a doorknob and seemed to be floating several feet above the floor with the most unearthly radiant look of ecstasy igniting his face. The audience loved it, understood it, and joined in. Cal concluded that they "had discovered a most potent and powerful way to make and revitalize theatre."[8]

Regardless of the applause he was receiving with his acting and directing, Cal became more and more interested in writing, where he felt he could express his own ideas and feelings more directly than by interpreting the ideas of other writers. In June 1970, he enrolled in an English class at Atlanta's Georgia Tech University. In one assignment where he was asked to write a self-description, he explained, "I am the tall thin type, but lately, I seem to be getting a bit paunchy—probably due to the beer, scotch, and vodka, which I drink too much of in an effort to de-sensitize by [sic] rather sensitive nature.... When I'm up, they tell me I'm warm, witty, and completely charming. When I'm down, my 'tongue is like an adder' and I seem more related to the iceberg that sank the Titanic."[9]

In yet another essay, he describes his mother as "a curious old coot." No longer the "uptight, Bible-touting bitch" that he viewed as a child, now, some thirty years later, he sees her as "eccentric as the day is long and totally unconventional, now she's just as likely to be in Hawaii sipping a wicked 'grasshopper' as she is to be piss-piously arranging flowers for the First Baptist Church. Quite a change, quite a nice change— because for the first time, I know that she is enjoying life. Enjoying it for herself and not trying to find joy in some sort of preconceived society-imposed strait jacket behavior." He writes lovingly about Miss

Vada's favorite pastime of paddling a small boat with her feet through the swamps and bayous, searching for oysters to harvest. One time, she was actually chased up a tree by a wild boar. She stayed constantly busy, making lap-robes for the nursing homes, canning jars of preserves and pickles, teaching retarded children, and making hats out of plastic Clorox bottles. "She used to be so serious about everything. Always trying to do the 'right thing,' to please everybody. I suppose trying to measure up to her self-imposed obligation to set me 'the right example.'...Now she doesn't give a good goddamn about anything. She just wants us all to be happy."[10]

He also sat in on a playwriting class taught by Raiford Ragsdale, whom Cal, Fred, and Tad had hired to teach at their school. For several years, she had been an editor with one of the major romance magazines in New York, but had returned to Atlanta and worked in the public library. Smart, eccentric, and entertaining, she and Cal became very close. She was a no-nonsense, straightforward kind of person who preached to her students: "Put the stakes out there; put the gun on the table." Cal had become interested in playwriting in recent years. In fact, he had written what he called a tragi-farce in one act, *There Ain't No Lemonade*, and wanted to write more. Under Raiford's guidance, he wrote his first play that was ever produced, *In a Garden of Cucumbers*.

Soon after Cal completed the script, Fred directed it with their students. In a copy of the play that he sent to a friend in 1981, Cal explained,

It's a Southern play and owes a certain debt to Tennessee Williams....The setting is all tacky, sleazy, ignorant Florida in the mid-Fifties. It's down-home-honey and RC Cola and Nehi and pink and black and plastic flowers and a lot of brightly colored dime-store rhinestones. It's late afternoon in an old heart-pine house (that has been cut in half) next to a new highway in a tiny almost deserted and nearly forgotten town in Central Florida. The sun is setting outside in an incomparable blaze of orange. A mockingbird trills one last evensong.[11]

The story concerns two lonely and horny older women, one of them played by Cal's student Patrika Darbo, who have nothing left to do but drink and watch porn on a broken-down television. This night they are watching the gyrations of a nude cowboy made clearly visible to the entire audience, and longing for the good ole days when the army guys during World War II would roll into town from the nearby base. "Oh, they knew what they was looking for honey and so did we," Carrie says. To which, her buddy Thelma replies, "We did our part for the war effort, didn't we?" By the end of the first scene, their prayers are answered when they begin to hear rumbling noises of trucks outside and discover that four hundred National Guard reservists will be camping in the city park every Saturday. Carrie ends the scene, exclaiming, "Let's get out on the porch and get to rocking!"

The second scene takes place in the very early morning hours and begins with Carrie bringing home a young, very naïve soldier under the pretense that she needed someone to accompany her through the dark streets. Just as she persuades the soldier, played by student Zacq Reid, to give her a hard back rub, Thelma enters with her catch, who is incoherent and very drunk. As Thelma starts to undress him, he vomits. The men soon leave, and the play ends with Carrie laughing, "We can be ready for them next time. There's still hope, Thelma!" Cal, Fred, and the cast were totally amazed that the congregation of the Unitarian Church where they performed loved it. Unfortunately, the one and only review of the play labeled it "fatuous, sensationalist and irrelevant."[12] Cal, however, liked the idea for the script, and he continued tinkering with it and hoping for another production for the next twenty years.

With aspirations to produce more fully mounted shows for the public, Fred, Tad, and Cal managed to convince Bernard Havard, the managing director of the Alliance Theatre, into renting space in their building for pennies. Fred directed in their studio a new script that he had coauthored with Cal, *The All-American Dreamland Dancehall*. Subtitled "An allegorical, political fling," it traces the history of the United States from the 1930s to the late 1960s in a series of scenes that take place in Miss Belle Liberty's dance hall. In an early scene that takes place just after the end of World War I, Belle stands on a pedestal, decked out in stars and stripes and looking like Mae West. As she bumps and grinds to music, she drinks, puffs on cigarettes, and shouts,

> The big war's won and over,
> Let's get fat and roll in clover.
> Miss Liberty will leave you, never—
> TODAY IS GONNA LAST FOREVER!

Then, a hot Charleston plays and the entire cast begins a wild dance until the emcee runs in to announce, "The stock market has crashed." The actors slowly move into positions as if they are sad, tired marathon dancers, and then eventually transform into a Great Depression breadline. Miss Liberty knows the solution: "War's the answer, loud and clear / Just as long as it's not over here." The crowd cheers as a jitterbug tune blasts and everyone dances again. Later scenes include vignettes about civil rights battles and women's lib. Belle tries to calm everyone down about all the country's domestic problems when she sputters, "In Asia, they're starving and not too bright / Let's go over there and stir up a fight." As Belle bumps and grinds with intensity on her pedestal, the crowd takes over the club. Acid rock begins to play, fights break out, police arrive, gun shots are heard, and people are dying.

The final stage directions read, "Sirens. Total chaos. It's the end of the world." After a brief blackout, the lights come up to reveal the dance hall in shambles and all the actors lying as if dead on the floor. Miss Liberty's pedestal is now a chrome pedestal with a large computer on it. Its lights are blinking. "It is alive with activity." Unfortunately, no reviews of the production exist.

The original script was very loosely written by Cal so the actors could adapt to audience participation. The plan had been for Cal to attend rehearsals and help shape and sharpen it. Unfortunately, Cal had other concerns at the time—his love for Grainger—and left it up to Fred to finish writing the script. Grainger, who came to be known simply as Brother, wound up leaving his wife and renting a tiny two-room apartment in the building at 20–13th Street NE, where Cal lived. For several months, Cal filled his journals with accounts of their relationship:

May 1971: "If he were to come to me and say, 'I am yours,' all the perfume in Arabia would be his for I would go to the grave fighting for it for him."

June 1971: "Whether Brother smiles or not…seems infinitely more important in the long run of things. Oh so much more important than the progress my career is making."

June 21, 1971: "Should I make the bed so nice and leave a little note demurely and prematurely pinned to his pillow—a note that says: 'Wake me if you want to talk or anything'—or whether to be bitchy and leave a clutter on the sofa so he would have to move it before he could sleep.…Or maybe this note would do: To B.F. Pinkerton, 'Fuck-off.' From: Madame Butterfly"

June 27: "He came home and we talked. I said, 'come over here.' [He replied], 'What I don't like is I guess what you would call 'love making.' In other words, I may suck his dick as long as I don't make love to him and don't touch him too much."

June 1971: "I do solemnly swear that I will never again attempt to buy love. Sex yes—love NO."

Brother knew how much Cal loved him. Although they had tremendous affection for one another, Brother reserved his judgment when interviewed.[13]

In spite of his feelings for Brother, Cal needed to connect with others. At the very time he was lamenting their relationship he was also seeing David Hayes. Like so many of his earlier affairs, this one did not last long. "I have love in me," he wrote, "but only for objects that hold their distance. I must learn to love—closely, fully, without reservation. I did not want him to fall in love with me, to fall in love has always meant pain. It has again. With a tawdry, distant object, I can control it—I can be in love with it, not vice versa." He continues, "I find my love for Brother much more satisfactory because of the utterly hopeless nature of the relationship. I know there is no hope. Therefore, I can indulge my every whim and when in bed he pulls away from me with a shudder, I can find great beauty. . . . I can find little beauty in the young man [David] who publicly professes his love for me."[14]

Before the 1969–1970 theatre season ended, Cal was cast in a play. Fred decided to direct Marguerite Duras's one-act, *La Musica,* in the studio of the Alliance Theatre and chose Cal and Catherine Calvert for the leads. The role may have been a stretch for Cal, since he had to play a man who comes to realize his lust for a woman. A couple who had divorced three years earlier meets at a hotel where they had spent the first happy months of their marriage. Although their relationship had turned hellish, their former love is now reignited. Although no reviews exist, Cal was moved by the experience. "That was such a lovely production," he remarked, "so deep and intense and mysterious. I do love to act. A pity it didn't work for me to do more. Intelligence—which Catherine & I both had an abundance of—is a rare thing on the stage—especially when coupled with emotion."[15]

A few weeks after *La Musica* closed, Cal surprised all his friends and took off for Florida. "Oh, you're just taking the summer off," everyone exclaimed when he quit his job at the Fashion Institute. "A few months away and you'll be back better than ever." No one could have guessed that gone for good was all the pseudo-chic finery and expensive clothes. No one really understood that Cal, at the age of thirty-two, needed time to retreat and to think about his future. "What do you suppose I was put upon this earth to do?" he asked himself. "I am so richly gifted in so many areas and remain . . . so completely frustrated. Perhaps these months of withdrawal & solitude—of nothing else—will help me discover mon raison d'etre."[16]

A young, nineteen-year-old man named Paul joined him for the summer at the modest, primitive, but charming cottage the Yeomans owned on Ozello Island, a few miles from Crystal River on the Gulf. Suddenly, without expecting it, Cal believed he had a lover. "It happened so stealthily I did not know. Not le grand amour, but nevertheless un tres enchante [sic] moment. Very pleasant, very fresh, very pure."[17]

But his euphoria about Paul was not to last. One night he awoke and overheard a conversation in the next room between Paul and an old friend, who was visiting them for a few days. "You know I'm very sexually attracted to you," his friend whispered to Paul. And then came the usual sounds "when a hot-blooded 19 year old boy is left alone with a very drunk thirty-ish homosexual." Cal sat quietly on the edge of his bed, tears running quietly down his cheek. He felt so alone, like he was back in Paris or London where he often sat so sad, so infinitely alone, and thought, "What is wrong, God? What is wrong?" His thoughts turned immediately to Fred Chappell and their attempts at building a relationship. "Oh Freda," he wept, "I wish you were here tonight....I wonder how many times you've sat alone—alone as only one can be when the heart has been stabbed by laser beams—and thought of me and a small tear ran down your cheek? I hope not too often, baby."[18]

Some time in the late fall of 1970, having no other prospects for employment, Cal reluctantly returned to Atlanta. One night when he was drinking at a bar, Tad Currie told him that he had heard a theatre wanted to produce one of Cal's plays. When Tad explained that it was not Georgia State University where he worked part-time but some theatre in New Jersey called Brecht West, Cal's spirits leaped—it was "like a wonderful bolt from the blue." His delight was dampened, however, when he started to share his news with Fred Chappell. He suddenly realized that Fred had known about the offer for days and had not told him.[19] He was badly hurt and never understood the reason behind Fred's silence. Was it jealousy? Didn't Fred want him to succeed? Was this punishment for not persevering in their relationship? Whatever the reason, the incident wounded their friendship and made Cal wonder if he should sever his professional ties with Fred, their school, and the Alliance Theatre.

Before he knew it, however, he was cast in another play to be directed by Fred in the studio of the Alliance. The play was *The Immoralist*, and Cal was cast as a character who has an affair with a young man, played by none other than Brother. Based on a 1902 novel by André Gide, the story is the author's recognition of his own homosexuality. The stage adaptation, written by Ruth and Augustus Goetz, was first performed on Broadway in 1954 and starred James Dean as an Arab teenager, Louis Jordan as Michel, and Geraldine Page as Michel's wife.

While on his honeymoon in Africa, Michel, played by Cal, discovers his attraction to a young Arab boy, Makti, played by Brother. Michel leads a double life, making love to his wife while having sex with the young man on the sly. When his wife becomes pregnant, she leaves him, but Michel follows, tormented by his guilt. Prior to the casting, Cal wrote, "Everybody leads me to believe that Brother and not I will play Michel in *The Immoralist*. It is as it should be. I *will* it to be. Why drag a dead horse across the stage when you've got a vibrant young stallion literally breaking the gates down waiting to get in. Just as Fred led me to Gide so many years ago, now he will lead Brother—to Gide, and then to me."[20]

To his surprise, Cal was cast as Michel. Working on the play must have been significant for Cal who had struggled with his own sexual identity and was tormented over his relationship with Brother. In one of his diaries, Cal penned, "The play should be about the struggle of a young man to find his identity as well as *meaning* in life. Perhaps the latter comes from the first?" In another entry, Cal reveals how he used the tense dilemma of his being in the middle between Brother and his wife, Ruthie.

> Put the conflict on the stage—Ruthie & me—confrontation scene—the whole bit. Ruthie: Alright you got him, but you will lose him too because he's his own being sufficient unto himself. When he's ready to move on, he will leave you. [Cal replies]: I know. . . . He will leave. It is right that he should. . . . He will move up the ladder up the stairway to destiny. He will go as far as he can. I will go with him as far as I can . . . and then unlike you, I will gracefully fade into the background and cherish what is left.

Shortly before the play opened, he wrote, "Do the Michel/Makti scenes as if you were Brother—what would you do if you were B?"[21]

A critic for the *Atlanta Journal* praised the powerful performance: "Yeomans' interpretation is one of such accurate fragility he manages to translate moods simply by being on stage. His work is impressive."[22] Grainger agreed that Cal was absolutely perfect for the part, since he fancied himself in the same role as André Gide, a gay man tormented by guilt.[23] The production was a huge success; all the reviews were excellent. Tad Currie recalled that it was a "very sensual production, done in the round, very simple yet with atmospheric setting, lots of sound and gorgeous lighting. I didn't know the play. While we worked on it and I watched rehearsals, I realized they had hit on something that was very provocative."[24]

Successful as it was, the Atlanta School of Acting and Workshop Theatre lasted only about eighteen months. Tad got a job directing at Georgia Tech University, and Fred became resident director at the Alliance Theatre. Cal was smarting from the success of his two partners. Proud of them, yes. But he wondered why he also had not profited from their project. He was especially envious of Fred, and perhaps a bit resentful. He had been Fred's mentor a decade earlier, and Fred landed his new position with the Alliance Theatre, in part, because of his successful directing of two plays, Cal's *In a Garden of Cucumbers* and Fred and Cal's *All-American Dreamland Dancehall*. Even more galling to Cal was that he saw Fred selling out, compromising his values, forgetting the dreams and goals they had for revitalizing theatre in Atlanta. "I hope you know what you've thrown away," he wrote. "I hope in what you've settled for, you find happiness. I hope you know what you have lost when you chose comfortable mediocrity in preference to our friendship."[25] With both Tad Currie and Fred jumping ship, Cal knew he must make some drastic career decisions.

In early 1971, two of Cal's Atlanta friends, Johnny Ferdon and Raymond Schanze, who were then working in New York at Ellen Stewart's prestigious La MaMa Experimental Theatre Club, encouraged him to apply for work at La MaMa where Schanze had just seen successful productions of two of his own one-act plays, *The Eye Ball Tomb* and *The Best Looking Man I Ever Saw*. A bastion of Off-Off-Broadway, the avant-garde theatre was known for starting the careers of young playwrights such as Tom Eyen, Jean-Claude van Italie, and Sam Shepard. Accompanied by Brother and their friend Dutch, Cal made a quick trip to New York to meet Ellen Stewart. What a thrill when Cal learned he was accepted! He was overjoyed and full of anticipation when he wrote to his new boss.

> The news of your permitting me to work at La Mama [*sic*] in the fall was greeted with great good excitement by all those in Atlanta....I am excited too! It will be so nice—so welcome—to be learning for a change. I am terribly tired of teaching—or perhaps have already taught what I have to teach. At any rate, I will arrive on or before Sept. 7 with shining school boy face (or reasonable facsimile thereof) and notebook and pencil.[26]

The notice of his acceptance came just days before the opening of *The Immoralist*.

Prospects of a New York career and acceptance by Ellen Stewart may have been Cal's main reasons for leaving Atlanta, but certainly not the only ones. During his five years in the city, he had continuously searched for love. Nothing seemed to work. Wearing his heart on his sleeve, he would quickly fall in love with a handsome young man only to find the relationship disintegrate. Cal always had to be in control, was attracted to men who needed him—his money, his guidance, his knowledge of gay sexuality. "I'm cursed with the ability (mother instinct) to see people not as they are," he realized, "but rather what they could be. I try to operate with them on the latter level."[27] He could never really accept a man for what he was, only for what he wanted him to become. "When I start seeking love in someone who can help *me* instead of it *having* to be someone I can help," he concluded, "then I will be well!"[28] He sought to mold the men into the image he wanted for them, but it never succeeded. Cal was now afraid of love.

Maybe New York was the answer; if not love, he could certainly find sex. After all, two years earlier the Stonewall riots had sparked the gay liberation movement, exploding the number of possible options for sexual encounters. Cal, who had visited New York just a couple of weeks after the riots to help Mary Will Woodard move into an apartment she was subletting from Johnny Mercer, fell into a virtual playground. Bars such as The Spike, The Strap, The Eagle, and Ty's invited horny guys into their dark back rooms where anything could happen—and did. Fist-fucking was on display at The Anvil. David Mancuso's The Loft in the East Village and The Sanctuary were attracting gays to the blaring sound of disco. The Beacon Baths, Club Baths, Continental Baths, The Barracks, and St. Mark's Baths were popular destinations, where men paraded narrow hallways wrapped in their towels, looking for a buddy they could plow in their private cubicle. Dark labyrinths in the abandoned warehouses along the Hudson River and under the piers drew those interested in more dangerous encounters.

He realized that in leaving Atlanta he would be leaving "the relatively safe, sane, & secure ghetto of bourgeois faggotry" and setting out "on an unknown journey to become 'a writer' and eventually 'a star.'" Once again, he could hear Mama Rose screaming in his ear, "Got the dream, yeah, but not the guts."[29] Looking back on his decision a decade later, he explained to a friend who was also facing major career choices, "I turned away from Maddox Drive [in Atlanta] because I didn't want to be like those people in Ansley Park and 13th St., because I didn't want to be like *anybody* in Atlanta...so I forged on."[30]

He left his twelve-room town house with its beautiful parquet floors, left his maid, his expensive clothes, his Buick convertible, his cocktail parties, and he traded it all for a one-bedroom apartment on the Lower East Side of New York City. As he explained, he "left the accepted confines of secure employment teaching in Atlanta in order to find freedom and learn how to be a writer."[31] But this time in New York he would have a job at Ellen Stewart's prestigious Café La MaMa. It was going to be his big break.

Founded in 1961, the theatre had always specialized in producing plays by emerging playwrights from around the world. At first, it appeared as if Cal's career was taking off. He was tapped to assist Andrei Serban on an innovative, flamboyant production of Euripides's *Medea*, with music composed by Elizabeth Swados. Serban combined Latin, Greek and vocal-izations, hoping to transcend the literal and arrive at the hidden dimensions of human consciousness. As critic Margaret Croyden noted, "It is an attempt to find a language identical to the emotion behind it."[32]

Six days a week for three months, Cal attended workshop rehearsals of what he called the "unknown tongue production of *Medea*."[33] Cal was not impressed with the director's approach. " 'The sound that created the world'—that is what Andrei is asking of his actors. How can you deal in such abstractions? 'A sound possessing the energy to create a world.' He says he has no idea what it is, yet says the actors are completely wrong in what they do."[34] Cal must have fumed when he learned that Serban received an Obie in 1974 for his directing *Fragments of a Greek Trilogy*, which included his production of *Medea*. Cal received no credit in the program for his part in the success.

While assisting Serban, Cal was also making plans to conduct an acting workshop at La MaMa. The class was to be limited to fifteen people and would meet on Sunday evenings from 7 P.M. to 11 P.M.. Unfortunately, the classes never materialized. In late December, a month before *Medea* opened in January 1972, Cal found himself forced to return to Atlanta. He had allowed David Hayes to stay in his house on 13th Street, but when David wrote that he was moving, Cal felt compelled to return temporarily and put the house up for sale. As he looked back on his few months in New York, he wrote, "Life at La Mama [*sic*] comes to an end—only a few days before I wind up my 'work' here. What a disappointment it has all been. It isn't all over yet, but God how it's failed me this go round." He realized he had "failed gloriously."[35] He felt unwelcome and dispensable. His dream of being caught up in a whirlwind of creativity remained just a dream.

His personal life had been equally disappointing in New York. He lived in a grim apartment, was abysmally bored, ate tons of Entenmann's sweets, was tied up with sofa fringe during a bondage scene, was threatened with a knife, and was robbed of $3,000 of his possessions by an ex-convict Puerto Rican hustler he had picked up in a gay bar. "Depression was my first, last, and middle name," he confessed. "Bleakness was the air I breathed....I was desperately lonely and totally sexually frustrated." Soon after he had moved to New York, Cal began to experience severe depressions and drug freak-outs that often led to hospitalization. Concerned friends, even Ellen Stewart, would rush him to the ER where young interns would jab him in the arm with what Cal called "the needle of tranquility."[36] After his panic ceased and he felt better, weary friends would cart him home. Time after time, he convinced himself that the nightmare was over, he could sleep it off, and then go back to work.

Even though he had momentarily contemplated establishing a new theatre in Atlanta—La MaMa Atlanta—his depression did not change when he returned to the city. Embarrassed and humiliated to have failed in New York, he sat for days on end in the empty house he was trying to sell, staring at bare walls. When cars slowed down and stopped in front of the house, he wondered if they had found out that he was a madman and were coming to get him. Finally, in late spring, he sold the house at a loss. "Anything to get away—flee death and boredom."[37] Since La MaMa was dark during July and August, he decided to return to Florida. With the help of amphetamines and white crosses, by mid-July he had managed to finish a play *Swamp Play #2: Earthly Chariot of Jesus Man, Inc.*[38]

Today, the script might be labeled "production dependent." When audience members entered the theatre, they were to sense that the theatre was "a graffiti covered cave in which grows a great forest of peters." The actors, costumed as huge phalli, were to be chanting and singing such lines as "For a free female blowjob, try the alley behind the bus station, rear-door American lunch. Ask for Ola," "Ola's her name and she'll suck the peter right off you." As the play begins, Ola begs a preacher to help her be released from the agony of her sexual desires. Instead, the preacher confesses that one morning when he was in church with a young boy "the evil that was in him welled up and cast a spell on me. I couldn't control myself and before I knew what I was doing, before I had time to pray it away, I had took my big blue hummer out of my britches and was whipping it up good when a voice that I took to be that of the Lord Almighty spoke to me and said...My rod and my staff will comfort thee." In the end, the peter demons condemn Ola, chanting fiercely

> Queen of the Greyhound and Trailways
> Rotten rubbers are your jewels...
> Rotten come-filled rubbers....
> Pubic hair is your crown of thorns
> Thighs caress your cheeks...

Ola, enraged by their condemnation, yells out "A blow-job for Jesus" as she runs up to a man who opens a "magnificent cape displaying the biggest, the most luscious the most dazzling piece of peter meat ever seen before on this earth....It is ablaze with rhinestones and spewing fire from its tip." Ola, then, surprises the audience that she is a man by pulling out her own peter "of equal magnitude."[39]

Cal had high hopes for the play. Since Ellen Stewart had encouraged him to submit scripts for her to consider, he sent her a copy, explaining,

"A birth has taken place and for better or worse a new grandbiddy is on its way to you. . . . I only hope it's not too retarded—it's what came out. . . . I remember—at our first meeting in reply to my 'I can't get it organically—especially my playwrighting.' you said something to the effect of 'That's alright. Come on up [to New York]—we have our ways of opening you up.' I feel with [this play] I opened."[40]

With the completion of the play, Cal's focus turned to his mother. He wished he could gain some kind of acceptance and approval from her, but knew it would not be forthcoming. "Look for the good in things, Calvin," she had always said, "Look for the good." He prayed that Vada could do that now. He saw her suffering from the hurt of the neglected, abandoned, lost little girl. It was the pain that she was her father's little girl, and not his son—her rage at being denied that, her hate at being deprived of that. And Cal believed that he was the object of her rage and hate. On June 24, he wrote, "Even if I achieve what I want so badly to achieve with this play—with my life—she will still be disappointed. My life will never please her—there is no way. . . . All that I've worked so hard for in an effort to achieve the childhood dream—stellar approval from mother—has caused its perpetual denial."[41] The next day, he added, "I am at the last straw with Vada. She is treating me like some kind of slime. . . . Lord what a woman, a sadly pathetic Medusa's head of unhappiness."

To celebrate completion of his play, Cal and Raymond Schanze, encouraged by Ellen Stewart, took off for a month for a vacation in Morocco. In the 1950s and even into the 1960s, the beautiful port city of Tangier was a holiday playground for gays and lesbians. Acceptance of homosexuality, easy access to drugs, and the proliferation of boy brothels were such a relief for anyone wanting to escape from the conservative and homophobic American society. Prominent visitors included Tennessee Williams, Truman Capote, Ned Rorem, William Burroughs, Jack Kerouac, and Allen Ginsberg. Authors Jane and Paul Bowles were permanent residents.

Because of a colossal mix-up at the Hotel Astoria when they tried to check in, Cal and Raymond were escorted deep into the Casbah to spend a night as guests at the palace of the world-renowned artist, Ahmed Yacoubi, who was a member of the royal family and a descendant of the Prophet Muhammad.[42] He and Raymond found themselves sitting barefoot on Moroccan carpets having mint tea with Ahmed Yacoubi when Cal became mesmerized by the Satanic charm of a rather peaked, spindly little Jewish boy from the Bronx who had crashed with a kind Arab family in the Medina in Tangier, a year or so earlier. Thoughts of visiting Arab boy harems were suddenly forgotten. Cal was in love! In a brief postcard to Ellen Stewart, he exclaimed, "I am in heaven."[43] He wrote to his mother that Tangier was "a most unusual place, very Holy, very spiritual."

Indeed, experiencing all the sex and drugs he could handle, Cal may have felt he was in heaven, but by the time he returned to New York "by the grace of God" three weeks later, he thought the trip "was hell." He had lost twenty-five pounds, was utterly exhausted and running a fever of over a hundred degrees.[44] It was at this point that he began to live with his old Atlanta friend, Johnny Ferdon, in a third-floor walk-up apartment at 193 Orchard Street in the East Village. Although today on the street level there is a very chic nightclub with a handsome outdoor patio and directly across the street is a four-star restaurant featuring French cuisine, in the 1970s the neighborhood was known for its spaced-out winos, drug pushers, and panhandlers. Before Cal could enter his building, he had to step over homeless drunks sleeping on the sidewalk and front steps leading down to the front door.

Mary Will Woodard met Cal and Johnny for dinner shortly after Cal returned from Morocco and was shocked to see how much weight Cal had lost and his hair hanging down to his shoulders. She knew he was on drugs. When she returned to her hotel room and looked out of her window, she could not believe she was looking at the man she adored— stoned, wrinkled, frazzled. She cried as she thought that night might be the last time she ever saw him.

Even though Cal wrote extensive journals through the years, he seldom mentioned what transpired in Morocco, only occasional, vague references. At one point, probably under the influence of drugs and alcohol, he was found wandering lost in a windstorm at the foot of the Rif mountains. A hunchback dwarf discovered him and led him back to his hotel in Tetuan. His most explicit description came three years after he returned to New York. When he looked back at his earlier, drug-related hospitalizations, he concluded, "Little did I know that all the real fun was yet ahead—the big time stuff would happen far away in a place called Tangier."[45] The most specific reference appears in the psychiatric evaluation written by one of his doctors, Tom Smith, several years later. Smith wrote about his new patient, "First paranoid psychotic episode in 1972, just prior to and during a vacation in Morocco [sic].... During the three weeks in North Africa, he slept little and had mounting fears and feelings of impending doom. He describes a well organized delusional system of agents against him."[46] At one point, Cal telephoned his mother in Florida that he was having serious troubles, and that strange things were happening to him in Morocco. She said she did not know how she could help, since he was so far away.

Actually, by the time Cal and Raymond got to Morocco in August 1972, the exotic 1950s no longer existed. Beginning when King Hassan II assumed the throne in 1961, the country entered a period of great political unrest. Dissidents were arrested, executed, or disappeared. Protests and rioting became so intense that armored tanks often patrolled the streets. On July 9, 1971, at the King's birthday banquet for 800 guests at the summer palace, 1,400 armed cadets invaded the palace, shooting indiscriminately and killing more than 100 people. The King hid in a bathroom until the firing died down and then ordered his troops to crush the revolt. They killed more than 150 rebels and captured 900 others. A year later, on August 16, while the King was returning from Paris aboard his private airplane, four local air force fighters fired on the King's plane. He landed safely, but the would-be assassins continued to attack the runway until the King was able to dispatch a radio message to them, saying that the King had been killed. The rebels ceased firing. Within hours they were arrested and shot. Clearly, it was not a safe time to be in Morocco. The only evidence of what Cal experienced during those weeks were a couple of brief comments in his journals: "The tension was electric in Tanger [sic] when that news [the attempted assassination] hit the town and oh! the excitement! the exquisite paranoia of it all."[47] "Having traveled to and from Morocco via Madrid and Casablanca at exactly the wrong time (toward the end of August, 1972) I am still terrified of airports and certainly military police in airports. I spent a night of terror in Casablanca that would have paralyzed Jesus."[48]

Immediately upon his return to New York, Ellen Stewart put him to work. He assisted theatre critic Henry Hewes, who was directing Bernard M. Kahn's *Our Very Own Hole in the Ground,* which opened on October 4. He then spent several tedious, boring weeks painting the first coat of red lead on the seven floors of the theatre's fire escape. By Christmas Eve, when he and Jim Sitton were visiting Vada in Florida, Cal had plummeted to new depths of despair and viewed the three of them as social misfits, abandoned to survive Christmas alone. Ten days later, he wrote, "I see a certain thread of mental disorder that has caused most of my trouble—paranoia & over reaction to difficult events. I seemingly have no where to go. Fuck it."[49]

Through most of the spring of 1973, his moods would swing dramatically from manic highs to depressing lows. By the end of January, for instance, he was beside himself over his sexual encounters and wrote at length about his "baptism by urine," the first time he had engaged in water sports. "The feeling of excitement, forbidden excitement was exquisite, a few moments of total ecstasy, a recapture of that wonderful adolescent feeling of total sexuality. A wonderful peak of soaring, singing, nerve-tingling, screaming heaven, and then that wonderful moment of guilt. The forbidden had been tasted."[50] Yet a month later, Cal felt paralyzed, catatonic. "Where is the up of life? It is all so down....I have been so completely destroyed—my ego, my confidence—that I can do nothing." During the high periods when he was feeling on top of the world, Cal often accompanied the journal entries of his sexual encounters with sketches of men's erections, often dripping with cum. As he wrote in one entry, "I am shameless about cock. I love it."[51]

He also began writing poetry that reflected his frustrations. One of them reads in part:

> i am not ordinary.
> i never was ordinary.
> i cannot conform to ordinary rhythms.[52]

In late spring of 1973, he began to work on a new play he was calling *One Two Boy Man*. Donald Arrington agreed to compose incidental music. When Donald was hired by Fred Chappell to perform in *The Fantasticks* for the month of July at the Sea Ranch Dinner Theatre in Ft. Lauderdale, Cal followed him there so they could continue their collaboration. Ironically, Fred wound up casting Cal to play the Indian. He had free board and room right on the beach, and, according to Cal, "fucked a lot"[53] before returning to New York in September.

Back in New York, Cal and Donald began immediately to peddle the play, giving one to the WPA Theater and one to Ellen Stewart even though Cal saw little hope in La MaMa's having any interest. He felt that during the four months that he had been gone from the theatre, it had become increasingly dehumanized. He thought Ellen was making a mistake by neglecting American playwrights, and he could see the truth in Raymond Schanze's observation: "La Mama [*sic*] has become a snob theatre."[54] As he took off for a two-month vacation in California, Cal penned a letter to her that he never mailed. "Sometimes I feel La Mama [*sic*] destroys people. It makes some, but many it destroys....I found it demeaning when you asked me if I would like to sand the floors of your new loft. I am an artist....I am now peddling a play....Surely this is where my time is best used."[55]

When he returned to New York, Cal seemed to take on a new, optimistic attitude. "After 3 years, I've shaved my beard, and it seems as if I've erased them," he beamed. "I want to start over again. This is my first year in NYC, etc."[56] It was probably one of his most productive years at La MaMa. He had been managing to scrape by with his $500 per month from the trust fund and the few dollars he earned working at the theatre, but since it was not enough to pay the bills and maintain his supply of booze and drugs, he took on a full-time position in the theatre's box office. During the day, "I work at La Mama [sic]," he chuckled, "afterwards—I dabble in promiscuity."[57]

Frustrated that Ellen Stewart had shown no interest in *Swamp Play #2*, the script that he had submitted to her two years earlier, Cal asked Jeff Weiss, well-known at the time for his own plays produced at La MaMa— *Locomotive Munch*, *And That's How the Rent Gets Paid*, and *Pushover*—to offer his impressions of the script.

> The rage, the terrifying pain and indignation, that bounds, vivid and sweltering, off every page is something I greatly admire.... You've managed to take your obsessions strongly by the back of the neck and force the face of it down into the shit of all our Christian origins.... It's a celebration of one's torments, externalized and purged.... You should direct yourself, I think, and not consign it to the well-meaning mits of the butchers that hang around La Mama [sic]. That would be death!... This play needs to be done.... Your vision touches me and, in some very personal way, breaks my heart.

Weiss ends his letter of support offering to speak to Ellen Stewart about it on Cal's behalf.[58]

But even after Jeff's intervention, she objected. He believed Cal's play was exceptionally good and contained deeply felt, emotional dialogue. Stewart, however, objected to the adjectives Cal used and complained of the play's "preoccupation with 'peter'—homosexuality." Cal notes in his Journal at the time that she "preached—beseeched—she begged for other things—saying 'there must be something else.' She said she had so much of it at La Mama [sic] and she was fed up."[59] Cal concluded that, regardless of her reputation as a forward thinker, Stewart's "actions...were frequently homophobic and guilt-ridden.... [She is] 'a Catholic' and personally very prudish and sexophobic, sexually dysfunctional and celibate by nature."[60] But, clearly, he was unaware that he had become obsessed with sex over the years. As he confessed in his journal, "At the moment, I have no interest in creative work in the theatre. I only want to fuck."[61] He had recently begun to experiment with sadomasochism (S&M). Years later, he and Ellen Stewart became good friends, but at this time, he had little good to say about her or her theatre.

By the end of February 1974, he was back in Florida, but when Ellen asked him a few months later to return and to direct an evening of readings from plays in progress and workshop scenes, he jumped at the chance. He selected scenes written by his roommate Johnny Ferdon, Jean Reavey, Sterling Harper, and Raymond Schanze. He was excited with the progress of the rehearsals, noting that it was taking "off like a sky rocket."[62] Ellen was out of town and unable to attend the three performances in mid-August, so Cal sent her his response. Something must have happened during the rehearsals. It succeeded, he wrote, "in boring the be-Jesus out of most everybody—me included.... Mostly because of some lousy playwrights—their insistence on writing *about* the event rather than writing the event itself."[63] Ellen must have disagreed with his observation, however, since she asked Cal to conduct a series of staged readings of new plays the next winter.

The first play he chose for the series was his *One Two Boy Man*. As the audience enters the theatre, two men are seen immobile, seated in silhouette at a table. The table is any table—restaurant, bar, kitchen, home. When the play begins, photographs of the two men from youth till the present appear behind them until there is a final click and the two silhouettes change to the two three-dimensional men, sitting at the table. In a typed memo attached to the script in the La MaMa Archives, Cal explains that the play

> is a simple dialogue that in reality would take only a few minutes to repeat, however with the inclusion of subconscious images, Proustian recall, and flights of fancy, it goes on considerably longer. There are shadow figures, silhouettes, echoes, reverberation.... It is a very simply [sic] play about two human beings.... There should be at all times an intense magnetic field between them.

Several years later, Cal admitted in a letter to Fred Chappell that the play "was a crystallization of trying to understand *you* and our relationship as I broke away from it in search of something else."[64]

The two men in the play were former lovers who meet after several years apart. The character named One has lived a completely homosexual life while the character named Two married and had a family. They talk about their lives with flashbacks in their respective journeys. The play is very sexual with a chorus of actors often assisting in creating a scene. In the first flashback, One seduces a very reluctant and young nude boy, who supposedly is Two. Another flashback reveals a Hell's Angel character who teaches Two the intricacies of fist-fucking. Later, One goes into a toilet at a highway rest stop and shares a glory hole with a truck driver.

A scene in a mental institution reveals a room that reeks of urine. "Men are curled, half naked in the fetal position. Others are splayed in rolling chairs, their mouths drooling, their heads lollingly helplessly back and forth. Some talk haltingly, half understandably. Others grunt and groan, and paw at the air. Some men's hands are encased in rags to prevent them from beating themselves. Many are toothless, horribly pimpled, or covered with running sores and black and blue marks....Next door, in a dormitory, a few men are sprawled on beds lined end to end....One naked man masturbates."[65]

The most memorable song that Don composed for the production was "Waiting." It was certainly appropriate for the script, since most of the scenes reveal characters waiting around for love—in bus stations, in hotel rooms, in empty bars, on street corners, in prison, and even in a mental ward.

After the first rehearsal, Cal canceled the workshop. All of the cast and production staff had been assembled at the La MaMa rehearsal studio on Great Jones Street. They read through the script once, and then Cal suddenly and with no warning dropped the bomb, "We're not going to do this." No reason was given, but more than likely, Cal suddenly realized that if Ellen Stewart did not like *Swamp Play #2*, she would never approve a public presentation of this script. He wrote in his journal that night,

> Canceled the play today. There will be no stars on my ceiling not tomorrow or the next day—or the day after that....In 1961 my mother cried tears as I left all that I knew for the big city—I thought the tears were selfish—bespeaking the loss of a treasured private possession. Now, 13 years later, I see they more probably were for all the pain she knew I was heading toward. It has been a ferocious struggle—that "flight from ignorance"—but I didn't know—I never knew—I had to find out.[66]

It was about this time when he began another desperate, hysterical search for sexual fulfillment, part of his lifelong journey for a true lover. He felt there was nothing for him to do when night came except get stoned, and then head to the West Village to get drunk. Nothing made sense to him—not movies, not theatre. There was the nightly ritual of a bath, dressing, rolling three joints, smoking one and putting two in his pocket for later. He was desperate to meet a person or, more specifically, "the person...who would stop the incoherence of everything and quietly take me in his arms perhaps and say 'I see, I know, I feel. Come with me. On the other side of the river is a golden land and it is my land and now, it will be your land.'" He needed to please anyone he met. "Piss is a precious thing," one of his tricks told him. "Don't waste a drop of it." "Beer piss is the best," another said. And so he began pissing in people's mouths. One of his unsuspecting tricks, whom he had escorted to the hollow tunnel under the West Side highway after cruising him at The Spike, gagged and puked, but remarked, "I don't like it, but it makes me hot."[67]

Regardless of Cal's failure with *One Two Boy Man* and Ellen's knowledge of his wild sexual promiscuity, she still proceeded to hire him to direct Paul Foster's *Rags to Riches to Rags: A Tale of Christmas Folly* with original music by Ned Levy and a cast that included Clio Young as Merry Christmas and Harvey Feierstein as Slush Fund, The B Girl. Foster had set the play on Christmas Eve and on the stage of a nightclub in Little Italy that he called the Singing Lady Bar.

One week before the scheduled opening on December 18, Cal wrote, "Directing Paul's shit Xmas play at La Mama's [*sic*]—trying to shape a monstrous cast of forgotten freaks."[68] What a catastrophe. Cal complained bitterly about the script that he had hoped would lead to more directing assignments. A poem he wrote at the time reveals his utter frustration.

> I sit
> bleary-eyed, unfocused
> in my kitchen.
>
> It has been a long descent
> to this place
> at this time
> in this chair
>
> "What happened?"
>
> Their eyes ask me
> I say
>   "look, don't ask, look.
> it's all there in the countenance
> in the opaque eyes of a too long
>   dead mullet...
> My face."[69]

Ellen Stewart had expected Foster to write a typical Christmas nativity story, appropriate for families, and was shocked and disgusted with the gay comedy she witnessed on opening night. A good amount of the farcical action took place on a Christmas crèche built on the nightclub stage, and with black actors. Horrified with what she saw, Stewart had a huge fight with Foster, and closed the production after two performances. Some years later, Cal pinpointed December 16, 1974, two days before the opening of *Rags to Riches to Rags*, as the beginning of his losing touch with reality. His manic depression was about to take control.

CHAPTER 4

"CRAZY AS A FUCKING LOON"

Depressed over his failure at La MaMa, Cal needed to get out of New York and in late January 1974 retreated to Florida, where he remained for several months. Nervous about making the journey alone, he asked Jeff Weiss to accompany him. While on board the Silver Meteor train heading south, he continued to grumble, "A piece of shit shit shit that Paul Foster had thought up no doubt to see how many people he could humiliate. Had I taken the whole thing seriously, I probably would have jumped off the Brooklyn Bridge very happily. It was all a gruesome joke from beginning to end. We all knew it and learned what ever paltry lessons that we could from such an asinine experience."[1]

Once he arrived in Crystal River, most of his time was spent helping his mother at the house by the river. He bought a new chainsaw and cut up a huge oak tree that had fallen on the property two years earlier. "Man against nature," he beamed. "Man won this round."[2] The discovery of a marvelous boggy, shaded area on the river's edge inspired him to plant a watercress bed. Whenever it rained, he worked on designing and creating a new kimono with a complex fabric patchwork. He enjoyed going to flea markets, especially The Green Door in Ocala, where he began a lifetime hobby of collecting such odd items as old scissors, staplers, bamboo-handled flatware, original Fiesta china, and other art-deco bargains. "What will become of all this shit I'm collecting," he laughed. "Somebody will have some fun someday disposing of it all."[3]

Although Cal pointed to the disaster of the aborted *Rags to Riches to Rags* as the start of what became his mental and emotional breakdown, he later came to accept the diagnosis of one of his psychiatrists—that the starting point of a psychotic breakdown is often a severe loss of some kind. That loss was the murder of his dear friend of ten years, Jim Sitton. Cal and Jim had been close friends ever since Cal had moved to Atlanta in 1965. Because of his wit, wry humor, and flamboyance, his friends called

Jim, the Contessa. A revered professor of art at Georgia State University, he had become known throughout the region for his technically exquisite drawings of aerial views of Atlanta. Cal and Jim had often partied together and had even shared sexual partners.

At about 2.00 A.M. on August 9, 1975, the Contessa and a couple of his friends walked out of a gay bar on West Peachtree Street in Atlanta. A stranger later identified as David Lee Berryman suddenly stopped them and asked for some travel directions. When Jim began to explain, the man pulled out a .22 caliber pistol and attempted to rob him. During the struggle that followed, Jim was shot in the right side of his head and was rushed to nearby Grady Hospital. Today it would be considered a gay hate crime.

At about 9:00 A.M., while sitting at his mother's house in Crystal River having his morning coffee, the phone rang and Cal got the news of the tragedy. He choked with tears and disbelief. Immediately, he then called Eglé Gatins Weiland, one of Jim's favorite pupils, and was told that Jim was alive but his status was hopeless. Cal was bewildered. Jim died at about 5:00 P.M. that same day.

The only way he seemed able to escape his sorrow was through sex. As he scribbled in his journal, "I fucked the night you died, Contessa, I fucked and I fucked and I fucked. It was the only thing that stopped the pain. I know you'd understand. You always said, 'Do a few for me, honey.' And we shared quite a few—over the years and all.... How you've changed my life, Contessa, in your death, in your life. I can't believe still—you're dead. I hurt so bad, Contessa. I hurt so bad.... I love you, Contessa, wherever you are."[4] Through the years, Cal composed many poems about Jim Sitton. One reads, in part,

> when love leaves
>   in the form of death
> and autumnal leaves fall
>   too early in August
> a hole.
>   just a great black dark
>   empty hole
>   ....
>   an historical event
>   encompassed by the dates
>   the beginning—1941
>   and, of course,
>   dismally so,
>   the end.
>   1975[5]

Just a couple of weeks after Jim died, Eglé invited Cal to her art-show opening at a little cooperative gallery in Atlanta, but he explained to her, "There isn't too much right now that I can deal with....There are some things I cannot do right now. I cannot attend any service or show. My spirit will be there, but I can't. Please understand."[6]

During the six or seven months Cal had been away from New York, he had come to the conclusion that he would never be able to work out for himself the kind of life he wanted and needed in New York. He decided he must "move on to some other turf and make a fresh start at a new life."[7] He planned to close his apartment and set out for California, but he would spend just a few days in New York prior to his move. His plans failed.

By mid-August, Cal, indeed, was back in New York, and it would be three years before he would make it to California. At first, he was appalled by what he saw in the city. Compared with the beauty and peaceful swamps of Florida, Gotham City seemed tawdry and soiled. He was overwhelmed with the seedy urban hell. It was "the land of dog shit and smelly, overflowing garbage cans....There was an almost necrophiliac air that shrouded everything in a pall of macabre gloom....An ecstasy of death had invaded the city."[8]

A few days after his return, he visited an old friend with whom he had collaborated on a musical. They both took hits of speed and then went out on the town, drinking at several gay bars. He and his friend closed one at 4:00 A.M. and then went to an after-hours bar where his friend left him. Cal blacked out. The next thing he remembered was being slapped in the face, and he then blacked out again. When he awoke later in the morning, he was told to get dressed. Eventually, though dizzy and bleary-eyed, he managed to stumble out of the apartment and hailed a taxi to take him to his Orchard Street apartment. He recuperated for a few days but soon was back in the bars again. He had wanted desperately to escape the city, but he found himself in the same rut that he had been in months earlier. Undoubtedly, it was a compulsion born of a deep-seated loneliness and boredom, plus a good bit of masochism thrown in.

He tried to justify in his journal how Jim's murder had affected him—his pattern each night of getting stoned, drinking beer, and searching for some faceless, soulless body to take home. Over everything, he wrote, "there has hung the dark, tear-stained shroud of my beloved Contessa. My grief has been omnipresent. Somehow—before I knew—without meaning it to happen, my behavior has become the most seriously self-destructive that I've ever experienced....I'm afraid I won't survive....I have met and begun to have an 'affair' with a physically masochistic but sadistically mind-fucking French man."[9] He had met a handsome, tall, bearded, dark-haired man in tight Levis, Jacques-Pierre Caussin.

Their relationship began on August 18, 1975, just nine days after the Contessa's murder. Very late that night at The Eagle, a leather bar near the docks, when Cal was almost too drunk to cruise anyone and was about ready to go home, he and Jacques suddenly eyeballed each other across a room crowded with macho men in leather, some sporting chains and harnesses. Jacques identified himself as a slave who was looking for a master to control him. This was not really Cal's type, but as he explained, "despair will drive you to the most casual arrangements for fucking."[10] Before he knew it, Cal was on his way to Jacques's pied-a-terre on West 74th Street. Once they arrived, Jacque slid on his expensive, silver cock ring and became Cal's slave for the night. In less than one week, Cal was tying him down with rawhide straps and handcuffs. "At last, I have a lover," he exclaimed, "who wants to eat my shit."[11]

Soon, they were seeing each other almost every night. Jacques had just broken up with a lover, was lonely, and wanted an affectionate person to share his life. Cal was also lonely and tired of the bar scene with its marathon of meaningless sex. Jacques had just purchased an old and crumbling but charming farmhouse deep in the farmland foothills on route 519 just north of Sussex, New Jersey, and Cal went with Jacques to share the first weekend he spent there. It was a rambling old homestead, isolated and completely provincial. Cal had always thought of New Jersey as an industrial wasteland with smoke blackened foliage, so he was amazed at what he found. At times, he could look out of the window of the farmhouse and see stray cattle grazing contentedly on the front lawn.

It was about this time that Cal became infatuated with the writings of James Purdy, whom Gore Vidal had called an authentic American genius. In one interview, Purdy had said, "When you're writing, at least in my case, you're so occupied by the story and the characters that you have no interest in what people may think or whether I should write to please anyone."[12] Another time, Purdy, who seemed to regard rejection as a badge of honor, told an interviewer, "I don't think I'd like it if people liked me. I'd think that something had gone wrong."[13]

Cal felt a close kinship with Purdy. Both had grown up in small, conservative towns and had moved to New York where they hoped to find more acceptance. Cal particularly liked Purdy's *Eustace Chisholm and the Works* where the author focuses on a group of displaced people who gather around Eustace in his run-down apartment. They are all searching hopelessly for love. Purdy's main characters were often like Cal, gay men who could not find love in their families, and who felt estranged wherever they lived. Cal was awestruck over Purdy's attitude about rejection, since it gave him a strategy in which to counter Ellen Stewart's rejection of his own scripts. Determined to succeed as a writer and to learn from his new idol, Cal arranged to meet Purdy at his tiny Brooklyn Heights apartment. The meeting was a disaster. In his novels, Purdy had written openly about homosexuality and what some critics considered perverted sexual activities. Cal, therefore, had assumed that he could discuss sensitive, sexual matters, but Purdy was shocked, became embarrassed and angry. Cal had no way knowing that the author was very private and reclusive. There was very little, if any, comfortable dialogue. Cal came to realize that Purdy was so alone in his sad little room with its efficiency kitchen, "sustained only by the drunken phone calls of faggots...and by the letters of appreciation that his work elicits....So alone and living only the most bleak and austere of monastic lives."[14] Cal had longed for some kind of verification of his work from this important writer whom he respected, but, instead, the meeting only added to his discouragement.

Before long, Cal and Jacques began to think of themselves as lovers and had no interest in sexual adventures with others. Their deepening relationship had started back in New York at a restaurant called One Potato. They had ordered dinner when Jacques, in the tradition of a romantic Frenchman, turned to Cal and said across the candle, "It's better when you call it love." While it was not exactly rose covered, the farmhouse in Sussex became their honeymoon cottage. Cal was ecstatic: "It was magical being in love and such a relief to be away finally at last from the tawdry and cheapening life I was accustomed to living." They spent every weekend thereafter at the farm, working and cleaning and searching the countryside for inexpensive antiques. "It was a pristine existence we lived on those radiant weekends full of love and fun and warmth and good clean country living," he beamed. "It was a magical time." Cal planned to give up his New York apartment, move his things to Sussex, and "settle in for a long winter of happy homemaking and...writing for the theatre in the perfect peace and quiet of rural N.J." He was happier and healthier than he had been in years. They cooked, ate well, drank many bottles of wine, and smoked lots of good grass—some of which Cal had grown the summer before in a secluded swamp in Florida.

Cal's decision to become a marijuana farmer had not been hard to make. There was no time spent deciding whether it might be right or wrong. He regarded marijuana "as a positive, stimulating, expanding natural agent and one whose good far outweighs any bad." He considered the legal ramifications, pondered the consequences of getting caught, and decided the odds were in his favor. "Free! All the pot you and your friends can smoke," he boasted, was too tantalizing and luxurious a promise to

turn down. And besides, he added, "he didn't have anything more meaningful to do."[15]

Jacques, who was a high-profile marketing director for Peugeot, had
business colleagues coming to the farmhouse for a weekend in early
October, and since Cal felt his presence would be awkward, he returned
to Florida where he purchased for $13,000 a four-acre island called Black
Creek Isle, formerly called Camp Pulaski Isle, just south of Crystal River
in a little community called Ozello. Very near where his parents had
owned a summer cottage, the island property had a sixty-foot mobile
home on it where Cal decided to create a cozy little hideaway all his own.
He had dreamed of returning to the island ever since his mother had sold
their family cottage several years earlier. The sense of peace and apartness, the harsh and unrelenting sun, the bleak and nearly uninhabitable
land, and the total isolation provided a "strange seductive voice that calls
to me," he admitted. After Jacques's guests in New Jersey departed, he
drove down to Florida and stayed with Cal about a week before returning
to New York for work. There was no way Cal could have known that in
less than one year his little vacation cottage would become his permanent
residence.

It may have been a magical time for Cal, but he began having doubts
about his relationship with Jacques. In late September, Jacques had left
Cal alone at the farmhouse while he went off on a "run" with a gay
group of California bikers, making Cal feel as if he were just some kind
of houseboy. He wondered how much piss Jacques would drink while
away, how much shit he would eat. Cal envisioned his lover "in the arms
of some sleazy, two-bit faggot biker." "I don't know who you are," he
wrote, "and I certainly don't know why we are.... We were hopeless
anyway from the start. Doomed and I knew it." Yet a few days later, he
wrote, "I love you, Jacques—even if it does all end today."[16]

Apparently, Cal knew in less than a month's time that Jacques was
starting to see someone named Paul and felt as if he were being shoved
aside. He sat drinking early morning coffee after Jacques left for work and
stared at the photograph of the person who seemed to be his replacement.
When Cal occasionally stayed overnight at his Orchard Street apartment
in the city, he envisioned Jacques bringing Paul to the farmhouse, and
their making love in front of the fireplace. More often than not, Cal
continued "to feel like a used car that has been taken back to the lot and
traded in for a more satisfactory model. It was so nice. For one month, I
was not alone."[17]

Because Cal was plagued with severe feelings of insecurity and inferiority, he could not understand what such a handsome man as Jacques
could see in him to begin with and needed constant reassurance of his

worth. The two were so different. Jacques was a very successful junior executive, rapidly on his way up in the business world. Cal was an unrecognized and unsuccessful, nonfunctioning playwright. Jacques's world was the coat and tie world of the expense-account luncheon and the stylish bars and restaurants. Cal's, on the other hand, was a world of small, out-of-the-way cafes, and downbeat establishments catering to artists. Jacques's friends were young, well-employed men, secure in their professional accomplishments. Cal's were like him, struggling artists who rarely knew where their next beer was coming from.

Yet another aspect of their relationship that bothered Cal was their sex life. About a year prior to their meeting at The Eagle, Cal had found himself drawn more and more into the world of leather sex, sadomasochism, and master-slave relationships. In no time at all, he and Jacques were using all the toys imaginable—chains, dildoes, whips, handcuffs, leather straps, ropes, wrenches, tit clamps, face hoods, hooks, cat of nine tails, amyl nitrate, candle wax, suspension devices. Afterwards, they would chuckle, "Now, my dear, we need a valet to come in and clean all of this up."[18]

While he often found such encounters exciting and quite a turn-on, they usually ended with his feeling guilty, cheapened, and dirtied. He yearned for what he considered the more conventional, innocent, simple, and pure expressions of gay sexuality. His conservative upbringing whispered to him that such kinky sex acts were evil and the work of Satan. When a new brand of poppers came out called Crypt, the signs were too clear. He freaked out. It was what he called "an ecstasy of death."[19] In his mind, Cal saw it as a great struggle of good against evil, light against dark, life versus death. Indeed, it was, in part, because of this struggle that he earlier had left New York for the first half of 1975.

When he met Jacques, he was desperate to have a permanent relationship. Jacques wanted Cal to assume the dominant, masculine, and masterful part of the duo, while he would become the passive, subservient, feminine one. Jacques was experienced in the role, but Cal, even though he had dabbled in such activity, was really a novice. He did not want to lose Jacques and went out of his way trying to please and satisfy his sexual tastes. He got into scat and enjoyed it, though he thought he shouldn't. With little previous experience at being a master, Cal felt awkward, bumbling, and terribly insecure. Would he do something or not do something that would make him look foolish and destroy the image that Jacques had created of him? "It was a stupid and improbable situation," Cal later realized, "and one that, one way or another, was doomed from the start." By early December, the turmoil and agony that Cal was experiencing was about to explode.

Cal, who had not cut his hair in about eight months and whose beard was long and bushy, had a rather fierce and discarded look to him. In fact, one of his friends complained that he looked like Charles Manson. Cal decided, therefore, that he needed to make a shopping excursion into Manhattan to buy some new clothes that he hoped would make him more acceptable in the social circles he was sharing with Jacques. He first went to Paul Stuart's, a posh men's store, where he purchased over $900 of stylish sports coats and trousers. When he handed the clerk his American Express card for payment, there was a problem in that the address he gave to the clerk was not the same as the billing address for the card. They did not want to complete the sale. He was taken to the stockroom to speak on the telephone to an American Express representative wherein he exploded. In a rage, he stalked furiously down the store's grand staircase and out the door.

About a week later, Jacques asked Cal, "Why are you watching each car that passes the house? You've never done that before." "Oh, I don't know," Cal answered. He could not tell the truth—he believed that the house was under surveillance not only by the John Birch Society, but also by a queer-hating vigilante group. An extreme right-wing group, the society's goal was to abolish Communism within the United States. Somewhere in the state, an entire black family had been murdered, and Cal concluded that the John Birch Society was responsible. He had heard that the antigay group did not want its rural atmosphere ruined by an influx of jaded New Yorkers, especially gays.

It was deer hunting season. Directly across from their farmhouse was a large, old barn that seemed to be a particularly popular parking place and departure for hunters, who could be seen with guns and formidable looking hunting paraphernalia. Cal believed that the ostensible hunters were in reality agents whose job it was to spy on him and Jacques. He suspected that the barn was their communication center, and they had all of their equipment hidden underneath the bales of hay inside. His paranoia began to sky rocket, believing that the so-called hunters were entering their house when no one was home. His fear was confirmed one morning when he found that a small framed portrait he had of Eleonora Duse had been moved from the downstairs sitting room to the floorboards of his car. He pleaded with Jacques to lock the doors, but Jacques boasted that they had never been locked in the past twenty-seven years by the previous owners, and he refused to do it now.

Cal's behavior became increasingly erratic. He and Jacques were invited to a dinner party hosted by David Barrett, a rich and well-known decorator and one of Jacques's former lovers. Immediately intimidated by the affluence and elegance of the sumptuous East Side town house, Cal became aware of David's attempt to play what Edward Albee called in *Whose Afraid of Virginia Wolff* "get the guest" with a barrage of demeaning verbal thrusts. "Look, honey, I know you are a quality act from Florida," he smiled, "but what really are you up to?" Cal dropped his fork onto his dessert plate and withdrew into himself with a careless kind of hauteur. Jacques wanted to leave, but Cal, who insisted on staying, began to match all of David's thrusts with equal venom. As he and Jacques drove back to New Jersey, he wept on Jacques's shoulder and made Jacques promise to never again subject him to such stress at the hands of one of his so-called friends.

When Jacques hosted his annual Christmas party at his New York apartment, he expected Cal to attend. Fearful of a repeat performance of the earlier social event, Cal asked his old friend, Grady McClendon, to accompany him. They first had a leisurely dinner and arrived at the party quite late, about 11 P.M.. Even though almost everyone had gone by that time, Cal was primed, ready for a fight, and soon began shrieking at "some old queen" who had been praising Maureen Stapleton's portrayal of Amanda in *The Glass Menagerie*. Cal yelled out that the performance was "vulgar, vulgar, vulgar." And then he turned on Grady, ridiculing him for his penchant for collecting autographed books.

Even with all these insecurities building up, Cal drove to Manhattan one evening to see La MaMa's production of Ada Amichal-Yevins's play, *Twilight*. In the rush to leave, Cal forgot his glasses. Being nearsighted, he could not read the road signs and got lost, only to find himself in Newark, where there was a large and active John Birch Society. With his paranoia, he naturally felt threatened. The next day, while eating at the Red Lantern, a neighborhood restaurant, he opened a packet of sugar to put in his coffee and panicked—he thought it was poison. He began to smell fumes from the gas stove that he thought were meant to kill him. As he rushed frantically back to the apartment, he passed a garbage compactor where he believed he saw dead Puerto Ricans. He ran to his apartment and jumped into the shower, screaming hysterically and beating himself, trying to exorcise the voices he was hearing. He threw on a pair of Levis and a sweater, bolted out of the apartment into the freezing weather, and ran up to the first policeman he saw. "I've been drugged," he cried out. He then ran to a nearby hospital but fled before he was admitted, fearing what they might do to him there. For a while, he barricaded himself in a deserted building. Then, as he ran down First Avenue, he broke out the car windows where he was convinced people were spying on him. He thought he heard a bomb explode. He ran back to the hospital and while in an elevator attacked a doctor whom he believed to be an enemy. He pushed on the alarm button of the elevator and rang and rang it until a dozen security guards threw him down and subdued him in a wheelchair with handcuffs and bandages. Cal began to sing an aria from *The Messiah* as a nurse injected him with Thorazine. When the police arrived, they threw him into a paddy wagon. He had only seven cents in his pocket, but he begged the police to call Ellen Stewart. When she arrived, she took him to Bellevue and had him admitted. Someone then went to his apartment building and tacked onto the outside door the following message: "193 Orchard St #12B, Notify Family of Lee Yeomans that he is admitted to Bellvue [*sic*] Hosp. Psychotic Ward. Call 17Pct for Details."[20]

Cal remembered being thrown into a large room with crazed zombies who had undergone shock treatments. The huge black women who supervised the pit would mop up the urine when the inmates wet the floor. After three or four days, when he was finally allowed visitors, the locked door buzzed open and, as Cal described it, "like a white calla lily appearing before a blue and white sky" stood loyal friend, Grady McClendon, an angel of mercy. Cal was then released and stayed with Grady at his elegant apartment on First Avenue and 49th Street.

What a contrast from the psych unit at Bellevue. He would sip tea from fragile Wedgwood china while sitting on an antique Louis XVI chair. Grady had a daybed in his living room where Cal spent most of the time resting and sleeping. When Grady left for work in the morning, Cal was in bed. When Grady returned home at the end of the day, Cal was often still there. Grady thought Cal was improving. He gave him some nice clothes to wear that improved his spirits. They would go for walks and out to dinner.

After about a week with Grady, Cal returned to New Jersey and to Jacques. Grady quickly realized that Cal's release from Bellevue was premature; his friend was not well, and his going back to New Jersey was a mistake. During the day, when Jacques was at work, Cal became increasingly lonely and depressed. He had macabre visions and revelations—he was surrounded by spaceships; Jim Sitton was not really dead, it was just a ruse; when he looked at electrical outlets along the baseboards of the house, he saw leering Egyptian cat faces. The face of the clock on the wall and the toaster were also cat faces. The sounds from the radio and television were cats. "Oh God, I can't stand it," he cried. "Now I know why some people like to live without electricity. It's the only way to avoid the cats, the omnipresent all-knowing ever spying devious Egyptian cats. Evil Gods incarnate! They and their electricity will rule the world."[21]

In no time at all, Grady received a telephone call that Cal had borrowed Jacques's car, drove some distance along New Jersey's Garden State Parkway, abandoned the car, and just started walking. When the highway patrol stopped to ask him why he was there, he admitted he did not know where he was. Eventually, they managed to find out where he lived, put him in handcuffs, and returned him to the farmhouse.

That evening, when Jacques returned to the farmhouse from his work in New York, he found the house in total chaos, windows broken, curtains torn down, furniture all thrown aside, dishes smashed to the floor. Cal had gone berserk and cried out that the John Birch Society was trying to kill him. Jacques was beside himself, but decided he had to get Cal to a hospital. Since Cal had twisted his ankle in his wild frenzy, it was easy for Jacques to subdue him and then drive him back to Bellevue Hospital.[22]

When Grady got the news that Cal had been readmitted into Bellevue, he telephoned Ellen Stewart for advice. After just a few days, they and the doctors realized exactly how bad he was and that Cal should be sent home to Florida. Grady was selected to inform Miss Vada. As he finished describing the recent events and told her that Cal needed constant supervision, she wept, "Why didn't you tell me?" Ellen then told Cal's friend, Raymond Schanze, she would buy airplane tickets and instructed him to accompany Cal back to Florida.

Miss Vada arranged to meet them at the Tampa airport at 5:00 A.M.. She thought Cal looked fine, so she took him grocery shopping before driving Raymond and him to his Ozello mobile home where she left them. A few days later, when Raymond was preparing to return to New York, he warned Miss Vada that Cal was not well—he had threatened to kill him. She found this impossible to believe. Her son was too sweet and good, she argued, so she did not pursue the warning. Soon after, however, she received a telephone call from Citrus Memorial Hospital in Inverness. The police had found Cal, who apparently had fallen on the island and was lying unconscious under a little bridge, and had brought him to the hospital. Dr. Brooks Henderson treated him, but after a short time decided that Cal was severely psychotic and not safe to be discharged. He was then, with his mother's permission, committed on January 10, 1976, to Anclote Manor mental hospital in Tarpon Springs, Florida—an involuntary commitment.

Situated on twenty-two acres of land, the hospital was known as a medieval house of horrors. Patients complained of being tied down to their beds for weeks on end and locked in their rooms with no connection to the outside world. Rumors circulated around Tarpon Springs that the doctors performed cruel and unnecessary procedures on the patients. Just four years before Cal was admitted, one of the psychiatrists was found guilty of engaging in sexual contact with a patient who subsequently committed suicide.[23] It was finally shut down in 1997.

When Cal arrived there in 1976, he was placed in the snake pit, the intensive care unit labeled C-1, where he was forced to sleep in an over-crowded hallway and deprived of adequate toilet and bathing facilities. He was subjected to a cacophony of noise—a blaring television, rock music blasting from radios, and freak-out screams from hysterical and frightened patients caught up in the clutches of madness. Like the others around him, he was a prisoner and could not escape. He was diagnosed as a paranoid schizophrenic and treated with antidepressant Elavil, antipsychotic Prolixin, and Cogentin injections to control muscle stiffness due to the Elavil.

He was not an easy patient to handle. It was customary that Cal would choose to drink coffee for his after-lunch beverage in what he called "the madhouse." But he changed his routine one day and asked for tea. As he slowly drank it, he "felt the world begin to slip away . . . the black woman behind the food window was one of them, [an enemy]." He began to hear voices from the dead—Isadora Duncan and Bessie Smith were talking to him. He jumped up and ran, slapping himself ferociously as he had done weeks earlier while taking a shower in his apartment. The orderlies grabbed him, and as he collapsed into their arms the head nurse gave him oxygen and a sedative. A doctor in the background kept shouting over and over, "You've come to the right place!" They carried him to his bed where a nurse sat by his side for several days.[24]

Cal survived the first month despite the care he received, not because of it. On February 10, after one month in C-1, he was moved to the relative sanity of C-2. As he wrote in his journal, "I can smoke a cigarette and shit at the same time. A great luxury after the guarded toilets of C-1."[25] But he was still imprisoned. There was no place to walk. "Restlessness cannot be escaped," he concluded. "It follows me around loosely circled as my soul shrieks 'Discipline! Discipline! Discipline!' [I] can learn to write in these beastly surroundings. [I] must. [I] have no choice but lunacy." What he wrote next on February 12, reveals his new realization about his relationship with Jacques.

> The fact that I must face is that it never existed anyway—our love. Perhaps that is what is depressing me so much. I was only a temporary diversion for "HIM." A concrete helper with the house. Another illusion gone—shattered. . . . I'm not a master nor am I a slave. I failed miserably at that game. Couldn't have gone on anyway. Hate it. Hate it all. . . . Jacques needs fun. I need peace. I thought it was love. He thought it was opportunity.[26]

Another time, he wrote, "My relationship with him caused my breakdown."[27]

His days in C-2 were very predictable. At 7 A.M., a nurse with an aide enters his room to give him 15 mg of Valium. He then dresses and walks upstairs to the dining room. He sits at an assigned table. After he eats, he walks out to the verandah. He sits and reads—first, F. Scott Fitzgerald's *This Side of Paradise* and then Françoise Sagan's *Scars on the Soul*. He chats with doctors, with his roommate, attends a leather craft workshop for the patients, participates in a group discussion meeting, returns to the dining room for other meals, tries to write, goes to bed at about 9:30 P.M., gets more pills from the nurse, turns in his cigarette lighter, and retires for the night. When he awakens in the morning, he is depressed at the return of reality and lies sluggish in bed until 7 A.M. when the nurse enters with his pills.

Anclote was expensive—about $150 per day. To make matters worse, Cal also owed the hospital in Ocala over $1,000 and Ellen Stewart over $2,000, since she had paid some of the Bellevue expenses and for his and Raymond's flights to Florida. Since Vada and Cal's inheritance was tied up in real estate and they had little real cash at their disposal, she contemplated selling their house by the river in order to afford the two-year treatment program. Cal objected strongly. After three months of negotiating about the costs at Anclote, the officials suddenly decided to discharge him. They claimed that he was cured, but in reality the real reason for his discharge was financial—Anclote demanded more money than Vada was able to pay. She paid them a little over $11,000 for his three months stay, but she could not afford to keep him there any longer.

The day he was released, April 14, 1976, Miss Vada drove him to Ocala to begin his psychotherapy sessions with Dr. Henderson. In addition to the once-a-week meetings that were a combination of individual and group sessions, the doctor continued the Anclote medications—Elavil, Prolixin, and Cogentin. As expected, Cal suffered from the typical side effects—drowsiness, decreased sexual ability, and weight gain.

While still at Anclote, he had written to Jacques, "I'm not going to be 'well' enough to head north for some time. Please know that unless I am some good to myself I can't be any good for you or anyone else.... I can't ask you to 'wait' or even pretend. In other words, your life must go on.... We will always be friends." Sometime later, Cal wrote at the top of his copy of the letter, "The hardest letter I ever wrote."[28] Cal then asked his cousin Van and wife Virginia to drive to New Jersey to retrieve his personal belongings.

He lived at his Ozello mobile home, beginning his day drinking three or four cups of strong coffee, writing in his journal, and reading—John Steinbeck's *Winter of Our Discontent* and D.H. Lawrence's *Sons and Lovers*. Lawrence's account of a young man who yearns for his parents' love and acceptance, yet seeks independence and searches to define himself sexually and emotionally, Cal found especially "relevant to me at this time."[29] Around noon, he would drive into town and have lunch with his mother. Sometimes Miss Vada would surprise him by driving out to Ozello with a homemade lunch or dinner for the two of them. He began to notice "there was a certain touching quality about her concern....My breakdown," he wrote, "may have strengthened our relationship."[30] Their conversation that often centered on their financial problems—how were they going to pay the mounting medical bills— depressed Cal, but he marveled at how remarkably strong his mother had become. "I guess Vada has won the battle. I am now totally in her control."[31]

He wrote to Florida State University to learn what he could do to complete his undergraduate degree. The answer was "nothing." Since fourteen years had passed from when he last attended and since he had failed several courses, the admissions office advised that it would be a long haul. On June 18, 1976, he drove to Central Florida Community College in Ocala, and after meeting with a counselor, registered for an English literature course. He was determined to go back to school and earn a degree, knowing full well the scheme would probably take two or three years. But he flunked the first test and stopped attending, confessing, "I have no discipline to guide me."[32] He skipped the final exam.

His dream of becoming a successful playwright had not disappeared. Just days after Cal was released from Anclote, Fred Chappell asked him to submit something for a play reading series he was planning for the studio at Atlanta's Alliance Theatre. The result was a play he titled "Fragments," which he had begun to write for director Andrei Serban before he was hospitalized. Since he had perceived his writing in this play was a real breakthrough in style, Fred's rejection was hard to accept. Only later did he come to realize the script was nothing but nonsense syllables.

Cal had decided to find a new psychiatrist. After four months of weekly sessions with Dr. Henderson, he had become bored and felt they were just killing time during his appointments. Furthermore, he wanted a doctor who would agree to stop all medications. On September 20, he drove to Gainesville for his first appointment with Dr. Phil Cushman, who would continue to see Cal for the next twenty-two years. Immediately, Cushman concluded that Cal, even after three months at Anclote and four months with Dr. Henderson, was still in very bad shape. He disagreed with the Anclote diagnosis, however. He thought that Cal suffered from a bipolar disorder, a mental illness defined by rapid mood swings from manic joy and excitement to deep depression. He was manic depressive and not paranoid schizophrenic.

Even with this new psychiatrist, Cal was impatient and questioned some of his advice. Didn't Cushman realize that just eighteen months earlier Cal was "crazy as a fucking loon?"[33] Cushman believed that Cal was becoming too reclusive and urged him to find ways of being more social. He auditioned for a play being presented by one of the community theatres in Gainesville, but he was not cast. When he drove to Gainesville for his weekly appointments, he always arranged to meet his friend Tony for dinner, and then spent the night with him, returning to sexual enjoyment after nine months of celibacy. Reluctantly, he agreed to attend family gatherings and even to host them. On New Year's Eve, for instance, he sponsored a big fish and oyster fry on the island with a large family group, including his cousins and their families. Nevertheless, he did not really enjoy the gatherings. "It was a loud and raucous group," he wrote after they had all left. "I sat thru it all on the fringes, waiting knowing they would all be gone soon enough and the island would be mine in all its solitariness—solitude—apartness—aloneness—oneness with oneself."[34]

By the summer of 1977, he had decided he needed to visit friends in California, not just for a relaxing holiday, but to escape. As he grew stronger, Cal resumed more of his former feelings toward his mother. He had never felt loved, never felt wanted. "The guilt of my birth," he insisted. "That is why I must get away from her. I must flee the guilt. That is the only way to obliterate it. I can't deal with it rationally."[35] He often said, "I must atone for my birth."

He arrived in Santa Monica on July 16, 1977, where he stayed with an old friend named Tommy and his partner Jim. His days were lazy and characterized by withdrawal. He would lie until late afternoon, reading Flannery O'Connor's *Wise Blood* and *The Violent Bear It Away*. His eyes would tire of reading, but still he did not move. He had no desire to go cruising at the gay bars: "The fun game that used to be has dried up and blown away."[36] He wanted to write, but his pen lay immobile on the table. He wanted to telephone his old friend, Grainger Hines (Brother), but he was anxious about how to explain his breakdown.

On July 29, he took a shuttle flight to San Francisco and was picked up at the airport by his friend and host, Michael Brennan, known as QUEEN MAB. They had met several years earlier when Cal was still in Atlanta. After dropping off his luggage at MAB's apartment and eating a fast hamburger in the Castro district, they took off for the leather bars where Cal saw masters, slaves, piss queens, and shit freaks. In one corner, a man urinated on a naked man lying in a bathtub. Across the room was an old-style shoe-shine stand with raised chairs and metal foot braces. Slaves were licking the shoes/boots of the men in the chairs. The odor of marijuana prevailed. They stayed until closing time and then, as they drove downtown past hustler's row, he was reminded of his New York adventures with a can of Crisco by the bed and a bottle of poppers in the freezer.

For nearly a year, Cal had avoided picking up tricks in bars, but that now changed. His second night in San Francisco, he dressed in butch attire, walked to a Castro bar, and shortly before closing time invited a young man back to the apartment. To Cal's dismay, after eighteen months of near abstinence, he remained impotent: "It is as if when the brain exploded the sexual area of my head (if not the heart) was completely burned out.... I've lost something that was very special to me and thus far have nothing compensatory to replace it with."[37] A few days later, he added, "I am impotent and like a sleeping prince I await someone's gentle kiss to awaken my slumbering libido. Will he find me? Will it come? Or am I condemned forever to be a barren voyeur?"[38]

Unlike his days in Santa Monica, Cal ventured out to explore the city. He and MAB drove to the Mission district to see all the Victorian town houses in their kaleidoscope of dazzling colors, rode across the Golden Gate Bridge, toured the Palace of Fine Arts, prowled around the Market Street bookstores, watched the tourists climb aboard the trolley cars, stopped by the flower vendors. On August 2, they saw Vincent Price performing as Oscar Wilde in the one-man stage play, *Diversions and Delights*. In an attempt to earn money, Wilde speaks to the audience about his life, his works, and his love for Bosie. Cal was enthralled, calling it "an eloquent plea for gay liberation."[39] In spite of his disappointing sexual adventure, Cal looked on San Francisco as an incredibly international and European city and contemplated spending the entire winter there.

He returned to Crystal River, however, in mid-August. Fred Chappell's ex-lover, Don Tucker, who was performing his one-man show at the Sea Ranch Dinner Theater, invited Cal to Fort Lauderdale for a long week-end. He stayed in an old 1940s type motel most of the day, enjoying air-conditioning that he did not have in his mobile home. Probably due to his medication, he felt no sexual despair or panic to drive out into the night to find a trick. Following one performance, they had a drink in the lounge and then went barhopping. Cal was disappointed that the Poop Deck had lost all of its former madness and had become just a dried-up gay bar with a clientele of old men and hustlers.

Waiting for him when he returned to Crystal River was a disturbing letter from his New York roommate, Johnny Ferdon. Cal had written to him previously about his plans to return to New York, but Johnny's response was ferocious. Cal would not be welcome to stay with him. Johnny wanted his privacy. Since the letter from Johnny does not exist, the actual contents are debatable. Was Johnny just trying to explain that he doubted if Cal was well enough to move back? Was Cal overreacting? In the same journal entry, Cal writes that he had also lost the friendship of Grady McClendon. Grady, he complains, deserted him after his break-down. His complaint seems baseless. After all, Grady helped him leave Bellevue, cared for him in his apartment for several days, telephoned Miss Vada about his breakdown, and assisted Ellen Stewart in getting Cal back to Florida. And one time, when Cal was at his lowest in New York and could not lift a finger to clean anything in the apartment, Johnny came over, saw the filthy toilet and proceeded to clean it as well as the mess in the kitchen—not the actions of a friend who would desert you. Probably Cal's response to Johnny's letter and his annoyance with Grady were just part of his recurring paranoia.

Energized by his trip to Fort Lauderdale, Cal turned his atten-tion again to playwriting. He dug up an old copy of his *In a Garden of Cucumbers* and studied how he might rewrite it for the dinner theatre circuit. Hoping to inspire his writing, he read all the plays of Bertolt Brecht and Sam Shepard, but it was Samuel Beckett's *Waiting for Godot* that helped him find his way back to writing. Beckett's "nothingness of everything appeals to me greatly," he admitted, "particularly at this time when my life is such a big nothing. Beckett has shown me how to take nothingness and use it in one's writing."[40] He began to work on a new script that he later called *Stool Play #1 (requiem)* and sent copies to Fred Chappell and to Ellen Stewart—neither were interested.

He was back in San Francisco by mid-October. Traveling with only a couple of satchels full of clothes and a bag of papers, Cal convinced himself that he needed "the stimulus of life, of the living of it, to spur me on to the next plateau—whatever that may be."[41] He had denied and fled from the sexual side of his nature, believing that it was the cause of his breakdown. Now, he was hopeful as he flew across the country on November 14, 1977—"I emerge after two years of hiding my life head-on again."[42]

And head-on it was! After his friend Michael Brennan (MAB) picked him up at the airport, they headed immediately for beer at The Rainbow Cattle Company, followed by a stop at The Bootcamp, and finally to The Leatherneck. At this point, Cal began to enumerate his sexual con-quests in his journals. Trick #1 was Tom, a typical slave, well-trained and very subservient. Tom wanted a master, and he definitely got one in Cal. Addressing Cal as "sir," Tom stripped him, worshipped his feet, licked his toes, sucked on his jockey shorts, and drank his piss while Cal slapped his buttocks with his belt as fiercely as he could. The next morning, Cal sat on Tom's face, while he sucked Cal's asshole. "My two year's long

sexual hiatus is ended," he cheered.[43] Indeed, in one day he was catapulted immediately back two years to the leather bars of Gotham. The
next night he returned to The Leatherneck and went home with trick
#2, Al. On day three, he purchased a lid of grass for $50 and stayed stoned
as much as possible. In one week, he had scored with five tricks. He
and MAB continued their relentless search for cock, sometimes with the
assistance of acid. On November 3, just about closing time at The Stud,
he met trick #9, a twenty-one-year-old Canadian by the name of Chris
Trohimchuk, otherwise known as Mr. Stealth Penis, or, as Cal described
him, "Canadian bacon of the finest and most succulent variety."[44] Cal
invited Chris to help him inaugurate his new apartment at 244 Hermann
Street that he had moved into earlier that day. In days to follow, there
were Rene, Jack, Roy, and Eric.

By mid-November, Cal was once again questioning his excessive
behavior of too many joints, too many late hours, too many nights spent
cruising desperate homosexual alleyways, and far too much sexual and
alcoholic debauchery. "The party's over," he insisted. "Reality enters the
picture and it is time to get to work."[45] One week later, on November
23, he began to see on a weekly basis Dr. Tom Smith, a psychiatrist and
director of the Alcoholism Evaluation and Treatment Center.

Cal's paranoid delusions, fears, and suicidal thoughts had returned.
Upon examining some of Cal's journals, Smith concluded that his writings revealed "obsessive thinking with marked guilt overlay and feelings
of low self esteem." He agreed with the original Anclote diagnosis of
paranoid schizophrenic and set clear goals for Cal—"increase sociability,
playwrighting and return to gainful employment"—and he prescribed
Elavil and Prolixin.[46] In less than three months, Smith could see marked
improvement in Cal's sociability and writing.

Indeed, following his initial meeting and diagnosis with Smith, Cal
became much more productive. He began once again to revise *In a Garden
of Cucumbers* and to work on several new scripts—*A Conversation for the
Duke and Duchess of Windsor, Berma Returns to the Stage, Poiret in Exile, Wet
Paint*, and a one-woman show about Flannery O'Connor for actress and
friend Dana Ivey. Tom Smith, who had become a good friend and was
not charging Cal for his therapy sessions, commissioned Cal to compose
dialogues to accompany images that he was creating for a slide show to
be presented in his studio. A few weeks later, Cal hand delivered several
of his scripts to Theatre Rhinoceros. He even ventured out to see a new
Sam Shepherd play, *Buried Child*, spending $4.50 for a ticket, which was
two day's of groceries. He left after the first act, "bored beyond any
remotely bearable degree of tedium."[47] Unfortunately, regardless of his
renewed interest in writing, no theatre productions materialized.

Figure 4.1 Tom Smith quickly became one of Cal's closest friends.

Source: Courtesy Cal Yeomans Collection, Special Area Studies, George A. Smathers Libraries, University of Florida.

At the same time, he continued his sexual and alcoholic debauchery. The fun and excitement of the party may have been over, but he continued to party. Unfortunately, the men he went home with began to seem empty and uninteresting. Even after taking a myriad of drugs, he could still feel no magic in the encounters. Very late in a dark school yard near Castro Street, he began sucking a dick that was sticking through the chain-link fence surrounding the basketball court. Suddenly, a giant spotlight exploded the night and like a cop show on television, they were exposed. It was the police, who took their drivers' licenses, called headquarters, and learned that Cal's trick was wanted for murder. After spending another night with a chubby, young boy in a tiny room of a dismal flophouse, Cal sobbed, "If I were to ever find myself reduced to having to live in such a rat hole, there really would be nothing left but suicide."[48] Yet this is exactly what he had been reduced to in his sexual pursuits.

On May 3, 1978, he was admitted to a detox house. Tom Smith wanted to start Cal on lithium treatments, commonly used for bipolar disorders, but Cal was terrified of the potential side effects—muscle tremors, twitching, kidney damage, and seizures. Instead, he agreed to being incarcerated, free to leave whenever he chose. He slept restlessly on an old single bed stretched with worn-out, old cotton sheets. Rather than staying tucked in around the plastic-covered mattress, the sheets writhed like insatiable snakes around his burned-out body. He would awaken often due to delirium tremens. "I'm burned out," he admitted, "really burned out. Being here is the only place I could get the rest I need."[49] He remained there for several days. A major result was his decision to abstain from all alcohol and eventually join Alcoholics Anonymous.

He was almost destitute. After paying his $230 rent each month, he had only $67.50 of his monthly allotment to spend each week for utilities, groceries, and other bills. Tom had recommended that Cal get a job. On July 24, 1978, Cal took the first step by visiting Connie Elliott at a state vocational rehab office: "Today I throw myself on the mercy of the state, admit I am a hopelessly floundering casualty."[50] But he had not worked in three years, could provide no references, and had no real job skills to speak of. To become self-supporting would give him self-respect and dignity, but he knew that he had always avoided assuming responsibilities. His decision to stop the job counseling was predictable. Just two days prior to his first session, he had concluded,

> I don't want and cannot accept the reality of getting a job....A small inheritance doled out over the years has made it possible for me to spend vast amounts of time doing only things which amused and gave me pleasure and encouraged the ludicrous notion that I am some kind of "star"

who is not subject to the normal and accepted requirements of society. I've come—spoiled child that I am—to believe vehemently that I am special and shouldn't have to endure the discomforts of honest labor.[51]

A few days later, Cal had a thrilling surprise. The old friend whom he thought he had lost forever, Grady McClendon, flew to San Francisco for a long weekend visit. They had a wonderful time. Cal invited several of his friends over for snacks. He was eager to show his old friend some of the bars he frequented, but mostly they just talked. "How lovely it was to have you here," Cal wrote after Grady left. "Truly it had been so long since we had shared that kind of communication and it was so very very exquisite to achieve it once more." He tried to impress on Grady that he was trying very hard "to reconstruct a good life from the rubble that was left" when he first arrived in San Francisco.[52]

No wonder Grady was as stunned as everyone else, when, on August 10, Cal flew back to Florida. He had told no one in advance, not even Grady McClendon, with whom he had just been having many serious, heartfelt discussions. His mental health and attitude were certainly improving, but he felt that there were too many elements about San Francisco that threatened his continued progress. He could see what was happening to Michael Brennan. Like Cal, he also fought against self-destructive demons within himself, had been in alcohol treatment centers, but was now returning to "demon-rum." Cal did not want that to happen to him. He had spent his ten months in San Francisco mostly stoned or drunk, and, as he later admitted, had "ingested every drug I'd ever heard of from Angel Dust to Kitty Litter." He had become increasingly desperate in another search for a lover. "This is not wise," he reasoned, "as the desperate make mistakes and in a world as tortured, demented, and drug-crazed as is the homosexual subculture, one mistake in the choice of a companion... can be fatal."[53] On August 5, Cal wrote in his journal, "I go away from all this soon; back to Florida and that is good." He was worn out from living in the "sordid sewer" of San Francisco and chose to flee for his sanity, if not his life. He was burned out, down and out, and broke. Soon after he returned to Crystal River, he wrote, "SF was all about getting out of the inertia and depression that had paralyzed me and that nothing here [in Crystal River] seemed to be able to cut.... I had the breakdown because the life I was trying to live was untenable.... I went to SF and I tried to live the same old way and prove that it could work. It didn't."[54] He knew that he was flirting with the mysteries of S&M just like he had done three years earlier and felt like he was "on an express train to a place that I knew I didn't want to go, but I thought that I would ride-on a bit further and get off somewhere before the last Terminal. I did," he realized. "At a stop called Bellevue."[55] With only one thought in his mind—stay out of a mental hospital—he went home.

For eighteen years, Cal had been running away from Crystal River and what he considered the ignorance and poverty of the uneducated, conservative people who had always ridiculed him. "It's been such a long journey. A young boy left—1961," he acknowledged. "An old man returns—1978."[56] What would happen to him now? How would he manage back in this town he loathed? Would he find a lover? Would he ever succeed as a playwright? Who knew?

CHAPTER 5

"I AM A NAME"

Cal recognized immediately that he had made the right decision in returning to Florida. The day he arrived, he found his mother sitting in a house with no heat, with a toilet that would not flush, a sink that would not drain, and eating little more than bread and water and gumdrops. He was needed "to hold an old woman's hand as she makes her slow walk toward the grave."[1] Days later, Miss Vada went outside to wash some turnips, forgetting that she had left a pot on the stove turned to high. Somehow she stayed outside too long, and the water boiled away, filling the house with smoke. She panicked, became terribly confused, and feared the house was going to burn down. Rather than turn off the burner, she pulled all the main electric fuses. When Cal saw her later in the afternoon, he was shaken with how depressed she was. "It wouldn't go off!" she cried. "It wouldn't go off!" She was convinced that she needed to move into a convalescent home. Cal wrote in his journal that night, "I must somehow stay well, on top of it, and keep my wits. *Somehow* she is going to finish her life in dignity, tranquility, and comfort. From now on out, ANYTHING I may need, desire, or want is secondary to that. It is the least I can do. And I will do it somehow."[2]

Complicating matters was their finances. Although Cal's father had managed to accrue quite a fortune, owning nearly half of downtown Crystal River as well as dozens of rental houses, Cal and his mother were actually real-estate poor. Their money was tied up in property, and they had little cash. In order to pay taxes and living expenses through the years, Miss Vada had been prey to any unscrupulous opportunist who came along. People would drive up and say, "I want to buy that lot for $100," and she'd say, "yes"—even though the lot was worth ten times as much. She would argue that she had to "whittle it down" in order to handle the properties they owned. Cal quickly realized that it was a miracle that anything remained of their wealth.[3]

He knew that his job of caring for his mother and the family business would not be easy. For one thing, Miss Vada did not trust him. Through the years, he had often come and gone. He had never stayed in town very long, so she naturally expected him to leave at any time. But now, Cal became his mother's constant caregiver. At eighty years old, she found that managing the house by the river and maintaining the four acres of gardens too burdensome, so he helped her move back to the house where he had grown up at 311 NE Ninth Street. The house and garden were both smaller, making it much easier for her to handle.

Although Cal approved of her decision and even helped her move—painting rooms, repairing the plumbing, and generally getting the house ready for her—he was uncomfortable in the old house. It was where he had slept in the same bed with his mother until he was eight and in the same room with her until he was in high school, it was next door to where his boyhood friend molested him almost daily, it was where he witnessed the odd and loveless relationship between his parents, it was where he yearned for love from his daddy, it was where he lived when he first felt unaccepted and teased, it was where he felt jealous and resentful of the attention his cousin Van received. To Cal, it was "a depressing old house filled with an atom bomb of memories."[4] The ever present, lingering ghosts convinced Cal that he could not live there permanently with his mother. He chose instead to remain at the house by the river, making frequent excursions to his mobile home on Ozello Island. The periods when he stayed on the island, he always went to town and had lunch with his mother.

He took care of the family business, cooked many of their meals, and doted on Miss Vada. He was able to see so clearly how his mother had suffered her entire life from the guilt of being responsible for her baby sister's death and had yearned for her father's love. He enjoyed seeing her and her "swamp buddies" put on blue jeans and boots and wade thru swamps once or twice a week, collecting driftwood, interesting sticks, and old scraps of iron. She would paint them bright, florescent colors and position them throughout her garden. Cal once chuckled that people might think she is a crazy woman, particularly during a full moon when they were especially eerie at night. Cal's Atlanta friend, Raiford Ragsdale, labeled them "Florida Gothic." It did not take him long to see that his mother was feeling more confident that he was going to stay with her. "A bit of our old closeness grows, I'm glad that it's happening in these last years. It's the only true affection I've ever known."[5]

By early November 1978, however, Cal was already feeling rejected by the townspeople and complained to Tom Smith: "Circumstances are fairly grim. I am all but spit on as I wander about THIS town. It seems

Figure 5.1 Cal often escaped to his mobile home where he could relax.

Source: Courtesy Cal Yeomans Collection, Special Area Studies, George A. Smathers Libraries, University of Florida.

they endured all of my 'PLAYBOY' antics up and through my break-down—even managing to conjure sympathy for me then, but fleeing to SF for one last party, leaving the grieving and increasingly senile mother cold all last winter...has finished me off in everyone's eyes....The general consensus of opinion in the 'village' is hostile and against me....I find people I've never met who...scorn my very existence. So I've lived now to become a despicable scum."[6]

One fall evening, Cal decided to drive out to Gulf Island Beach where he knew there was active gay cruising and a popular glory hole. After sitting for a few minutes at a picnic table near the men's restroom, a car drove up, parked, and the handsome, young driver strolled into the toilet. The man was very nervous. It was the first time he had visited the toilet, but it was the only place where he knew to meet other men. Cal followed. After making the right signals, Cal knelt down and looked through the hole in order to check out what was on the other side. It was dark, but as soon as Cal could see the man's face, he whispered abruptly, "I can't do this! Meet me outside." And he dashed out the door. The young man zipped up, exited, and then walked over to where Cal was leaning up against his car. "I couldn't do it," Cal explained. "I'm Calvin Yeomans. I went to high school with your mother!" Michael Parker, who was eighteen years old and searching for his sexual identity, found a mentor. He knew that he had "found one of the best friends of my life."[7]

That Thanksgiving, Cal and his mother were invited to nearby Sanford to share the holiday dinner with his cousin, Van, and his family. Cal was apprehensive about going. He had not seen his cousin for several years and wondered if the old tensions of their childhood would still exist. How would he be treated? Would his relatives be like the ugly folks in Crystal River? It was a classic feast, but Cal felt no family warmth or love and that Miss Vada "was being treated as an outcast because of her age and gentle senility."[8] No one felt comfortable, and Van was, indeed, hostile. When she learned of the incident, one of Cal's friends wrote to him that she thought Van was probably jealous of Cal, that Cal had usurped his place in Crystal River as well as some inheritance.[9]

For several months after his return to Crystal River, he had tried to avoid all writing. "I've been so down and out about writing lately. Abysmally so. Terminally so. I had convinced myself it was all a JOKE and I tried to stop, wanted to stop, wanted to end it never more to write again, but u-know I couldn't. It's habit now. Each day found me scribbling away in the journal. I couldn't quit. And now I don't want to. I want to write on & on & on & 'sing 'em all,' as Judy screamed so long ago in Carnegie Hall."[10] Playwriting became his therapy. His mother had often advised him, "Keep your hands busy and you will be alright." He took her advice. As he explained in a letter to Tom Smith, "It's write or die. So I write."[11]

A year earlier, Cal's playwriting had begun to take on a much more personal and autobiographical tone. What had originally inspired him to rethink his approach to playwriting was seeing Lanford Wilson's *The*

Madness of Lady Bright. Back in 1977, when he was visiting friends in San Francisco, he saw Wilson's play at Theatre Rhinoceros. "I was so struck by this fabulous thing," he told a reporter, "—you could write a play that didn't make sense for anyone but gay people. It was liberating."[12] As he recalled a few years later, "I wrote plays for years—or tried to—trying to pass for white and be heterosexual and nothing—absolutely nothing happened. Finally—after a long series of discouraging events and frustrating years—I said 'Fuck it' and started writing as honestly as I could—which meant, for me, frequently writing truthfully up front gay plays. Then and only then did my plays begin to be done. Then and only then did I become a functioning playwright."[13]

During those summer weeks in July in San Franciso, he had managed to finish writing a play, even though he complained that his writing was seriously reflecting the absence of grass. "I need it desperately," he confessed, "to free my pen and allow the words to flow like sensuous flesh-colored velvet. I shall try to fake my way through them without it."[14] The resulting play was *Richmond Jim*. But rather than send it off to Fred Chappell or to Ellen Stewart, this time he just set it aside, letting it simmer on the back burner for awhile. There is no doubt that he now felt more liberated than ever before. "I don't care really if they [my plays] make grown men puke or have hemoroids [*sic*] or apoplexy or the unending shits;" he wrote.[15] "I don't have to try to please anyone but myself and am free to make them [my plays] as homoerotic as I wish. For my own pleasure. God knows I have nothing better to do."[16]

He agreed to collaborate with Tom Smith on a new performance project. Known by his friends as Alma Rainbow, Tom, whose main interest outside his psychiatric practice was photography, came up with the idea to present four soliloquies, all to be accompanied with his original, projected, visual images. Cal agreed to write two of them, the first and last, which he titled *Poiret in Exile* and *Somebody's Angel Child*. Ultimately, the complete performance was titled *The Tenderloin Suite*, and was four monologues—*Poiret in Exile*, *Tony*, *Bernadette*, and *Somebody's Angel Child* that they described as "a series of photo poems, shimmering images of mercurial despair." All are set in rooms of San Francisco's Alcazar Hotel on Eddy Street. A fleabag hotel, it is "home to people on the move, people on the fringe—the poor, the bizarre, the lost....The aged get mugged, the punks get stoned, the czars make money, the Johns get canned and the alkies die."[17]

Cal's intent in *Poiret in Exile* was to suggest a day in the life of someone like French fashion designer Paul Poiret. Cal had become fascinated with the life of Poiret back in the 1960s when he was teaching fashion at Massey College in Atlanta. In the early 1900s, he had revolutionized women's fashions, introducing simple yet elegant lines of the Art Deco style and removing the rigid constraints of the corset. Although at one point he attracted a large clientele of famous women, he died in 1944, penniless and forgotten. Cal wanted the play to be about "the Poiret in all of us—the part of our nature that craves the wild, the exotic, the grand, the impossible. It is the tale of a man who, unable to adjust to anything else, was destroyed by his penchant for noble excess."[18]

As the play opens, the audience sees on an upstage screen an image of a sunrise on a barren beach while Poiret says,

> Sometimes, early in the morning before
> the sun has even thought of rising
> i awake and realize my own
> reality and...
> how welcome death would be.
> but then, as always, a bit of light dawns in the east.

A few minutes later, he asks,

> who would have thought...?
> who would ever have thought
> that the thing that is me
> could have become
> the thing that you see?

The image of the beach dissolves into his current prison, a dismal room in the Alcazar Hotel. He proceeds, examining and questioning his life and past actions,

> what did I do wrong I wonder
> but I know
> I pushed too much too far
> for too long beyond the beyond
> and I paused to pick too many flowers.

The play was a mad, insane monologue of an educated, artistic, cultured man who once had accomplishments, achievements, status, success, and contentment and lost it all, and in the process lost his mind. Cal admitted to a good friend that he was scared by how deeply into madness he had to go himself in order to write the piece.[19]

His character of Brandi in *Somebody's Angel Child* was a transsexual, perhaps even the first transsexual portrayed in a drama. The man was envisioned as "very beautiful, as close to looking like a beautiful young woman as possible, with ample buxom [bosoms] and a medium sized cock and balls (cock should get hard at one point)." She lives in the tenderloin hotel, drinks frequently, and makes voodoo type dolls out of wire, shells, bones, and black cloth. At the end, as she walks along the highway, a spaceship swoops down and carries her off.[20] "There is so much of my own experience to be used here," Cal wrote. "I understand being picked up by a flying saucer completely. . . . I did just that. . . I was running from THEM because I knew that THEY were coming to pick me up—well finally after a zillion miles THEY did, but it was a paddy wagon to Bellevue, but for all practical purposes, it might as well have been a flying saucer. . . . The pathology of emotional derangement seems to have certain motifs that recur and are rather universal."[21] Tom, who had counseled many transsexuals in his psychiatric practice, was ecstatic when he received Cal's contribution. "You have written a script that is consistent with their lives, their personal concerns. Your editing, your humor makes for extraordinary theater," he applauded. "I am overwhelmed by the genius of your work."[22]

Insisting on truthfulness and accuracy, Tom took risks in creating the necessary images. One evening, he and Michael Lundigan, a tough-looking hustler who was cast in *Tony*, ventured into San Francisco's tenderloin district to take photographs for the production, not quite expecting the filth and danger they encountered. Tom was shooting photos of Michael walking in the streets, peeing in alleyways, sleeping in cardboard boxes, and peering into shopwindows. As he was staring at a collection of vibrators in the window of a porn shop, the huge, 250 pound shop clerk, charged out the door with a baseball bat and yelled at them to move on. They then rented a sleazy hotel room, complete with filthy sheets, naked lightbulbs, and roaches—the kind of room where the characters of the play might have lived—and took pictures of Michael in the room and on the bed. Because of these incredibly vivid, projected visual images, the script was similar to Cal's earlier *Swamp Play #2* in being dependent on production in order to be fully understood. In May 1979, Tom presented *Poiret in Exile* for an invited audience, and the following October, Theatre Rhinoceros produced the complete *Tenderloin Suite* for a benefit performance in a church fellowship hall.

Audience reaction to the production was mixed, ranging from dead silence to verbose ambivalence. *Poiret* was the most misunderstood of the four scripts with comments "I hated it." "Too long." "I hate poetry." Several complained that they had trouble focusing on both the visual and the auditory at the same time. *Brandi*, the monologue of the transsexual, was the star of the evening, seeming to have more popular appeal than the others. Tom vowed that he would present it again—not in a church, but in an art gallery.

Regardless of Tom's enthusiasm, Cal did not go to San Francisco to see the performances. All he could think about at the time was his own survival and could not indulge in flights of fancy about his plays. Once Cal completed the monologues for *The Tenderloin Suite*, he wrote to Tom, "I truly think that will be my swan song to writing for awhile. It's all winding down around me. I've almost stopped writing in my journal. The need is no longer there. I don't think I ever had too much to offer 'literature', so it's no great loss."[23] Although Cal always appreciated Tom's encouragement to keep writing, he felt that it was a full-time job just finding a new, positive life to live.

Besides his writing, another important and healthy outlet for Cal was attending Gay Talk, a discussion group initiated by the psychology department at the University of Florida to provide an alternative to the bars for the gay students and the community. Every Tuesday evening, a core group comprised of students as well as community people would meet to examine a variety of topics—the biography of a gay author, steps in writing wills, religious perspectives, fears of coming out—and after the meeting regroup at The Ambush, a popular gay bar in Gainesville.

The day after a meeting on December 3, Cal noted in his journal that he had become "aware last night that young Jon—a member of the gay rap group I attend has grown interested in me. He made definite overtures so perhaps I will ask him for a date." Three days later, he vowed, "At the age of 40 I feel a new man trying to find his way into existence.... 'Cal' is dead. 'Cal' was born on the lips of Fergus Currie when I arrived at Flat Rock Playhouse so very long ago.... I am going to try to find my way back to Calvin: the person before and beyond Hollywood. The person outside the demented dream."[24] They must have had quite a date; Jon was smitten.

During the spring semester, when Jon was taking classes at the university, he found time to write Cal frequent letters.[25]

February 22, 1979: "You're terribly distracting! You keep popping in and out of my mind all the time."
May 1979: "You're a beautiful man Cal Yeomans and I'm so glad that our paths intertwine at these times. You have done wonders for me."

Jon Wesley Porch, a sophomore student at the university, was fascinated with Cal's worldliness and how he added a confidence of legitimacy to being gay. During the spring semester, he drove to Crystal River

Figure 5.2   Cal was thrilled to meet Jon Porch.

Source: Courtesy Cal Yeomans Collection, Special Area Studies, George A. Smathers Libraries, University of Florida.

every weekend and stayed with Cal at the house by the river. "For me it was most magical because I had the mere responsibilities of a child but was experiencing the pleasures of an adult," he recalled. "Our relationship was somewhat Greek in that he was the 'older' man teaching me about art and gay culture—and I believe he thought of it that way." As Jon later acknowledged, "We were lovers. The relationship had a strong sexual angle. I was a horny college student after all, and he was handsome. He was very free-spirited and natural about sex."[26]

They spent hours talking and listening to music, mostly opera and musical theatre—and smoking a lot of marijuana. Mostly it was idyllic, quiet days enjoying the stunning beauty and nature surrounding the house by the river. On their daily, long walks, Cal pointed out all the native plants that grew in the area—purple lizard flower, purple spike, red lobelia. A favorite was the potato vine that had giant, heart-shaped leaves that wound up and around tree trunks and produced large tubers on the vine that looked like potatoes. Another pastime was creating stories out of the photos in old albums Cal would buy in flea markets and junk shops.

As his relationship with Jon was developing, Cal received a surprise invitation. One reason he had left San Francisco and had contemplated winding down his writing was that it appeared that the plays he had submitted to Theatre Rhinoceros were all being rejected. Suddenly, out of the blue, he received a letter from Guy Bishop that had been mailed to his Hermann Street apartment in San Francisco and then forwarded to Crystal River. Bishop wanted to direct Cal's *Richmond Jim* at Theatre Rhinoceros.

Back in 1973, while Cal was working in the box office at La MaMa, "a little painfully young kid latched" onto him. Having just arrived in the city, the seventeen-year-old boy was naïve, awkward, and terrified. Cal took him back to his apartment and upon seeing the boy's ass remarked, "Baby they are going to be after that." Cal held him as best he could on his mattress on the floor. He held him "and caressed the satin skin...I sucked his dick and caressed and talked."[27] This incident became the basis for *Richmond Jim*, his first, major playwriting success. It premiered at the Theatre Rhinoceros as part of a double bill titled *Male Rites*, the other play being C.D. Arnold's *Downtown Local*. Cal's script was selected as the city's Best Gay Play of the Year (1979) and was later published in *Folsom Magazine*.[28]

It is the story of an innocent, young man from Virginia who goes home with an older man he had met at a leather bar on his first night in New York City. As the play opens in an apartment in New York's Soho district, a young and innocent Jim and an older and macho Mike, who is experienced in S&M, are nude and lying under a sheet on a mattress placed on the floor. They have just had sex. They smoke a joint, drink wine, and sniff poppers. Mike invites Jim to stay for the night and begins to discuss various sex acts such as fucking, bondage, and torture.

As they start to work each others tits, Mike's friend, Biddy, a burnt-out, fed-up, and flamboyant cynic, enters. He encourages Jim to try fist-fucking. "It's a riveting experience," he exclaims. "Simply riveting." He complains that the first thing his tricks want to know is whether or not he is into piss. "I have tried and I have tried," he confesses, "but I cannot stomach it. I'm tired of puking on their feet." Shortly before he leaves, Biddy warns Jim, "After so many years of the same thing, you find you become jaded and search for more and more complex and involved sensual thrills. One thing leads to another until one day you wake up and discover you are a jaded old thing no longer capable of a simple act of love.... You be careful, my dear. You'll end up with your peter cut off in this city. It is ruthless. But, you know, don't be afraid to experiment. You might discover an infinity of new heavens." Prophetic, autobiographical writing by Cal. It is exactly his own story.

Alone again, Mike and Jim resume their discussion of different ways to have sex. The climax of the play comes when naked Jim faces the audience and, catching his reflection in an invisible mirror, removes

Figure 5.3   The flyer advertising the evening of *Male Rites*.

Source: Courtesy Cal Yeomans Collection, Special Area Studies, George A. Smathers Libraries, University of Florida.

Mike's leather chaps, cap, and vest from a trunk and puts them on. The stage directions read, "It would be natural if Jim began to get an erection." He slips on a pair of black leather boots and attaches keys to the chaps. Mike, who is also naked, then, in full view of the audience, slides a silver ring around Jim's cock, hands him handcuffs and bullwhip, kneels before him, and pleads, "The rest is up to you." An incredible metamorphosis has taken place. The script notes, "No trace remains of Richmond Jim."[29]

Cal flew to San Francisco in early May to participate in the rehearsals, taking Jon with him. Cal became so frustrated with Guy Bishop's directing that he banned himself from the theatre until opening night. One of Cal's main objections was Bishop's decision to change the end of the play. In the original script, after Mike hands Jim the handcuffs and whip, he then holds up a double-headed dildo before saying, "The rest is up to you." Bishop argued that the play built to a beautiful, ambiguous, sensual, sexy end, but every time he introduced the dildo in rehearsals and preview performances, it resulted in laughter—and at the one place in the play where it shouldn't. Bishop cut the dildo from the production. Cal was furious over the censorship and concluded that at Theatre Rhino a playwright was just an extraneous nuisance who knew nothing about the play.

During these battles with Bishop, Cal was consoled by some of his friends. One of Cal's old buddies, Vance (Joe) Hendrix, a struggling artist who had moved from Crystal River to rural Tennessee, cheered him up. "We think it wonderful that one of your children has been born in S.F.," he wrote. "We struggle we grow as like grass through concrete and only the strong survive....I hope your babe grows wings and from a seed turns into a masive [sic] old shade tree where under you may spend many a pleasant day."[30]

As might be predicted, when *Richmond Jim* opened, it met with some criticism. Doric Wilson was outraged, so much so that he and cabaret performer Bill Blackwell even considered organizing a protest outside the theatre. A critic for the *Bay Area Reporter* labeled the play "little more than staged pornography....Mutterings and sputterings of words like 'gross' and 'stupid' filtered through to my ears from other restless audience members."[31] *Databoy*'s Lee Hartgrave called it an argument for S&M that was "dreary, neurotic, and depressing."[32] William Albright, a critic for the *Houston Post*, thought the play "offered a sympathetic glance at rough sex" but thought it was "unevenly acted."[33] Some critics, such as *The Sentinel's* Neal Obstat, Jr., despised the script's "relentless descent into grimness" and were alarmed that the play won the Best Play of the Year.[34]

Cal wrote to his therapist friend, Tom Smith:

> If *Richmond Jim* had been a porno film no one would have batted an eyelash but since it passes itself off as a serious play then it stirs up a furor....They [the producers at Theatre Rhinoceros] are depicted as some kind of daring courageous innovators who risked *ALL* by presenting it. Really dear! If the live theatre is THAT far behind the sexual and erotic developments of real life, then we are in trouble....I had no idea my work was so far removed from that which people can deal with comfortably. I guess I've always been obscenely naïve but I NEVER thought I was outraging any- one's sensibilities. I don't know. I'm terribly confused and guilt ridden about my writing....I wanted to take SEX out of the closet and bring it into the forefront where it could be enjoyed with the ease of a bowl of popcorn and the naturalness of a swim on a hot day. The "clouds of unknowing" that keep it obscured in veils of mystery have caused it to become unnecessarily twisted and perverted. It frequently seems it is more usually understood as an act of aggression than as a manifestation of love and pleasure. In my work, I wanted to demystify it into Freedom. But now I've become self-conscious about my work and guilt ridden and I can no longer write of the sexual with any joy or pleasure.[35]

Cal was frustrated that some critics thought that he intended to provide prurient titillation and to glorify S&M. "I don't know which is worse," he wondered, "1) the kind of agony you suffer when your work isn't being done, or 2) the kind of agony you suffer when it is being done."[36] In truth, the play illustrates the very private debate that Cal was having with himself concerning his own questions about the leather scene that he had embraced. "S&M and leather sex is an aberration of the '70's that a sexually oppressed minority latched upon to emphasize and dramatize their right to be MEN," he argued. "Before the macho gays, we all had to wear Gucci loafers or fruit boots and hair spray and jade east and mince & coquette like deformed women. Now we are free to be men."[37]

Other critics seemed to get the point. Carl Driver of the *San Francisco Crusader* recognized that the play "could easily degenerate into nothing but a sex show. Instead it is a powerful slice-of-life drama....There are deeper levels to the play; interesting statements about youth and inno- cence and how quickly both can disappear."[38] Robert Chesley, who went on to write *Jerker* and *Night Sweat*, called it "the first genuinely gay play" whose "context and subject matter are a world known only to city gay men."[39] A story in *The Advocate* noted that the play "probably provoked more controversy and fear than almost any other play written for the gay stage."[40] When Joe Hendrix learned of the attacks on the play, he wrote to Cal that he was lucky to be in Florida and not in San Francisco. "This way," he wrote, "perhaps you'll be spared social diesection [*sic*] as in to take you apart to see your intermost [*sic*] workings—ah hell he ain't right, and such."[41]

In spite of some good reviews, positive audience response, and the play's run being extended, Cal agonized obsessively over the negative reviews. He plummeted into another great depression, worrying about his mother, worrying about his old age, even though he was only forty at the time. "If I could only stop worrying," he cried. "If I could find a way of dispelling the devastating insecurity and fear that my world is soon going to end in a great calamity. Death is almost preferable to the knife-edge unknowing that is currently ruining my life."[42] He had hoped that *Richmond Jim* would be a major breakthrough, but the battles he had fought with the director and the attacks by some critics left him feeling desperate.

In an interview for *The Advocate*, Cal defended his play.

> I remember some fellow took his mother to see "Richmond Jim." In the midst of Biddy's scene where Biddy charts the treacherous urban gay scene, she just started crying. Gay people didn't cry, but she cried. She saw the sadness. She saw the pain....It's a lot more fun to go to the theaters and laugh and giggle and be silly—the escapist thing—and a lot of gay playwrights I know are very lightweight, giddy, glib. There's a place for that, but there's more than that....A lot of people have died in the battle for all these freedoms we have.[43]

Fortunately, once he and Jon were back in Florida, Cal's mood changed for the better. Rather than attend summer school, Jon decided to live with Cal in Crystal River until classes began in the fall. Cal was ecstatic. "I am now a produced and successful playwright (artistically if not financially) and I also have a beautiful lover here to share this summer with me. I am a lucky man indeed. And happier than perhaps ever before....Most splendid of all: there is HOPE."[44] Rather than live together in town and be spied on by prying eyes, Cal decided they would spend most of their time at Cal's remote mobile home on Ozello. In the evenings, they watched the sun set over the gulf or drove down a long road through the marsh, dotted with cedar hammocks, until they arrived at a small man-made beach on the gulf where they sometimes swam nude. Jon always wanted to explore the cedar hammock trees. Cal convinced him that wild boars were a real threat, so they seldom did it.

At one point, Volkswagon started making Beetles again, and Cal bought a big, lemon-yellow one that was also a convertible. He and Jon would drive all over the countryside, blasting opera on the tape deck. Cal especially enjoyed turning the volume really loud on the few occasions they went through a McDonalds drive-through, chuckling that he wanted to make the local people aware that there were alternatives in music. The house on the river had no air-conditioning. When they stayed there on hot summer nights with the windows thrown wide open, they would turn up the volume full blast on the stereo.

Sometimes old Atlanta friends would drop in for a few days. Cal cooked fabulous meals during those visits. Jon once asked him how he learned to be such a good cook, and he said that, once in San Francisco while on an acid trip, he realized how to cook and had been good at it ever since. Among his specialties were panfried pork chops sprinkled with chili powder, potato salad dotted with capers, corn pone pie, beef back, fried ocra, and corn bread in a skillet. Fred Chappell and his wife Agnes visited for a long weekend. They stayed up late drinking and catching up on old times the last evening, so Jon excused himself. The next morning, Cal told him that there had been a terrible argument between them. Agnes kept describing her husband over and over as being gay "past" and "present." Fred would adamantly add, "AND FUTURE!"[45] Jon did not know that Cal and Fred had once been lovers.

Cal was so happy with his new lover that he composed five poems dedicated to Jon. One of them reads,

> your love is
> everywhere
> around me
> here in this room
> in this sunlight
> in this sweet primitive air
>
> your love is here with me
> and I am here with it
> and I am yours and you
> can have me here
> in the love
> in your sunlight

One evening, Cal was visited with an awful moment of truth. After supper with Miss Vada, he said good night and departed for his mobile home. Enroute to the island, he stopped at a laundromat to shrink a new pair of jeans he had bought. Once he finished, he decided to return to his mother's to share a cup of coffee with her on the front porch. She did not hear him return. When he entered the living room, he found her sitting in front of a blaring television, reading one of his journals that he had left in the back bedroom. "It was awful.... I know now that she has probably been reading my stuff indiscriminately. Dear God! The ramifications blew me away.... At first I felt like suicide then the paranoia: 'She will use these as evidence and have me committed.'" They had coffee; nothing was ever said. Cal calmed down by the time he returned to his mobile home, but, as he commented, "The journals were not composed for my Mother's eyes."[46]

The incident might have triggered a bout of depression if it had not been for a letter he received. To Cal's delight, he learned that Theatre Rhinoceros submitted *Richmond Jim* for the First National Gay Arts Festival in New York City. At first, The Glines, a nonprofit producing company who sponsored the festival, rejected it. Luckily, Robert Patrick defended the play. And when the producers threatened to censor the script before it opened, Terry Helbing, who was considering publishing it in his anthology of gay plays, strongly objected and convinced them to leave the script intact.[47] Before taking it to New York, Theatre Rhinoceros remounted it in early May 1980 as part of a triple bill that included Robert Chesley's *Hell, I Love You* and Lanford Wilson's *The Great Nebula in Orion*. Cal was overjoyed when he received the news that his play had beat out Chesley's and Wilson's for the coveted 1980 Cable Car Award for Outstanding Achievement in Drama.

In their advertising for the Gay Arts Festival, The Glines promoted the play as "innocence meets leather" and booked it for five performances, June 24–28, 1980, on a double bill with Lanford Wilson's *The Great Nebula in Orion*. The only New York review, which appeared in *About Town*, was very critical. Liam Martin disliked the "blatant & tactile nudity & fondling," the sadistic menacing of Mike, and ended his review with a damning question: "Is gay theatre necessarily such a good thing."[48] Fred Chappell was amused when he heard that Cal chose not to attend the performances. He remembered all the years the two of them had been so desperate, at their wits end, for just a hint of recognition, and that Cal would have flown to Cardin's in Paris just to shop for the right clothes to wear for an opening. He had to chuckle now, thinking of Cal lounging in his mobile home in the swamps of Florida and letting the New York critics squirm and stew over his play.[49] In truth, Cal remembered the panic he had felt on opening night at Theatre Rhino and did not want to live through a repeat performance.

Apparently unaware of Cal's frustration with his directing *Richmond Jim*, Guy Bishop wrote to Cal that he was interested in directing more of his plays. In fact, he thought Cal's early play, *In a Garden of Cucumbers*, was hilarious, a wonderful gem, and staged a reading of it a few months after *Richmond Jim* closed.[50] Lanny Bauginet and Tom Hinde played the lead roles of Carrie and Thelma in drag. Ironic, this is the same

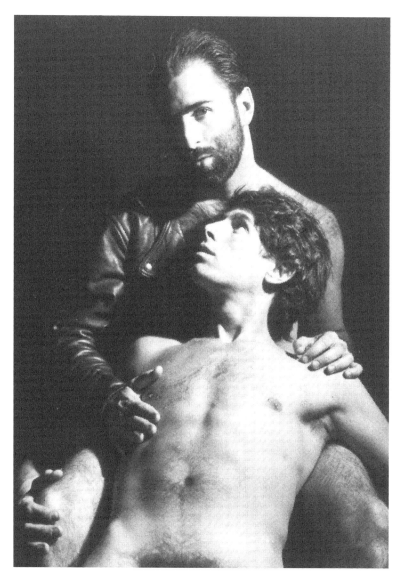

Figure 5.4 This photo of Jim (Randy Bennett) relaxing in the arms of Mike (Joe Cappetta) was used in New York for flyers, program covers, and souvenir T-shirts.

Source: Courtesy Cal Yeomans Collection, Special Area Studies, George A. Smathers Libraries, University of Florida.

play that Ellen Stewart had dismissed earlier as "pompous, fatuous and irrelevant."[51]

In the fall of 1979 and winter of 1980, during the months when Theatre Rhino was reviving *Richmond Jim*, and it was being rehearsed and performed in New York, Cal and Jon continued their relationship. Jon returned to the university, visiting Cal on weekends, and Cal moved more permanently to his mobile home. The letters Jon wrote to Cal never ceased being positive and loving:

February 11, 1980: "I miss the million dollar views at Ozello. . . . I want to feed the birds. . . . See ya soon!"

February 13, 1980: In a Valentine's card, Jon writes, "I remember last year about this time when I opened the mail and found a wonderful little card that said 'you're hot.' I was surprised. You had thought of me enough to send one. This weekend I get you! You're beautiful!! Be My Valentine, Cal. With much love, Jon."

Nothing in Jon's letters indicates he was questioning the future of their relationship.

The same is not true for Cal, even though he had seemed happy all summer. But after Jon moved back to Gainesville in the fall, he noticed that Cal "seemed to drink more during my weekend visits, and he would become increasingly negative." Cal had a little music box in the bathroom that played "Raindrops Keep Falling on My Head." When Jon asked him where it came from, Cal replied that friends had given it to him while he was in an institution. Nothing more was ever said. Jon did not take it very seriously, just assuming Cal had gone through some kind of difficult period that he did not want to share. Cal never discussed his bipolar disorder with Jon, nor did he ever mention his stays at Bellevue or Anclote Mental Hospital. Moreover, Jon did not understand Cal's decision to move to his mobile home in isolated Ozello. It was "a place that made ME sad and depressed—it just felt very lonely. . . . He had taught me to revel in being gay, and yet he was choosing to be more isolated."[52] Not until years later did Jon understand that these were symptoms of his mental illness.

They had a good Christmas together, but on January 1, 1980, Cal writes that he had spent New Year's Eve at a gloomy party with Jon in Gainesville. "Our affair probably won't survive much longer. The 20 year age difference looms as an insurmountable barrier. . . . Young Jon is just setting out on his 'Gay Life' and that has always been a difficult journey." The next day, he continued his observations. "When Jon is placed in the position of contrasting my aging and run-down carcass with the

Castro-type delights of the young men we were with New Year's Eve, he always encounters difficulty." Apparently, Cal had criticized Jon sharply and publicly for his excessive drinking and marijuana smoking at the party and now feared Jon was angry and would want to break up. "I miss you *so*!" he wept. "It seems I will learn to write…in lieu of you, Jon. I shall exchange flesh for words, touch for words, feel for words, but I won't forget how they really were when I held you close.…Did I teach you alright, son? Was it good? I'm sorry I wasn't number one."[53] And yet, three days later and after a weekend together with Jon on Ozello, Cal seemed more optimistic. "Jon and I were closer and more solid than we've ever been before.…He speaks of our future together in the years to come as if he plans for us to be together.…I will stay with him as long as he and circumstances will allow me to. He is the best thing, the most beautiful thing to ever happen to me."[54]

Cal's moods continued to fluctuate. Optimism for the future one day; fear of a split and being alone the next. By the end of January, he had come to realize that his relationship with Jon was over, and he sank into depression. Hoping to settle his anxiety, he began to take off unexpectedly for long weekends at a gay resort in Fort Lauderdale. "So the young man held the old man's hand for awhile," he brooded. "When the old man had been young, no one had cared enough about him to teach him anything. He had to learn about the mysteries of man to man love the hard way. When the old man was young, no one would make love with him more than once. He never understood why—still doesn't."[55] Valentine's weekend, Jon told Cal that he had taken on a new boyfriend. A few days later, Cal telephoned Jon in Gainesville and "broke down into uncontrollable tears" when he heard Jon's voice.[56] When Jon had returned to the university the fall of 1979, he had moved into an apartment with three other gay students who called themselves the "Screaming Foursome," and his life took on a whole new turn as he met new friends and developed a broader social circle. One of the new friends, Juan Carlos Morales who was a student in the university law school, became his lover. (As of 2011, Jon and Juan are still together, living in Houston.)

The fall of 1980, Theatre Rhinoceros presented another of Cal's plays. In *The Line Forms to the Rear*, again directed by Guy Bishop, a lonely, ex-drag queen named Henry, much like Biddy in *Richmond Jim*, insists, "I am not your average, run-of-the-mill glory hole faggot." Instead, he explains that he comes to the beach at sunset "administerin mercy sex to any and all comers. The man ain't walkin that I've turned down." He explains that "there's a mighty lot of sufferin out there cause people can't find nobody to touch em where they needs to be touched when they needs touching and I just said to myself.… Get out and do your part for the sufferin miserable and afflicted. Give all the pleasure you can and see what you get back in return." That is his mission—to "perform fee-lay-shee-oh on the masses." Just as he finishes his long monologue, an old leather queen enters and walks into the toilet. Henry turns to the audience and remarks, "Well, excuse me please. I got to get back to work." He heads for the toilet, turns back to the audience just before he reaches the door, and winks, "The line forms to the rear."

In a lengthy letter to Michael Brennan in San Francisco, Cal explained his motivation for the character of Henry.

> I wrote Henry...so that you urban gays would not forget that while you all are spending hard-earned cash-money buying your way into the lushly simulated thrills of plushly air conditioned, security guarded, completely authentically recreated TOILETS with padded, contoured, designer-created glory holes, that hundreds of thousands upon thousands of struggling, terminally oppressed rural gays still cannot *BEG* their way out of the real thing. We have no choice. I know you don't like Henry. Nobody does. That's the point. Henry has no place to go. He cannot get out of Podunk on the next Greyhound bus. He couldn't last 5 minutes in S.F. His I.Q. is probably 38. His education is somewhat staggering. Nevertheless he is a gay human being and therefore his needs need to be served—as do any human beings.... At the most Henry is waiting for a reason to keep living in a world that loathes his very physical presence and at the least he is just spanning and occupying that thing that terrifies us all out here so very VERY much: TIME.[57]

"Henry's great virtue," he explained, "is that he has been able to find a solace in the glory hole."[58]

The character of Henry shows once again that Cal was writing from his own personal experiences. He had explained to his psychiatrist, Tom Smith, the previous December about one of his new boyfriends, whom he had met at a glory hole. He was "a rather burned-out former drag queen from Jacksonville who's now a plasterer's assistant 3 days a week. He recently 'had to see a specialist' for his nerves who told him there was nothing to be done because his problems 'ran in the family.' He now lives with his mother in a small trailer."[59] Cal listened to his story and recorded it so faithfully that he was actually afraid of being sued. He admitted to Fred Chappell that he wrote the play "because I wanted passionately to tell all those stoned urban gays in SF just a little bit of how it was/is out here where 'Castro Street' (liberation) is far, far away."[60] The sold-out run of the play was a huge success, one critic describing it as "eloquent in its simplicity...solid and full of small observations" and praising Blaine Souza for his "touching" performance of Henry.[61] The play had been scheduled for only three matinees in November, but was so successful that Theatre Rhino added ten additional performances. Cal was thrilled to receive 5 percent of the gross box office receipts.

Cal did not attend the production, but became enraged when Tom Smith called him after seeing it. The artistic director of Theatre Rhino, Allan Estes, had allowed the show's director, Lanny Baugniet, to delete parts of the play without Cal's permission. His main objection was their cutting the entrance of the old leather queen at the end. When Cal complained, Baugniet argued that he had to consider the confines of the smaller space and budget.[62] During the run of the play, Allan Estes was initiating plans to tour Cal's *Richmond Jim* around the state of California, in part to capitalize on its just having played in New York a few months earlier. But Cal, who was fuming over their deleting long passages and even an important character in *Line Forms to the Rear*, refused permission. Once again, his artist friend, Joe Hendrix, supported what Cal was doing, "We were much delighted to read the scheme of *Line*. It sounds like a very realistic turn of events," he wrote. "I'm jelouis [sic] because I feel like you are carrying some type of banner for truth, and the truth shall set us free."[63]

Elated by his playwriting successes, Cal sent copies of *Richmond Jim*, *Line Forms to the Rear*, and *Somebody's Angel Child* to his old friend and former lover, Fred Chappell, who was artistic director at the Alliance Theater in Atlanta. His hopes for a production were dashed. Liza Nelson, the literary manager of the Alliance, thought the dialogue and the language were wonderful and original, but she found the subject matter dated and the plot development unrealized. Cal replied immediately to Fred.

> The fact that I am writing for a just-emerging minority theatre has helped my plays succeed. The minority is so delighted to see its ownself on stage that they will endure anything....JIM was not a big success in nyc—I think they mostly thought it silly....But you see in a community where its subject matter is of large concern as was the case in SF in '79, then if it is the only play to address such issues, then their [sic] ain't no competition. But I think there is something sort of sweet about JIM that may emerge someday in another production somewhere.[64]

Joe Hendrix learned of Cal's disappointment and tried to boost his spirits. "You know little trees that are often stepped on and broken make the most delightful shapes—people too I guess."[65]

When Theatre Rhino revived *Line Forms to the Rear* for ten performances the following February, Estes recognized his error—all of the earlier cuts were restored. Tom called Cal when he saw the revival and reassured him that the presence of the leather queen clumping across the stage with the aid of his geriatric walker while trying to appear macho "was indeed a powerful image."[66]

> Like a gunshot in a jungle and the ensuing dead silence, the only thing that could be heard were the deafening rattles of the chains on the walker and the steel driving pounding of the walker against the floor. Laugh, cry, scream—what to do. Embarrassment to the enth degree. Surely the play took on a new meaning. The compulsion of Henry (his mission) had to be seen in the light of the compulsion of the men (white shoes and leather man). All were (are) cripples with battle scars to boot.... We, the audience, saw the products of oppression and excessive guilt.... Yes the play needs to be seen, yes the play is frightening.[67]

Cal's old friend, actress Dana Ivey, was not impressed when she read the script. She insisted that the sexuality of his writing was repetitive and boring. She hated it, called it pornographic, and begged him to stop sending her his plays to read. Cal, however, could not comprehend her hostility. "It is very strange to me how controversial a subject SEX continues to be," he brooded. "The idea for the 80's seems to be 'of course it's alright to do it, but please let's don't talk about it anymore.'" In all honesty, he actually demanded the freedom and scope of the pornographer. Although he did not intend for his writing to arouse sexual desires, he saw nothing wrong if it did. He tried to explain to Ivey, "Sex is the powerful force which creates all human life. I'm so sorry you have been bored and offended by my obsessive use of it. It has always been to me one of the great mysteries & motivators of life, filled with humor & splendor & pathos."[68]

In spite of his disagreements with Allan Estes and Fred Chappell and the negative attitude of Dana Ivey, Cal was profoundly encouraged by these two back-to-back successes of *Richmond Jim* and *Line Forms to the Rear*. "I did learn how to be a 'writer'," he acknowledged, "albeit an awkward and erratic one and a homo-erotic one obsessed with the play of cock on cock and the struggle waged by men who sexually love other men."[69] "So many gay theatres opening that I do advise you to go gay quick if you want to get put on," he warned his old New York roommate, Johnny Ferdon. "I stay busy submitting all my old homersexual gay plays that used to be sneered at by various cunts like the WPA.... So thus we begin the '80's which is the first decade in recorded history when it is anywhere near o.k. to suck dick. Praise God Almighty, free at last!... Wonder if Ellen's ready?"[70]

One of the scripts he was working on was an adaptation for the stage of some poems he had penned a couple of years earlier. Tom Smith had begun supporting Cal's writing when he had been Cal's psychiatrist in San Francisco and had collaborated with him a couple years earlier on *The Tenderloin Suite*. They had been carrying on a marathon correspondence—at least one letter a week, often more—and frequent phone calls. Tom had read Cal's *The Daddy Poems* that had been inspired by his love for Jon Porch, had begun working on adapting them for the stage, and now turned to Cal for assistance. The plan was for a reading of the poems that would be accompanied by images from both movies and slides projected on a giant screen and by incidental music and sounds.

The intensity and shocking reality of the dialogue and visuals suggest Cal was once again writing from his firsthand experiences—this time with "daddy love." Certainly as early as 1973, when he was thirty-five and met the young man who became the inspiration for *Richmond Jim*, he had begun to enjoy occasional trysts with men considerably younger. By 1979, about the time he began his relationship with Jon Wesley Porch, Cal had come to realize, "For the last 20 years, I was looking for a Daddy. In other words: the masculine balance that has been so long missing from my life. Needless to say, I never found one."[71] But now, instead of searching for a daddy, he yearned to be a daddy himself. He wanted and needed a younger lover to teach, to mentor, to control and saw nothing immoral about such desires. In ancient times, he reasoned, sex with a slave boy or eunuch would have been regarded as unjustifiable carnal indulgence, "whereas with a boy of one's own (or near) rank or station it would have been regarded as a means of infusing the boy with the good qualities of the older man."[72]

As the play opens, viewers see a close-up image of four chrome tubes, standing vertically against a blue sky. They slowly dissolve into an extreme close-up of three nails, then to one nail, and finally into a stiff cock, shining with oil. As these images are dissolving, a voice-over is heard reading the first poem:

> thru it all
> like a
> steel nail
> your cock
> pierces
> memory tonight
> this morning
> the rain
> your cock

The cock image then fades into blackness, and the audience hears the word "daddy." Later on, a slide projects a hot, raunchy close-up of two men who are ass fucking. A little boy's voice is heard, pleading, "Daddy make me feel real good." When the lights come up on stage, a father and son are in bed together. The father says,

> you want it?
>   then open up and
>   take it, son.
>   take it.
>   i'm slippin it on down.
>   Daddy's comin on home.

A voice is then heard saying, "Daddy's comin on home." Toward the end of the play, slides reveal faces of famous men—Sigmund Freud, Abe Lincoln, Franklin D. Roosevelt, Walt Whitman—as a voice instructs,

> suck it kid, suck it.
>   get it
>   stand back
>   get it
>   on down
>   on down
>   slide it in
>   that's it
>   get it
> get it man, close up, get it
> daddy is goin to cum.
> swallow it son...
> take it. TAKE IT!
>   Be a MAN. Take it.
> OW!!!! TARZAN!
> I'm gonna cum.

When the words "OW!!!! TARZAN!" are heard, three sections of the big screen are filled with shooting dicks, fading into skyrockets bursting into a night sky, and playing over a sound system is the finale of Mahler's Eighth Symphony. It ends with the father and son lying nude on the floor, center stage. Their finger tips touching as the son says, "I love you Daddy."

Even as he was working on the script, Cal had serious reservations.

> I've grown tired of always resorting to scandalizing the page in order to energize it. There must be something else besides the homo-erotic night-mare to write about....I guess (it seems) the near terminal frustration and rage that my (homo)sexual oppression and confusion of the past 20 years

engendered has burnt itself out.... I've come to regret *ever* having committed THE DADDY POEMS to paper. They seem only to be a manifestation of my deranged mind that embarrasses people and that wasn't what I wanted.... The time has come to stop.[73]

Nevertheless, Cal was confident, perhaps unrealistically so, that this new, radical play would be grabbed up quickly by producers and become another hit. After all, Winston Leyland had published several of the poems in his *Gay Sunshine: A Journal of Gay Liberation*.[74] Cal was actually quite amazed at his sudden fame. "Sometimes I stop and think that I am a 'name' in the gay theatre in SF. *Jim* played there 3 1/2 months in 79–80 and my name was constantly before the public.... *Line* played a month last year and is being revived this February.... So I am a little bit of a something in SF." He then added rather darkly, "but what am I here [in Crystal River]? Just this afflicted prodigal son."[75]

CHAPTER 6

"PORNOGRAPHY? WHY NOT?"

As Cal and Tom continued working on *The Daddy Poems* for future production, Cal was thrilled when he got another offer—this time a world premiere in New York City! It meant he could thumb his nose at all those ignorant people in Crystal River. He had lost a lover, but his dream of becoming a respected and successful gay playwright seemed within his grasp.

For the most part, through the 1970s, New York gay theatres such as Meridian Theatre, The Glines, and TOSOS had produced "coming out" plays, gay sitcoms in urban settings, musical revues, or farcical satires. Even *Torch Song Trilogy*, which appeared in 1978 and whose first act features a backroom of a bar where men engage in anonymous sex, focuses on the life of an effeminate gay man longing for love and family. Credited at the time for its breaking new ground in gay theatre, it really seemed to be just another gay sitcom in an urban setting. Frustrated with such narrow perspectives of the recently liberated gay society, Evan Senreich and three of his buddies—Tom Starace, Larry Hough, and Billy Cunningham—founded Stonewall Repertory Theatre in the fall of 1980.

Although none of them were theatre professionals, they had a keen interest in theatre. Perhaps inspired by the movie *Cruising* that had come out that year with its explicit portrayal of the gay leather scene, they wanted something edgier than what gay theatres had been presenting. By pooling their resources, the four managed to rent the Courtyard Playhouse at 39 Grove Street. To prepare for their second season, Senreich put out a call in *Village Voice* for new scripts by gay playwrights. Seeing the opportunity, Cal sent him *The Line Forms to the Rear*, as well as his not-yet-produced *At the End of the Road*. In this new play, *At the End of the Road*, another man, who is just as lonely as Henry, the ex-drag queen in the first play, does not have his sexual needs satisfied in his marriage.

Manny brings his wife, Leona, to the toilet at the beach under the pretense of finding men for her to suck and to fuck her. What she does not realize is that when her husband is in the toilet supposedly arranging men for her, he is actually engaging in sex with them himself. In one scene of overlapping dialogues, the audience hears Leona rambling on about her disappointing sex life and her several abortions while at the same time they see men's feet under the wall of the toilet and hear Manny sucking Prince Charming, a sexy macho stud. At the very moment of his climax, when the stud gasps, "Jesus Christ! Here it comes, man," Leona ends the story about her abortions, sighing, "All the babies that will never be." The play ends with Leona begging Manny to fuck her and suggesting that he buy a couple of large cucumbers on the way home.

Cal remarked that he had learned a lot from writing the character of Leona, "most especially the device of revealing major changes taking place in [her] life without her knowing but the audience being in on the knowledge."[1] Like his other plays, this was also based on his personal experiences, having seen frequently the real Manny and Leona by the toilet at a beach near Crystal River. On one of the walls by the glory hole, Cal had seen their advertisement:

> If you like hot free female sex, my wife and I are here 4 or 5 nights a week 6 PM to 8 PM. I'll meet you in here—show hard—I'll ask you what you like. You tell me women. My 40 year old wife loves to suck, be sucked, and fucked. I love to watch. We will go to the end of the road where she will take care of you. Bring along 1 or 2 of your friends. She will take care of them too. But only 1 at a time—the others will have to wait in their car till one is done.[2]

What the ad leaves out is that the husband services the men at the glory hole before they leave the toilet to meet his wife. At first, Cal had resisted writing about this strange and sad situation; it was so tawdry and pathetic. But in the end, he decided "the sufferings of these poor pitiful forgotten people" will show that "everything is NOT alright and good about our world as we live it and I don't try to pretend that it is."[3]

Cal was enthusiastic about attending a meeting of Gay Talk, since his new play about Manny and Leona was to be among the subjects of discussion. He certainly did not anticipate the audience reaction. They pronounced it "sick." Shocked by their response, he wrote, "Suddenly I understood why my plays achieve no real popularity. . . . I will always pine in inferior positions because I can't feed them up beat, positive inanity."[4] Luckily for Cal, Senreich did not agree with the members of Gay Talk. He was very interested in both *Line Forms to the Rear* and *End of the Road* and promised Cal a production if he could add a third script to allow for a full evening's performance.

The result was *In the Shadow of a Rainbow.* His inspiration for the play was meeting Bill. In early January 1981, Cal had begun working three days a week at the Crystal River Library. Though not a fancy job, shelving books and waiting on patrons kept him busy, and at $3.00 per hour it gave him an additional $65 per week. One afternoon, a local stud electrician by the name of Bill walked into the library while Cal was working at the front desk. Bill wandered over to the fiction section of the library. Cal soon joined him. They chatted and agreed to meet at the K-Mart parking lot the next evening and then drive to the woods at the edge of the beach on Fort Island. Tingling with lust, life, and desire, Cal was as hot and horny as a teenager. There in the car with the cranked down seats and the rolled up mosquito windows, there in the hot, dark, just-rained Florida night, Cal was happy "beyond the realm of even the hoped for." "I am reborn," he sighed.

A few weeks later, Bill returned to the library, and they agreed to meet later that night. Since Miss Vada was out of town, Cal took him back into his bedroom of the old family house and to the luxury of a bed. As they were putting their clothes back on, Cal suggested, "You know, Bill, you could just call the library when you want to see me and I could meet you. You don't have to come by if it's inconvenient."

"Well," Bill hesitated. "Uh… This is the last time. I don't want to do this anymore." Dressed, they moved into the living room. Bill sat on the sofa and began to talk about his wife and his six-month-old son. He hoped they could be friends, but he did not want to have sex with Cal again.

"There's more to life than sex," Cal said bravely. "Keep in touch about the wiring at my house."

"Uh," he blurted out, "My name's not Bill—I ought to tell you. I lied to you at the beach. Might as well tell you. I'm Tom. Good night."[5]

In the Shadow of a Rainbow, the final act of the trilogy, dramatizes a similar situation. John, an intellectual gay man, yearns for a romance with Dan, a married, working-class man who is baffled and fearful of his homosexuality. Cal confessed that this play "is just me and a man—a man I know—and is mostly all of the things we didn't say when we met and touched. I think they were all in our mind, yet…, and now they're spoken."[6]

When the play opens, John is sitting alone at a picnic table near the toilet, dreaming of the times he had been there with Dan. The first time they met, he had invited Dan back to his apartment where "thank God, the expected, the hoped for happened." Dan just blurted out, "O.K. You want to suck my dick?" "And when he came," John remembers, "it was the most unified of communication in that kind of moment that I've ever experienced." But suddenly, Dan had jumped up and left abruptly, muttering "fuckin queer shit."

Subsequent encounters between them became longer and more intense, culminating in another session at John's house. Dan strips, flexes his muscles, and suggests they Indian-wrestle. As they wrestle, John reaches up to kiss Dan on the mouth, but Dan pulls back, demanding, "No kissin.... Men don't kiss." The stage descriptions read: "What follows is a carefully choreographed struggle that uses many of the traditional movements of classical wrestling. It is a struggle to the truth. Its purpose is for John to rape Dan with a kiss. They struggle for some time, their bodies forming many beautiful and erotic physical arabesques.... Dan's struggle against John's affection weakens until finally, with a great moan, Dan gives into John and starts passionately returning his kiss." As the lights fade, John begs, "Now fuck me."

The setting of all three plays in *Sunsets* is a place Cal often visited—outside the public toilet at the deserted beach on Fort Island. Because of the setting, Cal had toyed with the title of *Glory Hole 3*. After all, he argued, all three plays are "about communication in and around and thru a certain energy focal point that is a glory hole."[7] But Senreich and Cunningham thought Cal's idea for the title was too sensational and might put a wrong spin on the plays. They are "about loneliness, not getting your needs met," Cunningham stressed. "We see different kinds of people who come to the rest stop—very vivid."[8] In the end, they agreed on *Sunsets: Three Acts on a Beach.*

Senreich was thrilled to produce *Sunsets,* since it fulfilled his vision—to present new scripts by gay playwrights that were more risky and daring than usually offered. As director Billy Cunningham described it, "This play was different. It was outrageous. The material in the play is so off the wall. But when I read it, I believed it—its honesty."[9] Even though he liked the script, Senreich worried during rehearsals if people would tolerate it.[10]

The first act was the play that Theatre Rhinoceros had already produced successfully, *The Line Forms to the Rear.* In the Stonewall Rep production, Henry, the ex-drag queen who administers mercy sex to any and all comers, carried on a bag with his props. At one point, when he began to describe one of his drag performances, the lights changed, Henry removed a long lavender glove from the bag, slowly put it on, and sang *My Funny Valentine.* At the end of the song, he held up his hands as if accepting applause, froze, the lights switched back to the present, and he wept, "And they laughed at me." It was a heartbreaking moment. At the very end, a leather queen walks into the glory hole. Henry held up his arms again, this time as if to hug or embrace the audience, winked

Figure 6.1   Program cover for world premiere in New York of *Sunsets*, illustration by Tom Starace.

Source: Courtesy Cal Yeomans Collection, Special Area Studies, George A. Smathers Libraries, University of Florida.

at them, and then quickly broke out of it and into his last line, "The line forms to the rear," as he crossed to the toilet.

Since male nudity was not common on the stage at that time, the director "had trouble casting the bloody thing." At auditions, actors "totally freaked out," Senreich recalled. "They would read the first long monologue of the ex-drag queen and then leave. We could find nobody for the last two plays."[11] Finally, he persuaded two members of Stonewall Rep to play Dan and John. Since the two actors (Larry Hough and Tom Starace) were lovers at the time, it made it easier for them to play the roles. Nevertheless, the first third of the performances, they were reluctant and wore towels and underwear. They knew that the director wanted them to play in the nude, so one Sunday night before they went on, they spontaneously decided, "What the hell, let's do it." They played it in the nude from then on. Although the script calls for the wrestling scene to be like a lyrical ballet, their rendition was much more violent. John removed his briefs first and then tried to rip the underwear off of Dan. Hough recalls, "Eight years later I would be on the subway and somebody would come up to me and remark, 'I remember you in a play that ended up with you wrestling in the nude.' "[12]

Cal did not attend the New York production. Instead, the week it opened he booked himself into the lavish Marie Antoinette Room of the Gideon Lowe House in Key West and spent his evenings at the cruisy Monster Bar. "I guess I would go to see my plays in NY if any body would ask," he explained to Dana Ivey,

> but nobody don't and I don't really *want* to be there anyway. It's a heap easier (I guess) not to be there and I'd much rather contemplate it all from beneath a moonlit coconut tree in Key West than face the gothic horrors of that inate new york superiority that must first put everything down in order, it thinks to elevate itself....I do so very much hope they *are* SHOCKING. I hope that all of NY finds them nauseous and vile. I pray they won't be politically correct. I hope they are unflinchingly presented in utter realism. I hope they make people urp in the aisles. I hope grown men faint....I hope anything ANYTHING to make that ossified dying city see and feel and know a breath of truth and humanity.[13]

Figure 6.2   The final scene of *In the Shadow of a Rainbow*, John (Tom Starace) on top, Dan (Larry Hough) on bottom. Copyright © 1981 by Billy Cunningham.

Source: Courtesy Cal Yeomans Collection, Special Area Studies, George A. Smathers Libraries, University of Florida.

But his smug bravado may have been only a façade. He wrote in his journal yet another thought, perhaps more honest: "I hate it when I gross people out."[14]

When *Sunsets* opened, it connected; audiences loved it. Ironically, the *Village Voice* ad for *Sunsets* was next to an ad for a production at Ellen Stewart's La MaMa. Most nights there were mob scenes as the staff tried to shoehorn theatregoers into the small, seventy-five-seat theatre. It was scheduled to run for five weekends, starting September 18, 1981, but it was extended two additional weekends. Cal received 5 percent of the gross box office receipts thru the first sixteen performances and 10 percent after that.

Reporting in *The Advocate*, James M. Saslow called Stonewall's production "intriguing, fresh and a welcome change of focus from the predominant urban (and urbane) subjects of gay theater."[15] Nearly thirty years later, Saslow remarked that the play

> did break new ground at the time, because it was about inarticulate ordinary people who were out of the loop of the developing gay urban culture, which they knew nothing of, at a time when most gay theater [in New York] was of the two-clones-are-clever-Village-or-Castro-roommates-and-have-zany-adventures-with-campy-dialogue genre.... In 1981, it was novel and important to look at the lives of those who were still untouched by what was still a small, relatively little-known minority urban subculture that was articulating a whole new approach to life, leaving the closet behind. Those people were sad, and un-self-aware, like many gay people in the pre-Stonewall era.[16]

Robert Chesley was equally ecstatic: "The play is a landmark.... It's concerned with what *really* happens between real people; it jogs us out of our cozy, complacent ghetto reveries and reminds us that gay liberation is more than a matter of fun shops, fun discos, fun drugs, fun restaurants, and fun sex.... The audience at the performance of *Sunsets* that I saw was noticeably disturbed by the sexual frankness and explicitness of the play. But, in my view, this is as it should be: theater *should* shake us up and give something to think about.... Hooray for the Stonewall Rep!... They're doing the plays gay theater *should* be doing."[17]

A negative review came from Robert Massa in the widely read *The Village Voice*. Lukewarm on the first and last plays of the trilogy, he railed on that the middle play about the woman who visits the glory hole with her husband "left a bad taste in my mouth, so to speak."[18] Cal's first playwriting instructor and friend, Raiford Ragsdale, agreed. She read the plays and told Cal that they were just "a collection of sexual acts." Infuriated, he argued that he had made the conscious decision that whatever he wrote would be just for him: "Just what I wanted to write. The way I wanted to write. That I would proceed without compromise with the writing....I will write...that which is in my heart—be it fucking or sucking or the new nun embroidery—with all the strength and truth and beauty that I possess. I have no interest in pleasing you or anyone else with my writing. Let the chips fall where they may."[19]

About a year earlier, Cal had received a response to a fan letter he had sent to poet, novelist, and memoirist May Sarton about her new book, *Recovering: A Journal*. She had confessed that she was scared to death how readers would react to her honesty. He never understood what she meant until he wrote the last act of *Sunsets*. Sarton writes of her aging days as a lesbian author who has just had a mastectomy, knows there will be no more lovers, is being scoffed at by the mainstream press, and describes her frustration and despair. "It is I guess—like my play," he reasoned, "in the long run embarrassing but nonetheless somehow you can't stop thinking about it. That's a funny thing about the truth."[20]

Cal was becoming more and more critical of other playwrights. He saw a Mabou Mines touring production of Lee Breuer's *The Saint and the Football Players* in Gainesville and thought it was "singularly devoid of genius and / inspiration [and] lacked heart & soul and was almost as tedious as what it set out to spoof: football & the USA."[21] Before the final curtain fell, Cal stormed up the aisle, grumbling at the top of his voice about the awful production: "No wonder I can't get my plays produced if that's what people want to see!" And then there was Harvey Feierstein's *Torch Song Trilogy*, which Cal likened to a Neil Simon sitcom. "What is all the hoopla about. Is it the fact that it's *acceptable* gay theatre? It is *not* the usual kind of play to come from La Mama [*sic*]."[22] At least with this last observation it must have been galling for him to see the success of Feierstein when he had actually been the one who catapulted Feierstein's first acting success back at La MaMa when Cal directed *From Rags to Riches to Rags*.

Almost the same day of Chelsey's rave review for *Sunsets*, Cal learned that his and Tom Smith's *The Daddy Poems* had been rejected in a play contest sponsored by Theatre Rhinoceros. Cal was furious with the news. "It is censorship by stupid and self-righteous creeps. What does Allan Estes know about theatre? Nothing as he has conclusively proven time and time again," he screamed. "He does however know how to kiss ass."[23] Cal should probably have realized that he was treading on danger-ous ground with the script. It would have been risky enough to write about older men loving younger men, but this portrayed sex between a father and son.

Nevertheless, when Mark I. Chester read *The Daddy Poems*, he cried. A radical sex photographer known for his powerful images of S&M, Chester wrote to Cal, "In many ways we are following similar energies. We are putting out energies that one is not even supposed to discuss in polite society and we are putting it out to the public. [The script] brought up a lot of feelings about my Dad," he remarked, "and the relationship that we had and the kind of relationship that I wish we had had."[24] Chester specifically noted the Daddy's last line of the play, spoken as he and his son are dressing: "Make peace at home first / between your legs, son / then there'll be no more war." Cal acknowledged that the line had been spoken to him by his own father and was "the only thing I've ever heard him say to me since he died."[25]

The notoriety Cal was receiving for his playwriting did not relieve his depression or his paranoia. Homophobia was still rampant in Crystal River. His young friend, Michael Parker, whom Cal called "Bag Boy," told him that his grandmother overheard him talking about Cal one day and remarked, "Oh, you mean Sissy Yeomans." One day when Cal and Michael were walking downtown, a truck slowed up near them and yelled out, "You fucking faggots!" Another time, Cal's cousin saw them together and whispered to Michael, "Your mother don't know you're hanging around with Calvin, I'll bet."[26] But Miss Vada did know. She had invited Michael to join her and Cal for a hamburger cookout. When she obviously thought that Michael could not hear her, she said to Cal, "It's just pitiful that Michael is gay and having to grow up in this little town like you did." Cal knew that Michael's opulent beauty and bleached hair proclaimed his sexuality for all the town to see. "Together we must make quite a statement," he noted. "I'm sure they all think we must be fucking."[27]

"I am become 'the town nut'," he wrote, " 'the one that works in the library,' 'the one that you see all the time down there at the beach,' 'the one that looks at you so funny with those round rimmed glasses,' 'the one that always makes you think your fly is unzipped when you walk past him,' 'the one who don't have no friends and is all the time by himself.' "[28] The rage and the hatred Cal felt for the people of Crystal River was sometimes overwhelming.

The longer he stayed in Crystal River, the more depressed he became. He continued taking thioridazine regularly to combat his depression, but his challenges were enormous, especially for someone with a bipolar disorder and with tendencies of paranoia. Although the house by the river was rented out, Cal was still responsible for the upkeep of the four acres of garden. In the spring, the blue swamp iris, bright-red azaleas, blooming orange trees, and the wisteria glowing from the old, grey oak trees were magnificent, and it was Cal's responsibility to care for it all. Collecting rent from their tenants, maintaining the rental properties, supervising repairs, and caring for his mother took its toll on his energy and patience and led him to contemplate suicide several times.

With all of their wealth tied up in real estate, Cal and Miss Vada's day-to-day financial situation was bleak. As Cal would try to scrape together enough to pay their living expenses, his rage toward Miss Vada was building up. "I despise Vada more each day as more clearly I perceive the magnitude of what she did."[29] "All the fortune in property she gave away after Daddy died just to get rid of it," he seethed. "Vada in her pitiful ignorance has destroyed me. She has completely ruined my life."[30] One major error was her selling 1,500 acres of farmland to a Yeomans' relative for a mere $1,500, a fraction of what it was worth at the time. But in spite of his anger, Cal continued to look after his mother. He saw her almost daily. He took her shopping, and took her out into the country to pick blackberries, having to follow behind her because she passed over so many due to her failing eyesight. Sometimes they would take picnic lunches to eat at Ozello. One evening, he invited her to accompany him to a party hosted by his boss at the library and made sure that she was dressed to the hilt, wearing a new, pink pantsuit adorned with a crocheted pearl, rope tied in a knot, and a pleated nylon collar of lace ruffles surrounding her face.

Yet he knew that somehow he had to find a way to escape, to retreat if he was going to prevent his rage from exploding. In 1980, Cal had begun renovating the family rental property at 650 Citrus Avenue with the hope that he and Jon Porch would live there. A typical Florida "cracker" house only a few steps from the main downtown intersection, it later became a yarn/knitting/sewing shop and even today houses a gift shop. With the help of his cousin, Sid Kennedy, Cal painted all of the interior walls white and bought a crystal chandelier from Sears that he hung in the front room. It was still hanging in the foyer in 2009. As one of his old friends remarked, it was "a sly nod to 'grandeur'," a nice surprise in that fairly basic setting. Eventually, he painted the front louvered door a glowing Bahamian pink, knowing that it would proclaim to all passersby that "a Queen lives/resides inside."[31] Cal managed to squeeze into the little house an old, monstrous, eight-foot long turquoise sofa he had purchased at a junk shop. Zacq Reid, Cal's artist friend from Atlanta, installed several large planters around the house. After Jon and he had split, Cal had rented out the house by the river as well as his mobile home on Ozello. His memories of Jon were so vivid, Cal did not want to live at either place. His only choice, it seemed, was to live at the house on Citrus Avenue.

And as his depression worsened, his rage toward his mother would regularly peak, and he would blame all his troubles on her. Cal realized more clearly that he had to find a way to get out of town more often. On February 6, 1981, he signed a contract to purchase 1.03 acres—51 miles north of Crystal River, 16 miles south of Gainesville, 7 miles west of the historic town of Micanopy—in the middle of nowhere. Surrounded by enchanting woods, eight acres of farmland, and miles from any neighbors, it consisted of a two-bedroom mobile home, rabbit hutches, a chicken house, storage shed, and gas generator. The only sounds came from cattle, cicadas, birds, the scratching of a passing armadillo in the leaves, and wind through the trees. About twice an hour a car might pass down the gravel road in front.

Located on an old Indian trading path at the edge of the tall grass of Paynes Prairie, running from Micanopy to western Florida, Cal called his new home-away-from-home "Center." Supposedly, there was a marker on the property designating the spot as being the actual center of Florida. The little town of Micanopy with its quiet, dirt backroads was the oldest inland town in the state and had become an artist colony, filled with ancient, towering pines and enormous, old, moss-draped oaks. He loved walking along the old roads and devouring the bright-magenta azaleas, dogwood, wild hog plum, and the yellow swamp jasmine.

The only alteration he made to the trailer was to install a six-foot, sliding glass door at the back of the dining room/den that gave him a beautiful vista across the back of his property into the unobstructed forest of long leaf pine and oak and palmetto trees that edged his property. Zacq Reid presented Cal with a housewarming gift of a very imperial, artificial eagle that he mounted atop a gate post at the entrance. "All who pass are now aware that someone weird lives here," he laughed, "and I am quite pleased with that."[32] On lazy days, he could lie on his Mexican hammock stretched between two oak trees, swinging naked as a jaybird and listening to all the sounds of nature. His only constant companion was, Wilhelmina, a stray, black cat that stumbled upon Cal and stayed.

Now that he had set up this hideaway retreat, away from Crystal River and his mother, Cal spent considerable time at Center. It certainly made it easier to check out the men at the Gainesville gay bars and to attend the weekly Gay Talk meetings. It was there where he met and befriended a university student. Bruce McCoy, an ambitious and energetic eighteen-year-old freshman studying advertising and communications, began attending the Gay Talk meetings off-campus as soon as he arrived in Gainesville. Cal was forty-three years old—old enough to be Bruce's father, but that was no obstacle to their friendship. They hit it off immediately. Bruce enjoyed hearing of Cal's experiences in Atlanta and New York, was curious about his playwriting successes, and was fascinated with Cal's intelligence, wit, worldliness, and southern charm. Unlike most of the relationships Cal had with bright and handsome, young men, this one was platonic. Any sexual connection that he enjoyed was purely vicarious.

They spent lots of time together, going to movies, scrounging around antique shops and flea markets in the area where they looked especially for Roseville pottery and Syrian, octagonal inlaid tables. Cal was a bargain hunter and always looking to add to his collection of staplers, old scissors, and bamboo-handled flatware. A regular stop was at the Green Door in Ocala. Another was in Micanopy where they would spend hours browsing in Marlene Oberst's shop called The Shed and sometimes have lunch or a treat across the street at either Old Florida Café or Shady Oak, both specializing in huge deli sandwiches and Key Lime pie.

On weekends when Bruce stayed at Center, they went on long walks through the countryside, often accompanied by Wilhelmina. Bruce urged Cal to keep writing, but, instead, Cal seemed more interested in reading and in exploring a new hobby of photography. On one excursion together, Cal took dozens of photos of Bruce wondering through the maze of the Waldo flea market debris.

They shared a love of books and attended regularly the meetings of Gay Talk. Shortly before they arrived at the group's Valentine's party in 1983, a bomb threat was telephoned to where they were to meet and police surrounded the building but found nothing. After being warned of what might have happened and the risk involved, the party proceeded. Cal won a prize that night for the most creative Valentine's card. It had a tongue sticking through a lace doily on the cover. Outside was written, "Love It!" Inside, "And if you can't love it, Lick it." His card the year before had also won the prize that bore the sentiment, "Lo Cal, No Cal, Tonight I'm yo Cal."[33]

Cal continued occasional meetings with Bill, his married friend, picked up one-night stands at The Ambush, met men at local glory holes, and played with guys he met at Gay Talk. Cal was disappointed when these trysts with young men did not develop into long-term relationships. He wanted each of them to last, but sensed that the young men were increasingly embarrassed to be seen with him. "They kiss me in a sweet delusion that I'm the Daddy of their dreams," he wrote, "then reality ... & they find they've kissed the pig of their nightmare."[34]

During the summer of 1981, Cal learned that the Hippodrome Theatre in Gainesville was sponsoring a play contest with the first prize of $1,000 for a play set in Florida and written by a Florida playwright.

Upon reflection, he sent *Cucumbers* and just the first two acts of *Sunsets*. "I hope they don't turn me in to the police," he chuckled.[35] He did not win.

The next year, Stonewall Rep was selected to present *Sunsets* in Chicago as part of the Third National Gay Arts Festival. Howard Casner, critic for *Gay Life*, was overwhelmed by the play, especially the third act, calling it an "exhilarating experience." The play is "one of the highlights of my Chicago theater experience," he wrote. "Its erotic detail, direct language, deceptive simplicity, all combined into a beautiful study of melancholy—of two men who ask nothing from life but who grab in childish awe when life exerts itself and offers them something."[36]

Although Cal always seemed to need such praise and acceptance, he could not bring himself to brag about his achievements. His old friend, Fred Chappell, on the other hand, was not so shy. He telephoned Cal several times to tell him that he was being presented with an award by the Governor of Georgia. Fred "has fallen for it hook line & sinker," Cal complained. "I can remember the day when we laughed at the kind of people given awards by the Governor."[37] A few days later, he admitted, "I don't know why I loved Fred—many years ago when we were both sort of strange grown-up children. Perhaps because he allowed me to.... He has always been sadistic toward and destructive of his friends."[38] Cal could not comprehend how Fred could continue stuck in a bourgeois, heterosexual marriage and tolerate playing the game of working for a large mainstream theatre that exploited him.

In early May 1982, Cal and Tom Smith had one of their very few angry exchanges. Tom had phoned Cal that he wanted to present *Poiret in Exile* at a major conference focusing on alcohol and drug abuse, but more importantly, he wanted to show how the play reflected Cal's personal life. Cal was outraged!

> Perhaps *Poiret* is one of the few nice things that resulted from the drugs and booze....I have been sober & drug-free for 2 ½ years now. Must we drag thru it again?...Do I have to keep wallowing in the guilt and regret of it all.... Must it be publically discussed and pointed out like a freak in a circus....I transmuted my pain & suffering into a verbal art work of shimmering beauty. Must we tell the world—destroy one of my few accomplishments.

Cal ended his letter with a plea to Tom. "I *want* you to discuss *Poiret* but not in light of the alcohol & drug abuse that produced it....I am not yet strong enough to *survive* such a discussion."[39] He eventually allowed Tom to use the play, but insisted that he not mention Cal's family in any revealing or graphic way. "I don't mind what you say about me," he cautioned, "but leave them out."[40]

A highlight of his summer of 1982 was an interview published in *The Advocate*, featuring Cal along with playwright C.D. Arnold. The editor, Mark Thompson, was impressed with Cal's work because he seemed so committed to his craft, especially at a time when so much gay theatre was slapdash, and viewed Cal as "certainly among the most talented gay playwrights" at the time.[41] "Their plays," wrote Dick Hasbany in the article, "may take some of the most poetic, ambivalent and exploratory looks at being gay we've yet seen on the stage, and they have not always been easy to take." He proceeded to blame the squeamishness that many gays experience on the fact that they are so used to their theatre entertaining them and presenting "benign or stirring images of gay life" that are fun and politically useful. "Political usefulness and reality," he insists, "are not always the same." When questioned about the goal of his writing, Cal explained, "I'd like to demystify sex into freedom. I think we should have the freedom of pornography if we need it for artistic purposes. Why not?" In the end, Hasbany proclaimed that their plays "may be helping to create a gay theater that is at once more personal, more idiosyncratic, and more universal than most gay theater has been."[42] The national publicity from the article certainly drew interest in Cal's plays.

San Francisco's 544 Natoma Performance Gallery chose to open their fall season of 1982 with *Sunsets*. When Peter Hartman founded 544 Natoma in 1977, it was the first openly gay performance and gallery space in San Francisco. He had worked with Judith Malina and Julian Beck in their Living Theatre in the 1960s and was determined to present contemporary, radical art. Drag star Ethyl Eichelberger performed there before she became a name, so did Whoopi Goldberg. At one point, Hartman sponsored a photography show that included the full range of erotic images, from pederastic fantasies to the extremes of S&M. Later on, he hosted the weekly gatherings of San Francisco Jacks, a safe-sex club where the primary outlet was masturbating. It was a lights-up, pants-down sharing of sexuality. The performance space was long and narrow, with two rows of bleacher-type seating on one side. For *Sunsets*, Hartman, who directed, had the wood-paneled stage covered with three tons of sand. At one end of the stage was a set of shoji screens that provided an entrance and exit for actors.

Hartman's production, in keeping with his goal for the theatre, was even more outrageous than Stonewall Rep's in New York. Every night during the San Francisco run, when John Ponyman entered the toilet as Prince Charming in *At the End of the Road*, he "pulled out his dick and got it hard and then stuck it in Manny's mouth and truly got it sucked."

The action was behind a scrim, but there was no wondering what was going on. When Prince Charming "exited the toilet there was no more mystery because a big old hard dick was snaking almost out of his cut offs and every eye knew they'd watched a blowjob."[43]

From the beginning of his long-distance communication with Hartman, Cal was encouraged. "To do your plays next is going to be such a fucking turn on!!!!" Hartman wrote. And he reassured Cal that he would never "edit out material because it might prove 'offensive.' Never."[44] Hartman paid for Cal's flight so he could attend the opening night, and Cal was thrilled with what he witnessed: "The honesty (not the pornography) of it was what just blew people away. The beautiful damned honesty of it. . . . I saw the audience . . . all of us, collectively, flood the theatre with a radiant godlike pink light that was the flame of our joy because the truth of the ecstasy of man to man love had for once (and maybe the first time) been captured and honestly and beautifully and sacredly portrayed live on the American stage. . . . I knew I (we together those at the theatre and me) had expanded and ennobled the range of truth."[45]

Following the run, Hartman confessed to Cal that he was so pleased that Cal was satisfied. "You have been given such a rotten deal, I think, out here, [at Theatre Rhinoceros], and I wanted to show you that you *are* much loved and appreciated, and, perhaps, most importantly, *understood*."[46] Indeed, Hartman seemed to understand that for Cal "*Sunsets* was a great outcry to the world, a great wail of sexual loss & despair & absence & need."[47]

Mark I. Chester, who was in a relationship with Robert Chesley, attended several performances and was hired to photograph Cal and C.D. Arnold for the article that was to appear in *The Advocate*. "What blew me away," he recalled, "was the honesty of ALL the sexual interactions and speeches by the characters. No one talked about sex this openly and honestly in a play. And if they even approached it, it was much more in the vein of situation comedy and sexual farce, not serious theater."[48] Mark Tomkin of the *Bay Area Reporter* raved about the production and praised Cal: "He has an erotic sensibility to his writing, and his use of overt sex acts to illustrate the powerful draw of man-to-man sex is both fitting and exciting."[49] A critic for *The Advocate* praised the play as "a fine work, expanding the typical gay play into a study of the sexuality and frustrations that constitute both the gay and straight worlds. Quite rightly, Yeomans never defines the line between the two worlds, because often there is none: We are, simply, sexual beings."[50] Robert Chesley had raved about the play when he had seen it in New York, and now wrote, "I saw *Sunsets* this weekend and was *very* moved. It's one of the *best* evenings in theater I have ever had. When I say that I mean it, but it does mean that there is something in the plays which appeals to me very personally."[51]

Regardless of his annoyance with Theatre Rhinoceros, while he was in San Francisco, Cal attended their production of Doric Wilson's *Street Theatre*. Wilson was in attendance that night, and at the curtain call, Cal was stunned when Wilson acknowledged his presence to the audience and dedicated the evening's performance to him. Cal had never met Wilson. "It was so strange," he admitted, "to have the feeling again of being somebody other than just this reclusive nonentity of a faggot-casualty who works in the library and lives in a mutilated trailer in the woods."[52]

When Cal learned about five years later that Dennis Yount, who had played Dan in the final act of *Sunsets* in San Francisco, had died of AIDS, he wrote, "I can't help but wonder what he would have done, what he would have become if he had not had the heavy burden of homosexual oppression to weight him down.... When Dennis dropped his pants & swung that big old dangling dick with its great hanging swag of delicious looking foreskin at the audience we all gazed and saluted.... It was a dick to dream about on a man to die for. Dennis was a rare angel who some of us were graced to witness." After one performance, Cal, Ponyman, Yount, and the director, Peter Hartman, went to the Eagle bar where Cal told Yount "how rare & incredible his heartbreaking sensitive & accurate portrayal of the young 'straight man'" had been. He felt that he and Dennis had hung out in some of the same rest stops and admitted rather shyly, "If I'd known you had such a gorgeous uncut dick I would have written some lines especially for it." Dennis laughed, "Well, it's not too late." Cal could not forget his friend's "beauty and grace—or the sad feeling that he never really found his rightful & deserved place.... Some people," Cal conceded, "are too beautiful, too gentle for earthly reality."[53]

While Cal was in San Francisco, Tom Smith arranged an interview for Cal on a local program called Traffic Jam. During the course of the interview, Cal was questioned about the graphic sexuality in *Sunsets*. "My sexuality has always been a terribly important & prominent part of my life—as it is I think of any healthy life," he argued. "Exploring, expanding, coming to understand my sexuality has been a wonderful, exciting adventure. It is natural that some of this extraordinary experience would find its way into my work."[54] To Cal's amazement and embarrassment, a few weeks later, when he returned to his job at the Crystal River Library, his boss remarked that a friend of hers in California had heard the interview. He nearly passed out when told but quickly rallied and viewed it as just another aspect of his closet dynamited away.

February 1983 found Cal back in San Francisco, this time to participate in play readings that he hoped would result in productions. His dreams were dashed. During the reading of *The Daddy Poems*, the lesbians in attendance revolted and refused to let the actors proceed. A riot ensued and many people stormed out in a rage. John Ponyman who had played Prince Charming in 544 Natoma's production of *Sunsets* wrote Cal soon after he had returned to Florida. "After all the brew-ha in San Francisco last time you were here I can well understand why you lost the taste to write. But let it go, Cal. Write. *Sunsets* was wonderful. Keep it up. We all run into minds like Ann and Wendy [the lesbians at the reading]. And we must go on."[55] Cal summed it up bluntly: "My work remains as controversial as ever."[56]

After much coaxing, Tom Smith visited him for the first time in late March 1983. They spent time together at Center and Ozello before touring Epcot and then staying in Key West for a couple of weeks. Nothing seemed to go right. Tom felt ill most of the time. Their one trip to The Ambush in Gainesville was a devastatingly off night with no "discodorables" present and terribly loud music during the drag show. Cal had thought that Tom would dance the night away, but it did not happen. The weather in Key West was irrationally cold, making any beach activity nearly impossible. Epcot, or as Cal called it, "Urpcot," was the real disaster, the lines were beyond tiresome. Cal's morale was boosted when he met Ralph Haddix, a young, bisexual construction worker, at a men's room. Cal was washing his hands when Ralph entered, sauntered over to a nearby urinal, pulled out his gorgeous, blond cock, and began to stroke it. "Nice dick you've got," Cal said.

"Glad you like it," Ralph replied and flashed a perfect Richard Gere smile.

"Need a ride?" Cal asked, as he slowly dried his hands. It was the beginning of an intense, four-month romance. They often spent weekends at either Center or Ozello, Cal's Temple of Love—the weekend branch. "He is a radiant love child," Cal wrote, "perhaps the most beautiful of my entire life."[57]

He admitted to Tom Smith, however, that "Ralph wants cock & to eat pussy, too. It's a hard act to balance.... I can't handle Ralph.... He doesn't really want me; just the Daddy security I represent."[58] Hard to understand, given Cal's background, they did not engage in any sexual activity until late August. One night, Cal instructed Ralph to go into the bedroom, take off his clothes, and lie in bed. After a few minutes, Cal walked in and shut the door. "Alright," he said." "The door is closed, what happens from here on out nobody will know about but you and me.... We don't have to have sex if you don't want to; do you want to?

I'm willing to just be your friend if you want it that way—although it will break my heart....Do you want to?"

"Yes," Ralph replied.

Cal turned off the light and whispered gently, "Tonight I'm going to teach you to hug. Don't be afraid to touch me.... You can fist-fuck me if you want to." Cal then reached out and held Ralph in a great bear hug. Cal understood Ralph's hesitation, since he was raised in the Church of the Nazarene, but he was sure that Ralph wanted sex. Eventually, they "went quite a ways beyond hugging." Ralph had enjoyed reading some of the masturbation (J/O) tales in the San Francisco Jacks newsletters that Tom Smith had sent to Cal and told Cal he should tell Tom that they had ended up the night forming the Ozello chapter of a J/O club.[59]

Cal knew that Ralph continued to sleep with women, but he always thought that if he held out just one more day, another week, another woman, that eventually Ralph would be his. One night when Cal was waiting for Ralph to return from seeing one of his women, Cal composed a poem, which he titled "For Dolly Parton."

> Sometime tonight my Man is supposed
> to join me here in this warm bed, but...
> with him you never know and I'm trin'
> hard not to set it up too big and just
> be here and take it
> as it comes. Might as well, it's
> the only way I ever get it anyhow.
>
> But oh I wish he'd come home
> soon high-spirited, horny, and happy
> and throw my legs in the air
> and fuck me and make a baby of
> love to flood my soul and keep me
> company when he's in that old mood,
> needful of arms that ain't mine
> and hearts that are hollow and use him.
>
> My Man ain't faithful
> but by God when I
> corner him and get it
> he's good and better and
> Lord he's worth the wait.
>
> Please, honey, don't stay out too late.

Through September, Cal took literally hundreds of photos of Ralph, some nude. His favorite was Ralph standing in the morning sunlight at the top of a neighbor's cattle loader with the sacred oak trees in the background. He is nude, facing away from the camera, revealing his youthful, bronzed legs and back, accentuated by his pearly, white ass. Looking at Ralph's beautiful body enraged Cal when he thought of the women Ralph had sex with. In early October, Cal ended the "summer romance / madness," confessing that he had "prayed it might work—knew it wouldn't. But I'm out of it now by the skin of my teeth."[60] Ralph returned to live with his wife in Fort Lauderdale. Cal rationalized that the one beautiful picture of Ralph, the glowing golden picture, was worth all he had been through. "The picture has in it what I was hoping for when I came home" to Florida in 1978.[61]

By this time, his playwriting success had become so well known that the University of Florida Federation of Lesbian and Gay Students, funded by the University student government, invited him to present a major address as part of their Lesbian and Gay Society Speakers Series, billing him as a "nationally acclaimed playwright and poet." In describing his writing, Cal pointed out, "The largest kernel of truth I can find is my life. Everything I've ever written has been about my life to one degree or another. Frequently it is a literal rendering; often it is not. It's always a combination of real life, seen—observed life, and imagined life. But it is my life. *Ma Vie*, as Isadora said. Living my life is my *business*, my work."

He proceeded to urge the students to come out. No one would be free, truly free, until they did. "We must not stop our struggle for freedom until every gay and lesbian human—wherever he or she may be—is totally free." Just as he was finishing his introductory comments and was about to begin reading from his writing, hecklers set off the fire alarm in the hallway outside the auditorium. For a few minutes, there was bedlam. After calm was restored, Cal caught the eye of one young man in the audience. "You see," he said. The man nodded in complete agreement. Everything Cal had been preaching had been validated.

He then read some of his poetry and selections from his plays, ending with a challenge to the students.

> Too long have we contented ourselves with second class citizenship
> Too long have we been jokes
> Too long have we hurt
> Too long have we died—frequently at our own self-loathing hands
> Too long have we been casualties
> Too long have we been victims
> Too long!
> It's time to move it on up, to take the next step
> To live fully and healthily—*proudly*
> as members in good and full standing of the world community.

It's all or nothing
First class or nothing
Full human rights or nothing
THERE ARE MANY BATTLES YET TO BE FOUGHT.
I challenge you the youth of Amerika, to fight them.
I'll help all I can.[62]

No one was offended when he read scenes from his plays and his poetry. They all gave him a standing ovation.

Cal became so energized that he decided to quit his job at the library and devote more time to his writing. His first goal was to write a sequel to *In the Shadow of a Rainbow*, which he called *Banana Summer*. It begins two months after *Shadow of a Rainbow*, with John coming home from work and lighting a joint. As he relaxes in a chair, the audience sees images on the back wall that suggest his humdrum life, his carnal dreams, his nightmares, and as the script reads, "dick, dick, Dick, DICK." The doorbell rings, jolting him back into reality. Dan enters and they quickly begin to share their frustrations. Dan reveals that his wife has moved back with her parents, taking their children with her. John relates his growing distaste for meeting men at glory holes and then discloses the story of his being institutionalized at Bellevue Hospital. They discuss their sexual preferences and then John asks Dan, "Are you going to run away this time when you've cum?" Just at that moment Juanita Allen, a seventy-nine-year-old lesbian who works at the library with John, rushes in, carrying a bag of books. Cal did not finish the script, but his plan was to have Dan and John live together for awhile, but, eventually, Dan's wife would get him back. Clearly, the plot was based on Cal's own story. Pat Bond, a lesbian actress whom Cal met when she was in Gainesville performing her one-woman show on Gertrude Stein, was very interested in playing Juanita. She was on the board of Theatre Rhinoceros, so it might have been a good opportunity for Cal if he had managed to complete it.

Interest in Cal's work was exploding. Robert Chesley, who was just beginning his career as a gay playwright, asked Cal for advice on several of his new scripts, including *Nocturnes*, *Night Sweat*, and *Stray Dog Story*. In turn, Cal sent Chesley drafts of his *Daddy Poems*. Evan Senreich of Stonewall Rep was so encouraged by the success they had with *Sunsets* that he begged Cal to send him *Richmond Jim*, *The Daddy Poems*, and *Conversation with the Duke and Duchess of Windsor*, as well as two new plays he was working on, *Wet Paint* and *Malibu*. Harrison Pierce saw *Line Forms to the Rear* at Theatre Rhino, had read about *Sunsets*, and considered producing one of them for Gay Pride Day in Portland, Oregon. Blaine Souza, who had played the role of ex-drag star Henry in Cal's *The Line*

Forms to the Rear in San Francisco, pleaded with Cal for another script he could act in and was especially keen on *Poiret in Exile*. Peter Hartman of 544 Natoma Performance Gallery flew to Florida twice to discuss presenting Cal's plays in New York.

In just four years, it was clearly confirmed: "I am a name!" Although his playwriting had begun while living in Atlanta in the late 1960s and had continued during his years in New York, prior to 1979 only two of his plays had been produced—*In a Garden of Cucumbers* and *All-American Dreamland Dancehall* that he had coauthored with Fred Chappell—and both of those productions were a decade earlier. He had written eight more plays during the 1970s—*Swamp Play* (1972), *One Two Boy Man* (1974), *New Hope Farm* (1975), *Stool Play* (1976), *Conversation for the Duke and Duchess of Windsor* (1978), *Somebody's Angel Child* (1978), *Malibu* (1979), *Poiret in Exile* (1979)—as well as several brief sketches. But no productions, no nibbles of interest for ten long years!

In 1979 it all changed. *Richmond Jim*, produced in 1979 and 1980 at Theatre Rhinoceros in San Francisco and in 1980 in New York as part of First Gay Arts Festival; *Tenderloin Suite* (4 one-acts, including *Poiret in Exile* and *Somebody's Angel Child*), produced in 1979 in San Francisco as a benefit for Theatre Rhinoceros; *Line Forms to the Rear*, produced in 1980 and revived in 1981 in San Francisco by Theatre Rhinoceros; *Sunsets: 3 Acts on a Beach* (3 one-acts including *Line Forms to the Rear*, *End of the Road*, and *In the Shadow of a Rainbow*), produced in 1981 at Stonewall Repertory Theater in New York City and in Chicago in 1982 as part of the Third Gay Arts Festival, and at 544 Natoma Performance Gallery in San Francisco in 1982. His plays were being seen along side those of Doric Wilson, Robert Patrick, Harvey Feierstein, and Lanford Wilson. Gay audiences were viscerally connecting, and even legit theatres were becoming interested. Clearly, Cal was at the top of his form and gaining recognition for the graphic sexuality and reality in his plays.

Glowing, perhaps gloating, with pride, Cal wrote to his old friend Raiford Ragsdale, "I read the other day that the 80's are going to be a decade of sexual discovery in the USA. Well, if so, I am already there (I guess)."[63] But his enthusiasm was tempered. In April 1981, the Centers for Disease Control in Atlanta began to notice an increase in the number of cases of a rare lung infection called pneumocystis carinii pneumonia. Their published report in June about these cases is sometimes referred to as the beginning of AIDS. More appropriately, it was the beginning of the country's awareness of the disease. On July 3, 1981, the *New York Times* published the first article on "the Gay Cancer," the first widely distributed, public news of what was to become AIDS. Panic set in as the number of deaths each year grew astronomically—from 234 cases reported in 1981 to 16,000 in 1985. Many linked the disease to its initial occurrence in gay men, calling it "gay compromise syndrome." Others called it GRID (gay-related immune deficiency) or the "gay cancer."

As concern grew about the calamity attacking so many gay men, the public grew fearful of the so-called gay lifestyle that they now felt was threatening American society. Panic set in. Landlords began to evict tenants who had AIDS. Stories circulated of gay men ousted from their apartments and left to die on the streets. In 1983, the Food and Drug Administration barred from donating blood to any man who had had sexual contact with another man since 1977. In October 1984, San Francisco closed all their gay bathhouses and private sex clubs; cities around the country followed suit. Cal came to realize that the sexual liberation he had anticipated for the 1980s might not occur, and he became alarmed over the future of his plays. It never occurred to him that this might be the least of his worries.

CHAPTER 7

"GET RID OF THAT GAY STUFF"

The AIDS panic had a devastating effect on gay theatre. Soon after John Glines accepted his Tony Award for *Torch Song Trilogy* in 1983 and identified his coproducer as his lover, ticket sales for the show plummeted. Even closeted gay celebrities such as Liz Smith and Bobby Short attacked him for being so public about his sexuality.[1] When openly gay actor/director Michael Kearns was rehearsing James Pickett's *Dream Man* in 1985 at the Los Angeles Actors' Theatre, he was instructed by the producer to "get rid of some of that gay stuff,"[2] particularly the metaphorical death of one of the characters by autoerotic asphyxiation—cutting off air supply to intensify orgasm. Homophobic heterosexuals insisted that there was no such thing as safe sex; all gay sex was deadly.

Even San Francisco's liberal newspaper, the *Bay Area Reporter*, changed its policies. It had always reported coming events of the South of Market leather community as well as running a regular porn column. At one point, editor Paul Lorch had decried the closing of the gay baths, but suddenly he announced that the newspaper was accommodating to the AIDS crisis with a responsible journalistic twist toward health and away from sleaze. This shift astonished Cal. "Isn't sex a component part of health?" he questioned. "Sex can be unhealthy, but so can sports, sleep, meditation, 'good' nutrition and all the other aspects of health. I'm getting angry....This is frightening, regressive and senseless. The fresh air of San Francisco is becoming polluted with self righteous, profit motivated, restrictive toxins. I am starting to suffocate. Internalized and externalized homophobia will cause more damage and deaths than AIDS. Guilt and self righteous aggression and violence will punish us for our transgressions. All we did wrong was love men and be jubilant over dick."[3]

As the plague raged, some theatres began losing their audiences. Evan Senreich, founder of Stonewall Rep, recalled that it was a bleak period because many theatregoers chose not to see edgy, sexually explicit plays. The AIDS epidemic kept audiences away; after six seasons, the theatre folded. The problems that Senreich and others faced were not just with straight, conservative theatregoers. Kearns points out that gay playwrights and producers "were vilified by their own. Many gay men went to great lengths to clean up their image.... They didn't want their secrets revealed in public."[4]

"The problem," Doric Wilson concurs, "comes from our fellows in our culture." As he writes on his web site, "Our worst adversaries most often are us."[5] Once the AIDS scourge entered the scene, gays, especially closeted ones, feared that portraying gay lives publicly and realistically on the stage would prejudice heterosexuals and lead to a rise in hate crimes and gay bashing. Gay plays changed. As late as 2002, historian John Clum noted, "Since *Torch Song Trilogy*, the majority of gay drama has centered on AIDS."[6] Gay characters were usually portrayed as politically correct with their sexuality "distorted, denied, or diminished."[7] This new focus stifled many rebellious playwrights such as Cal. Doric Wilson lamented that AIDS more or less wiped out gay theatre in the 1980s and stopped him from writing plays.[8]

Robert Chesley, who had been inspired to write plays after seeing Cal's sexually explicit dramas, deplored that "gay theater [in New York] seems to have fallen on evil days; and, anyway, to my knowledge the only controversial gay play ever produced in New York was your Sunsets. 'Controversial gay play' almost seems like a contradiction in terms, alas, when it should not be."[9] A year later, Chesley complained again: "I find myself without a theater, and therefore don't know whether there's any point in continuing to write plays. [My director] is more than a bit up tight about eroticism, and I remain very concerned with erotic theater, or with the erotic in theater."[10]

To Cal's surprise, a leather bar in Portland, Oregon, called The Cell produced a revival of *Richmond Jim* in September 1983. About a month prior to the opening, the director, Jerry West, asked Cal if he would rewrite the script to encompass the problem of AIDS. Cal wondered where he would start rewriting? Where would he stop? Thinking the whole play would have to be revamped, he declined, explaining,

I think there's enough foreboding of the whole thing there: when I wrote it, I knew <u>something</u> was going to happen—I just didn't know what....Just before I left NYC at the very end of 1975...so often I thought—so often I felt—so often I said: 'It's as if there is an ecstasy of death everywhere.' ... That's the way I interpreted the freedoms/excesses that were already getting so totally over the line and out of hand. At some point sanity was lost. At some point it became not freedom, but death-wishing self destruction.

Instead of rewriting the play, Cal suggested that they insert a couple of sentences into the last speech of Biddy's, the ex-drag queen, so that he would say, "My dear, there is an absolute ecstasy of excrement. It's almost pure necrophilia. <u>An ecstasy of death!</u>" Since Biddy is something of a prophet, Cal felt the foreboding might be enough.[11]

Because the city vice squad in Portland would not allow nudity, thus preventing Mike from slipping the cock ring onto Jim, West had the actor playing Jim wear a large, leather codpiece that suggested he had an erection. Doric Wilson saw the play for a second time in Portland and revised his earlier opinion. Better directing and acting allowed Wilson to see that it was a brilliant little play.[12] Although no reviews appeared, the audience reaction was so enthusiastic that the producers contemplated reviving it in a legitimate theatre in town. Cal feared that the request by Jerry West to rewrite the play because of the AIDS crisis was a prediction of his own future as a playwright. Four years would pass before another production of his plays.

In early January 1984, Cal, who had been encouraged by Tom Smith, made plans to direct two of his plays in San Francisco later in the spring. Most likely it would have been *Autumn Dialogue* and *Line Forms to the Rear* under a new title of *Wet Paint*. By the end of the month, however, he changed his mind. After going to Atlanta to see Fred Chappell's production of *Crimes of the Heart,* he wrote, "It was a grim trip. ... I find myself so very happy to be back home in the woods, but filled with anger at (I guess) my inability to accept & deal with an alien world."[13] He canceled all plans to direct. Anna Freeman, the executive secretary of Gainesville's Acrosstown Repertory Theatre, expressed interest in producing *Sunsets*, asked to see more of Cal's scripts, and invited him to attend their play-reading nights. But Cal, relishing the solitude of his home in the woods and dreading the thought of being forced to compromise his writing, could not muster enough energy to even consider returning to commercial theatre. Cal was heartbroken over the loss of his friends to AIDS. In 1984, Dennis Yount and John Ponyman, actors in the San Francisco production of *Sunsets*, as well as Allan Estes, the founder of Theatre Rhinoceros, died of AIDS. Cal penned a poem to Ponyman at the time, part of which reads:

> you'd hoped I'd take you
> back to Florida, John,

but I was helpless and
even if I'd taken you
away, it was too late

You said my words and my mind exploded.
You said my words and my heart ignited.
You said my words and the play was beauty.

Who'll say them for me now, Son?[14]

Cal was bewildered whenever he thought of a sexually restricted and repressed San Francisco. Cities, he wrote, have become "charnel houses of the dead & dying. Sex is no longer recreational or pleasant relaxation, but rather a terrifying game of carnal Russian roulette. Fuck and die."[15]

A year earlier, Cal had driven Ralph out to the glory hole that had inspired his play, *Sunsets*. Amazing, the Manny and Leona of the play were actually there in their bright-red truck with a large confederate flag hanging in the rear window. Ralph went into the restroom to check out Manny who had just gone inside. When Leona got out of the truck, Cal was stunned, shaken, and frightened. Leona, who was never too much overweight, had lost not only her teeth, but at least fifty pounds. Her legs were spindly toothpicks with "a definite shrouded aura of death hanging about her." Leona had AIDS.

As Cal sat on a nearby picnic table, a station wagon drove up with a plainclothesman behind the wheel. They were now everywhere on the beach. "So what used to be innocent and unknown, hidden and unremarked is now, like so much else, fodder for the fascist oppressors," Cal complained. "Chalk up another one. The old easygoing beach of SUNSETS is now a thing of the past that will never be again. I'm glad I captured it in a play. No one will ever forget."[16] Just two years earlier, Cal had boasted to Johnny Ferdon in New York that the decade of the 1980s was going to be the "first decade in recorded history when it is anywhere near o.k. to suck dick."[17] How quickly the world had changed.

Obviously, in this atmosphere that viewed gay sex as deadly, Cal's kind of play was out of favor. When Cal offered Theatre Rhinoceros more scripts to consider, they refused. They sought to become more mainstream, less edgy and radical. According to photographer Mark I. Chester, sex was always suspect on their main stage. As Chester saw it, "At Theater Rhino, you always knew that some hot young gay man would take off his shirt, parade around the stage and show off his body as part of the play, but that was the extent of any sexual activity."[18] They were really drawing room comedies. The plays were popular, but very safe. Often referred to as "apartment house" plays, they featured young, cute men in underwear, living in San Francisco apartments and going about the new lifestyle that gays were then creating. Clearly, Cal's plays were something different.

Actually, Cal was more comfortable at 544 Natoma. Founder Peter Hartman, with his background in New York's Living Theatre, insisted that gay artists not hide their sexuality in their art. Although considered a genius by many of his friends, Hartman definitely walked the line between madness and genius, fueled by the use of drugs. But after only three years, he had run out of money and could not keep the theatre afloat.

Cal had received outstanding reviews and awards; his plays had been sought after; theatre producers had begged him for scripts. Yet the negative criticism and the fear that his voice would be muzzled were damaging and intimidating for this sensitive, lonely man with a bipolar disorder and lingering paranoia. "My career as a playwright—indeed: a theatre person—is over," he admitted. "Can't tolerate the sham of it all. Can't stand the people."[19]

He continued to write lengthy journal entries each day, but also turned his attention once again to writing poetry in collections he titled *10 Poems for Luna Park* and *The Glory Hole Poems*. Although most are quite sexually suggestive, three were published in *Amethyst: A Journal for Lesbian and Gay Men*. One reads,

> i reach for my pen,
> the urge to write a poem having
> seized me, but before I have
> it in my hand I know no
> poem, the act of creation of one,
> is going to slake the passionate
> hunger these fancy words are
> wired-up in hopes of obliterating...
>
> No, this hunger is for the boy
> himself, for the man to be
> here hot bedded with me underneath
> this squishy fluff warm comforter.
>
> i want the man,
> the whole being in the flesh.
>
> No poem can take your place.[20]

He did not intend to have his poems published. Just as he had despised reviews of his plays, he knew he could not endure the smug rejections and censorship that he would face with his poetry. "I'm just going to file it all & let some 'pale English major' sort it out.... If it gets published let it be posthumously. If it all gets burned up—who cares. I've never written anything for anybody but myself anyway and only what I needed to survive."[21]

His fear of censorship was realized. He was asked by officials at Georgia State University to provide a poem for the exhibit they were mounting in honor of Cal's dear friend, Jim Sitton, who had been murdered in Atlanta ten years earlier. The first six lines of "Fragments for Jim" read:

> too heartbroken it seems to write much of anything
> still, ten years after, only fragments come, pieces of
> jim Jim JIM: Jimmy:
> > precious Parisian bisque,
> > crushed, all ruined
> > in a fucking parking lot.

When Cal attended the show in Atlanta with Fred Chappell and Raiford Ragsdale, the poem appeared in the exhibit program, but the sixth line was changed to read "in a f-ing parking lot." Amused by their editing, Cal wrote to Johnny Ferdon, "They don't want us there [in Atlanta] and never did."[22]

Cal's friendship with the young and handsome Bag Boy, Michael Parker, continued. Although they did not have sex, they often slept together at Cal's mobile home near Micanopy. Michael seemed to enjoy being nude around Cal and showing off his sculpted body. Their both being Crystal River "boys" and sharing a common heritage made for a curious bond. "It is like I found a son," Cal beamed, "a boy, a boy, a boy, a boy to love."[23] Cal compared their relationship to the thirty-year difference between the older Christopher Isherwood and his much younger lover, Don Bachardy, and prayed it was a sign that he would not have to grow old alone. Eventually, Michael met a cute, young man who moved in with him, and Cal gained a better perspective of their affair. What he saw happening to Michael is what he always knew would have happened to him if he had not escaped from Crystal River.

With only a few relapses, Cal managed to maintain his sobriety, but to combat his bouts of depression he turned more heavily to drugs. Soon after he had returned to Florida in 1978, Cal's old-time friend, Joe Hendrix, who lived just outside of Red Boiling Springs, Tennessee, began supplying him with indica seeds, a kind of cannabis plant known as a relaxant and an effective antidote for anxiety. Cal planted the seeds in the fields at Center and mailed Joe monthly payments for more grass. Intrigued by the isolation and freedom that Joe described living in what he called his Hippy Holler, Cal spent several weekends there and gave poetry readings for the more enlightened of the area. Encouraged by Joe, who wanted a partner to help him with the planting, harvesting, and distribution of his cannabis, Cal even considered for a brief time purchasing property near Joe and joining him in the trafficking business.

Convinced he had no future as a playwright, in the spring of 1984, Cal jumped at the chance to participate in a three-week poetry workshop conducted by Allen Ginsberg at the Atlantic Center for the Arts in New Smyrna Beach, Florida. The Center was founded for the purpose of giving talented artists the opportunity to work with master teachers, hoping the experience would propel them into the top ranks.

From the time Ginsberg had published his scandalous poem, "Howl," with its raw and explicit language in 1956, he had been, along with Jack Kerouac and William S. Burroughs, one of the leaders of the "Beat Generation." Cal naturally felt a kinship with him. Ginsberg also was openly gay, talked frankly about sexuality in graphic detail, refused to compromise his style, and advocated the use of marijuana. As he wrote in his application to the workshop, Cal explained that he wanted to study with Ginsberg because he was feeling, "the art leaving me. I'm not sure I want it to leave me."[24] He yearned for artistic stimulus and feedback from functioning writers and from someone with Ginsberg's reputation.

Sadly, Cal found the experience to be an absurd debacle. During one of the workshop sessions, Cal read a fragment of a poem he had composed that included the word "prick." Ginsberg interrupted him and "pounced like a proper offended 50's faggot," insisting that Cal should be discrete. "I don't have any interest in being discrete," Cal retaliated. It dawned on him that this legendary man was "afraid of us, closed-off, out of touch, remote—and New York City snotty." Cal concluded, "he's missed most of the sexual revolution—been so busy chanting STOP THE BOMB that he has not stopped to consider <u>why</u> the bombs are dropped. He also seems to have forgotten MAKE LOVE NOT WAR."[25]

Cal was so angry that he considered dropping out of the workshop. Instead, he remained and submitted to Ginsberg at the close of the workshop two poems that sum up his opinion of working with the radical guru.

> Faraway in cavernous falling
> cities, my friends and brothers
> are dying one by one.
> As any good Jew will
> tell you: there are more
> ways, Mr. Ginsberg, to
> obliterate

a people than with the
Bomb.

★

victims of sexual
genocide, the rare
butterflies of
night fight
hopeless odds
drop writhing
dying shameful
deaths in Ward 5B
alone
most glad they're
gone.

The workshop did nothing to bolster his self-confidence. As he contemplated his future, he wrote to Johnny Ferdon, "I get nothing but discouragement for my writing....I have almost no spirit left. I'm completely beat down—silenced. Hokum & Hogwash have won hands down."[26]

Miss Vada died on January 23, 1985. A few days earlier, Cal had found her lying on the floor. "I don't even feel tired no more," she wept. She

Figure 7.1   Cal with his mother in 1982.

Source: Courtesy Cal Yeomans Collection, Special Area Studies, George A. Smathers Libraries, University of Florida.

had suffered a heart attack and had fallen with a horrible thud, facedown on the kitchen floor. Blood poured from her nose and from the cut on her lip—a dark, awful, growing pool on the cream of the marbled linoleum. Cal rushed to her and took her limp body in his arms. "Poor baby," he said as he cradled her in his arms. He was stunned, terrified, and felt utterly helpless.[27]

Her funeral was one of Cal's biggest challenges. His cousin Van and his wife, Virginia, sent flowers; Virginia attended, but Van did not. Cal paid hundreds of dollars for Rayford Meeks, a gay cousin of his who owned a florist shop in nearby Inverness, to make two large floral displays for Vada's casket. Tom Smith sent flowers. The pallbearers included Cal's cousins, Sid Kennedy and Bobby Wilder. Out of respect for his mother and their prominent family, Cal knew he had to behave properly and "do it right." His old friend, Grady McClendon, helped him select a sport coat that he wore over a black turtleneck.

It was a real concession, since he almost always wore jeans and flannel shirts. He wore dark glasses that helped to distance himself from the respectable crowd. Many of those in attendance were people who had always been critical of Cal. Grady stayed with him the entire day. While

Figure 7.2 Grady McClendon, always a loyal friend.

Source: Courtesy Cal Yeomans Collection, Special Area Studies, George A. Smathers Libraries, University of Florida.

at the gravesite, one of his mother's friends bent down and whispered in his ear, "Now that she's gone, you better not bring any of those men into her house. I'll be watching!"[28] When everything was over and everyone had left, Cal broke down in uncontrollable sobs.

Shortly after her death, Calvin composed several poems in her memory. One he titled "Fragment for Vada."

> Time is slipping away—
> my time
>   (yours too)
> I remember Vada that
> last afternoon that last
> sunset as we drove past her
> her beloved church, past
> the A.D. Williams house toward the hospital
> and the cold Florida winter sun
> setting low behind the trees
> of the old swamp flashed
> thru the Pinto windshield
> and I looked at Vada—my
> Mother's tiny frail body
> so diminished with age
> and saw her take one
> last look toward the spot
> where her old church
> used to stand—the one
> they tore down—and saw
> her look sadly away again
> straight ahead down the
> road and together we knew
> then she'd, we'd never share
> another ride again.
>
> I cry now alone in this
> Key West night, so tired,
> so frightened, feeling my own
> body grow old—knowing what
> lies ahead and[29]

The final eight years of Vada's life, the relationship between her and Cal had improved dramatically. He could never forget her face when, moments before she died, she pulled him down so he could kiss her cheek good-bye. Her face, despite the pain of a failing heart, was radiant with love as she whispered to him, "You'll be alright, son."[30]

It was so difficult for him to shake the melancholy. Four months after her death, he wrote in his journal, "Sweet Vada gone. And with her the main restricting obligations which governed & dictated my life. This is good in many ways. But in many ways it is frightening, disorienting, & hurting. Vada had become so much all there was of my life in recent years. Now she is gone & there are huge holes, enormous vacancies, great voids that must be faced & filled....A New Life must be found to live. My life after Vada. My life alone."[31] And a few weeks later, he wrote, "I wish Vada was in Crystal River, missing me, wanting me home."[32] In letters to his friends, telling them of her death, he wrote, "Nobody loves you like your mother does."[33]

Even though actress Dana Ivey had been extremely critical of his writing, after Miss Vada died, Cal gave her the AAA quality diamond ring his mother had purchased in 1945 for $695. It was now valued well over $1,000. Years later, Ivey wrote to Cal that Vada's diamond brightened her life every day. She felt so very special wearing it.[34] In spite of the generous gift, she would not grant any interviews for this book.

In early January 1985, he had asked Grady to go with him to Key West to help him pick out a house to buy. He knew his mother was failing and that he would need to escape from Crystal River once she died. He settled on an old cigar maker's cottage at 1215 Newton Street. It cost $72,000 for the small working-class house—about all any bourgeois, gay man of modest means could afford in Key West at the time. Sometimes feeling terribly isolated from creative artists and the steamy gay world of San Francisco, Cal encouraged visits by his friends.

They were not always a success. When Tom Smith visited him in 1985, he brought along his current lover, Jeff Hamilton. The first few days, the two of them stayed out all night and argued nonstop. Hamilton wound up moving into a hotel, and Tom suddenly flew back to San Francisco. Cal was shattered, since he had cleaned and cooked for a week in preparations to host his old friend. A few weeks after Tom left, Cal learned what motivated his hasty departure. Tom had discovered a lesion on his tongue that he feared was a sign of AIDS. "If, as he believes, he has AIDS and is dying, how will I feel?" Cal grieved. "More loss. Loss. Loss. Loss."[35] For seven years, Tom had been one of Cal's major champions, literally a lifesaver. Miss Vada had been so comforted with how he helped her son that she kept a photograph of him stuck onto her refrigerator door. Cal had often commented that he doubted if he would have lived without the support Tom managed to provide so generously.

Although Cal was still enjoying his friendship with the Bag Boy, he was bowled over when he met a young, university student in early

Figure 7.3   Vern Gransden was Cal's personal Richmond Jim.

Source: Courtesy Cal Yeomans Collection, Special Area Studies, George A. Smathers Libraries, University of Florida.

February 1985. One night at The Ambush, Cal was approached by a very hot, short, butch, young man, wearing his keys on the left, which meant he was a top.

They went outside to the back patio, smoked a joint, and shared their sexual likes and dislikes. Cal was excited to discover that Vern Gransden was looking for a daddy master to teach him. He was especially fascinated that Vern was attracted to him because he had gained so much weight, now a forty-two-inch waist. "Teach him I will if he wants," he wrote. "Or maybe we'll learn together."[36] They made a date for the following weekend. After about a year of seeing each other, Cal realized that Vern was his Richmond Jim. Cal photographed him in several hot, bondage poses that prompted Cal to think "it is time for man to man love to be reactivated strongly 'one more time'—this time of course within the framework of safe."[37] Although their relationship changed through the years, they remained close friends and saw each other often. Vern, who referred to Cal as "Il Papa," came to view Cal as his dearest friend, mentor, father-figure, buddy, and fuck-buddy.

The summer of 1985, Cal enrolled in a playwriting workshop in Key West, wanting to give his writing "one more whirl," as he put it.[38] The result was a one-act he titled "Hibiscus," Cal's only play about AIDS. It takes place in a little Key West bar that originally opened as a leather bar.

A fashionable, heterosexual couple enters, and they sit near a man who is very drunk, steadily crying, and sniffing poppers. When the drunk takes a huge hit and begins to cough and gag, the couple starts to talk about the alleged dangers of poppers—they are lethal, they can impair the immune system and contribute to contracting AIDS. "And people still do them?" the woman asks. "Sure," her companion replies. "Self-destruction is as fashionable as it always was." The drunk inhales more, begins to retch, gags with dry heaves, and runs into the men's room. "I don't understand it," the woman says. When she asks, "Why would any-body sit in a bar—or anywhere—and do that to themselves," he answers, "Who knows? Maybe he just found out he has AIDS."[39] At that point, the couple decides to leave for a disco bar where they can dance and forget. When he sent the script to Tom Smith, Cal admitted that he seemed to be suffering from some kind of sickness or malady that prevented him from finishing the script. "If I don't write then I won't have to share and that is the only way I have I guess of getting back at the world."[40] There is no indication that Cal ever sent the script to anyone besides Tom.

For some time, Cal had refused to acknowledge that Tom had AIDS. But just days after Tom informed him in February 1986 that the test results were positive, Cal flew to San Francisco and found his friend depressed and very pale. "How will I survive with all my friends gone?" he wrote. "Their deaths used to scare me so bad. Now they've become commonplace."[41] With Tom's impending death on his mind, Cal had taken lilies to his mother's grave before he left to see Tom. As he stood at the family plot, he thought, "Vada's gone. Buried beside Daddy. My slab's on his right. He's between us as he always was. If I could do it over I believe I would have put Vada between us."[42] Tom died a year later, on July 27, 1987, at the age of fifty.

While he was in California visiting Tom, Cal was invited to a lunch with Robert Chesley. They had met briefly a few years earlier when Cal was in town to see *Sunsets*, but they had no opportunity to really talk at that time. Cal was excited to see Chesley, since he knew that Chesley had been so fired up about his plays. They talked nonstop. Chesley told Cal that when he had dated Mark I. Chester he often participated in all-night bondage trips. They discussed the status of gay theatre and agreed it needed to become more sexual. One thing Cal remembered clearly was his saying that safe sex is not sex, it's masturbation, which made Cal wonder if Chesley was practicing safe sex.

Most of the men that Cal connected with were considerably younger—Ralph Haddix, Bruce Emerton, Michael Parker, Vern Gransden—and were appealing because of their youth and inexperience. He could be their mentor and help them learn how to cope with being gay in a homophobic culture. Michael Haykin was quite different. Born in 1954, he was younger than Cal by sixteen years, but still not a youth. When they met at The Saloon bar in Key West the fall of 1985, Michael had already started to make a name for himself as an accomplished painter and had exhibited in several galleries. Cal drooled over him. With his long, curly hair and slender but sleek frame, he was sexy with a raw allure.

The night they met and went back to Cal's house, the sex was fantastic. "You turned me on," Cal raved, "with the fire of nuclear fission and hardened my joy-stick as it pierced your ass-hole into steel."[43] Cal took several photos of Michael, and posed for one of his paintings, sitting nude, his tormented countenance staring out, cold and unknowing with a woman at his side, dressed to kill—staunch and strong. When Michael went to New York for a show at the Limbo Gallery, he took the painting, titled "Perfect Strangers," as part of the exhibit. Cal wrote to Johnny Ferdon in New York, "If you need a chuckle, stop in to see it."[44]

Once again, Cal was hopeful for a permanent relationship. After about a three-month, intense affair, however, Cal wrote the following poem.

> michael, michael, michael,
> with the fire between us,
> we could have done so much
> good stuff together. with the
> fire between us, we could have
> lit-up the world.[45]

They continued to see each other for the next few months, and then the affair was over. When asked about their relationship nearly a quarter century later, Michael simply replied that he did not know Cal very well and that their relationship was brief.[46]

Living adjacent to Cal outside Micanopy was a young, straight couple, Martha and Tim Hoggard, along with their two children. They often invited Cal to join them for Thanksgiving and Christmas dinners where they usually exchanged small gifts. On one occasion, Cal gave the children little wooden rocking chairs, another time, pieces of pottery he had picked up at the local flea market. After Miss Vada died, he found one of her handmade quilted pillows and gave it to little Molly Hoggard. He loved playing with the children and taking them on long hikes through the countryside and into the woods. When Martha was baking pecan pies or banana bread, she often made extra to take to him. During one particularly hot summer, they even lent him one of their window air conditioners so he could manage the oppressive heat beating down on

Figure 7.4 Cal hoped for a permanent relationship with Michael Haykin.

the metal of his mobile home. "With their customary exquisite sensitivity," the Hoggards always seemed to understand his moods. It reminded Cal of what his mother always said, "Good neighbors are one of God's greatest gifts."[47]

On April 8, 1986, Cal met a man at a poetry reading he presented at Gay Talk in Gainesville who would become a very close friend, Eric Garber. At first, Cal thought he was interesting but just another older graduate student. Eric did not divulge who he was until later at the bar when he indicated he was a writer. When Cal asked him what he had written, Eric answered, "I write under the pseudonym of Andrew Holleran."[48] Cal was stunned, flabbergasted. He was so pleased that the author of *Dancer from the Dance* and *Nights in Aruba* was so impressed with his poetry.

Cal enjoyed talking to Eric about writing and appreciated how attentive he was to his ailing mother, whom he called "mummykins." Cal recognized that Eric had a lot of unadmitted anger and a New York bitter bite, the typical fag put-down that he tried to suppress. "But all considered," he wrote, "he is a lovely person and we are strangely 'good' as friends."[49] They often went to The Ambush together after the Gay Talk meetings and sometimes met up at the gay baths in Jacksonville. Cal always joked about how very white and skinny Eric looked at the baths, and how he "spooked" many of the guys as he walked down the narrow, dimly lit hallways in his towel.

Later in April, Chesley visited Cal in Key West. This was the first time they had spent several days together, and they got along famously. Cal took several photos of Chesley, some in the nude. They talked endlessly about the theatre and about Chesley's plays, especially *Pigman: A Comedy in Three Acts*. A gay man who goes by the name of Boy loses his partner to AIDS and discovers that his partner knew who infected him—a sexual pig who has AIDS and is having unsafe sex with every man he can find. In his quest to find the pig man and make him stop having unsafe sex, Boy comes across all kinds of gay men—a queen, leather man, fister, speed freak, a wealthy doctor. When he finds the pig man at the end of the play, the confrontation focuses on the fear surrounding sex at the time and that gay men should not renounce their sexual desires during the plague. Cal liked the play but advised Chesley to "use himself more. Write more from personal experiences."[50]

Knowing that Chesley was heading for New York, Cal gave him Ellen Stewart's telephone number and arranged for him to meet with her to discuss the possibility of her producing *Pigman* at La MaMa. Cal harbored many complaints about Ellen, but, even so, he recognized she was an important force in American theatre and that a production at La MaMa

Figure 7.5   Cal took several photos of Robert Chesley in Key West.

Source: Courtesy Cal Yeomans Collection, Special Area Studies, George A. Smathers Libraries, University of Florida.

could be a major boost to Chesley's career. Chesley, who, like Cal, longed for more approval of his writing, was extremely appreciative of Cal's support and endorsement.

> Every contact I have had with you and/or your writing has been important to me.... I am alienated from the current wave of neo-antieroticism which is sweeping through the gay community.... You are important to me—not because you have ever said my writing is good and I can rest easy, but because you see what I am trying to do, what my goals are, and consider that seriously.... I find [your writing] illuminating in areas of human experience previously undocumented; I think you are stating truths which <u>need</u> to be stated, doing so very directly and very beautifully, and doing so when nobody else is.[51]

Chesley's meeting with Ellen Stewart was predictable. Her first remark to him—and which she stuck to for the entire meeting—was that she did not do his type of play, especially one like *Pigman*; she did only experimental theatre. Chesley found it ironic that Ellen was celebrating the silver anniversary of La MaMa by doing revivals and nothing the least bit experimental. "There is a gap in her theater," Chesley complained. "It has not, at least yet, addressed [sic] the current ghastly tragedy of gay men."[52]

Chesley's reaction to Ellen Stewart gave Cal ample reason to respond. "She thinks black plays always have a kitchen sink in them and she thinks gay plays are always about 'me and my lover.'...She...thinks gay plays somehow second rate....We are part of something that won't be understood in our own time and perhaps never," he argued. "It doesn't have to do with gay or straight, but rather with the liberation of the human body and mind and the realization of its capabilities and the expansion of its limitations in order to realize full human potential."[53]

Having returned to his home at Center, Cal began the emotional and arduous task of clearing out the house where his mother had lived in Crystal River. A year had elapsed since her death in 1985. He had consciously avoided the task earlier but had finally decided to put the house up for sale. With Grady and Michael Parker's help, he took much of her furniture to his mobile home. As he walked out the door the last time, he paused to look at the light in Vada's corner, where her chair sat in her last years and where she spent so much of her time watching television and making her quilted pillowcases. He could see her sewing basket on the floor to her left, her scissors on the table to her right, but now it was only space, empty space awaiting a new family to give it life. Although it was the house in which he had been conceived, he never felt he had a place there, no room of his own. And the circumstances under which he and his mother returned after his breakdown were so horrendous, he had nothing but bad memories of the house. He knew he could never live there again, did not want to, and knew that he could not have survived it. "So I turned it loose," he sighed, "but not without a certain sadness, a tinge of regret."[54]

Undoubtedly pumped up from his conversations with Chesley about the challenges of writing for gay theatre, Cal sent a lengthy letter to Robert Massa, theatre critic for *The Village Voice*.

It was <u>always</u> difficult to write plays for gay theatre because the very nature of the genre is innately so controversial—even for gay people. We may be quite accustomed to doing certain things in our lives, but we are not accustomed to seeing them depicted on stage—or ready to accept it....I could go on writing hoked-up, half-assed situation soap operas, nice little plays about "me and my lover" and I'm sure these would be gobbled-up as quickly as I could turn them out. This does not interest me and it certainly does not excite me....

Shock, fear, traumatized silence, confusion, paranoia were my first reaction to AIDS. But what, as a writer, should be my appropriate reaction? Silence is no good. How could I write about it when no one really even knew what it was, how it started, where it was going, what caused it, how long it would last....What to do? I have several unfinished scripts that had been begun as a follow-up on what we had tried to begin with "Sunsets": a sexual performance theatre. Needless to say these can't now be produced as originally conceived, in our time or in the conceivable future. What was exciting, hot, sexually electric yesterday is now either fatuous or unmistakeably ghoulish. Jokes that <u>were</u> funny are now horrifying or at best tasteless. What to do?...

I was talking to another gay writer [Eric Garber] the other day and he turned to me and said, "Well, if we can't use humor, what then can we use?"

From some wisdom I didn't know I had, I instantly replied, "Rage. We can use rage. We can step to the edge of the stage like Diana Sands in James Baldwin's 'Blues for Mr. Charley' and just tell it like it is."

"But I'm not very good with rage," he replied.

I laughed and was surprised to hear myself say, "Well, I am." We *must* "utter what we suffer".

Powerful, exciting plays <u>will</u> come out of this time. But only when existing gay theatres and the control figures of gay theatre realize that time is short and that it is much too late to worry about whether a play is correct or incorrect, palatable or unpalatable, healthy or unhealthy. It is time to speak. To speak anything you can. To speak as much as we can. To say all we can. To let everyone know all they can of our experience—of the right side of it, of the wrong side of it, of the goodness of it, the badness of it. We must let the world see the full range of our experience, the full range of our struggle and <u>certainly</u> the full range of our suffering and despair—which was gargantuan <u>before</u> the advent of AIDS and is now, well...: it would be easy to say that there are no words for it. But we must find some.[55]

Although Cal was discouraged about the status of gay theatre in general and Ellen Stewart's production choices specifically, he agreed to participate in the silver anniversary celebration of La MaMa. Following lengthy discussions with Ellen and her staff, Cal proceeded to prepare a reading composed of his poetry and selections from his plays, which he titled "Pieces of a Way." Contemporary psychologists might call this a counterphobia tactic where a person searches out those things or situations that cause them apprehension and is drawn to what scares or repulses them. Just as a phobic person takes drastic measures to avoid what they fear, a counterphobic person seeks out those situations. Trying to overcome what is feared, the individual overcompensates and pushes toward it, which becomes the person's attempt to cope with internal anxiety, leading to an almost constant state of "fight or flight."

While Cal certainly feared more rejection and disapproval from Ellen Stewart, he hid behind a grandiose social mask, projecting the aura that he did not care what people thought of him and proceeded with his preparations. In reality, he was terrified he would receive negative criticism. Regardless, he longed for her approval and acceptance, just as he had from his mother; it would justify his existence. In fact, through the years he continued to send Ellen gifts—a coral necklace, a handmade quilt, a crocheted blanket that he made, an alligator handbag, a painting by Joe Hendrix, a necklace of glass beads made by Miss Vada—as well as birthday cards almost every year.

He worked for several weeks on what to read—the poem about his mother's death, selections from "The Daddy Poems," speeches from *Richmond Jim* and *Sunsets*—and rehearsed his reading as if he were heading for Broadway. As he prepared, he recalled something Miss Vada said so painfully a few months before she died: "I can't do *nothing!*" Her fingers were too gnarled to pick things up, she could not see well, it was so difficult for her even to walk. He was feeling the same, seeing his life as a damaged and highly emotionally handicapped person's struggle to function. Once again, he contemplated just throwing in the towel and giving up and sinking under the knowledge that he was a perpetual ne'er do well and a worthless misfit. But, as usual, he hoped the reading might be of some worth for someone and therefore justify his existence.

It had been ten years since Cal had been back to La MaMa, ten years since Ellen had him admitted into Bellevue Hospital. As he stood before

Figure 7.6   Ellen Stewart wears the coral necklace Cal gave her.

Source: Courtesy Cal Yeomans Collection, Special Area Studies, George A. Smathers Libraries, University of Florida.

the audience on October 10, 1986, Cal was comforted to see so many faces he recognized—Johnny Ferdon, Agosto Machado, Raymond Schanze, Donald Arrington, Eric Garber, Robert Chesley, Bruce Emerton, Doric Wilson, and, of course, Ellen Stewart. Robert Patrick had a conflict and could not attend the reading, but he still showed up before it began to congratulate Cal in advance. Regardless of the many supporters in the room, it was difficult for him, especially suspecting the material he had chosen might raise some eyebrows. He knew he would have trouble reading "Fragment for Vada," but was totally surprised when he lost control reading "The Daddy Poems." When Ellen handed him flowers during the final applause, all she whispered to him was, "Some beautiful images, but the subject matter: No."[56] He did not learn until later that the flowers were not from Ellen. She had removed the card that indicated they were from his old Atlanta friend, Raiford Ragsdale.

The reading left him with a nagging sense of shame, "a metallic edge of regret at having embarrassed others. . . . I did what I wanted to do," he wrote, "but somehow I wasn't prepared to take the consequences." Many were stunned. Doric Wilson's horror-stricken face haunted Cal for years after. When he went to bed that night, he cried himself to sleep and awakened the next morning still crying, "I don't think I can risk doing what I did at La Mama [sic] too often."[57] Soon after Cal returned home to Florida, however, he confronted Ellen about her complaints. "The subject of my reading is the very life of 10% of the world population. Our sexuality is the aspect of our humanity that makes us different from the rest of mankind. . . . Suffice that it was extremely meaningful to all gay people that you allowed me to speak in your house. As you well know, gay men are quite effectively being silenced these days. As you say, gay plays are 'passe'. But you might ask yourself why."[58]

A few weeks later, Cal was delighted to be part of the packed houses at Seven Stages theatre in Atlanta, seeing Chesley's *Jerker*, directed by Michael Kearns. Set in the Castro neighborhood in 1985, the play dramatizes via phone sex the relationship between two gay men, who are terrified by reports of AIDS. Sounding much like Cal, Chesley explained that he wrote the play because he believed it was "important to remove the stigma against sex that AIDS has created, and . . . to remove the stigma against gay men."[59] The play, which included simulated orgasms, was at the center of an obscenity controversy after a radio station broadcast excerpts of it the previous summer. Chesley had responded at that time, "Prudery kills, on the radio or anywhere else. . . . Nobody ever died from being offended by what they see or hear."[60] Ultimately, the FCC ruled that the broadcast was indecent and possibly obscene, sanctioned the station, and implemented new, more stringent broadcast indecency guidelines.

Before Cal drove to Atlanta, Chesley had informed him that Kearns had read Cal's *Sunsets* and was keen on directing a production of it. Though reluctant to discuss it with Kearns, Cal was certainly flattered by the prospect, especially after seeing his direction of *Jerker*, and hoped the folks at Seven Stages would produce it. Rebecca Ranson, the executive director of the multi-arts organization that had invited *Jerker* to Atlanta and who founded Seven Stages, had written the successful AIDS play, *Warren*, so Cal thought she would be receptive. There is no record indicating why it was not done.

About the same time, Kelly Hill, who had directed three Chesley plays and performed in two, met Cal and was keen on directing *Sunsets* as well as *Pigman*. He pitched both of them to Theatre Rhinoceros and to The New Conservatory Theater in San Francisco as well as to SAME in Atlanta but to no avail. "Producers in those years," he discovered, "didn't want to take the risk with [their] plays due their overt sexual imagery and AIDS themes. Bottom line was the theaters were fearful of losing money."[61]

Although Cal continued to dabble with playwriting—but seldom with the thought of a production—he had developed additional creative outlets. For several years, he had toyed with photography, but in 1983 he began to explore it more seriously, mainly because Ralph Haddix, his love du jour, liked to have his picture taken. After Ralph returned to his wife, it did not take Cal long to realize there were other men who enjoyed being photographed. He wrote to Ellen Stewart at the time, "I feel myself increasingly called to make pictures and less to write and am just going along with that instinct."[62]

If a man interested him, and he saw beauty—spiritual or physical or both—Cal would ask to take his picture. Most of the men consented. He soon discovered that "my pictures say it better than my words ever did."[63] His plays always illustrated aspects of gay life that often made people uncomfortable. With his photography he was able to convey much more without a large audience, without a production. He could simply set up the picture and let the viewer read meaning into it, let the viewer create the story behind the picture.

Although most of his photos were of nude men, many were not. But even with the nudes, they were sensual, but never offensive, even though he experienced sex with most of his models. They were usually unposed, candid, and almost always black and white. Cal's photographs were personal, private, nonstudio, environmental types of shots. For one of his collections, Cal traveled all over Florida to capture the fascinating fronts of dozens of beauty shops, ranging from impressive buildings in larger cities to makeshift storefronts in forlorn little villages. In another collection he called "Men of North Florida," he captured men in various settings—leaning against a feed store in Keystone Heights, descending a majestic circular stairway, rehearsing with a French horn, repairing plumbing, exiting an outhouse, scrubbing down an armpit, lounging in a garden chair, walking nude along a beach. He was a great voyeur and an observer of people, which gave him the opportunity to see and to interpret in his photographs.

His first exhibit was at The Ambush gay bar in Gainesville in December 1986. One of the photos was of his friend, Frank Regan, who had given Cal permission to include his photo, but assumed they would be exhibited in New York or San Francisco, certainly never in Gainesville. What a shock he had when he entered the bar one night and saw his genitals hanging on the wall for all his friends to see. Cal was aware that some of his photos did not meet common decency standards, but he argued that it was to his taste. "I don't have no guilt," he explained. "From here on out...my work is to my taste....There's them that thinks my work good art....[T]here's a larger number that don't think it's nothing but filth. I don't know and don't care too much."[64]

The following July, Cal was asked to show his photos at The Ambush again, this time for an art show that was to include works of other artists, including pottery, erotic drawings, and tie-dyed T-shirts. When Cal told Eric about the show, Eric remarked, "Oh, the first Cal Yeomans Art Show." Cal quickly replied, "No. The first Gainesville Gay Art Show!" Although their friendship continued, there was often tension. Cal would stress the importance of writing truthfully, and Eric would immediately change the subject or leave the room. "He can be *so* New York," Cal complained.[65] He wanted to discover if there was enough between them for the foundation for a serious friendship—if not a love affair, but it made him "feel like Cecil Beaton whumping up Garbo."[66] And yet, Cal felt lucky to have Eric living nearby. He was the only person in the area with whom he could totally communicate.

A few years earlier, Cal had met Ernie Mickler and his partner, Gary Jolley, while on one of his trips to Key West. Ernie had been living there for several years, working mainly as a caterer. Cal often invited him to cook at his house where the guests usually were houseboys, bartenders, and pals of Ernie's. Cal and Ernie became fast friends; they entertained together, frequented the bars, and cruised men on the beaches. Not surprising, Cal photographed Ernie extensively, sometimes nude on the beach. When Ernie was putting together his 1986 book, *White Trash Cooking*, Cal often helped him with the layout and text. Some of the photos that Ernie used to promote the book were Cal's.

Mid-March 1987, Cal was back visiting Joe Hendrix in Tennessee. Joe had known that Cal was continuing with his photography, often of nude men, and informed Cal that, even though he was straight, he was interested in posing for some. Cal jumped at the chance, since he had lusted after Joe ever since they had met in the early 1970s when Joe and his family lived in Crystal River. During the course of the photo session, Cal was overcome with his desire for Joe and later confessed, "I was certainly aware that this was a good time—if there ever was going to be one—a possible time—when I might be able to physicalize the love I've had for you since I first met you. I've *always* wanted to worship your temple. I've always wanted to suck your dick. . . . I do intend to suck your dick every time you'll let me. But, by the same token, I'll certainly do my best to respect our love and friendship if you don't want to physicalize it. . . . Making love to you was a dream come true and like an exquisite taste of heaven on earth."[67] Cal was relieved to get Joe's response: "I love and respect you and it's much to [*sic*] early or I'm much to [*sic*] confused to say I'm deicated [*sic*] to homolove. I'm apprehensive about possiblity [*sic*] of changing yrs of relationship being a good friends lover."[68] Cal hoped that when Joe saw the photos that he would not freak out. They were a mixture of nude, partially dressed, and fully clothed—both black and white and color. Since they were so beautifully erotic, Cal considered putting together a special boxed set called The Joe Suite.

When Cal was in New York for his reading at La MaMa, he and Ellen had talked about Ernie's new book, *White Trash Cooking*. She loved it and suggested that Cal and Ernie should adapt the book into a musical. In no time at all, Cal arranged a meeting on April 5, in Tallahassee to include himself, Ernie, Gary, and his longtime theatre friend, Fred Chappell, who was teaching at Florida State University. The actress, Collin Wilcox, who had played the raped girl in the film, *To Kill a Mockingbird,* was running a theatre in Highlands, North Carolina, so they invited her to join them, thinking the play could premiere at her theatre. Although she did not show up, Cal thought they had made a good start and planned to stir up interest in New York.

He was unsure, however, how much he could count on Fred. They all had a rather elegant sit-down dinner with Fred and his wife, Agnes, complete with a huge bouquet of pink roses as a centerpiece. Fred, Cal realized, was "off the wagon," drinking heavily again, and proceeded to entertain them with an astonishing monologue of a character named Martha, who apparently inhabited his body when he was drunk. Cal found himself transported back to what he had tried to escape from twenty years earlier. "Fred is a mess," he wrote, "and it is sad to see him drinking again."[69]

Ernie spent the next several months working on both the script and on a second cookbook, sending drafts to Cal. In one of his responses,

Cal warned, "Be cautious or...you'll find you're writing about a cliché rather than about REAL experience. Ground your work specifically in the real you've really <u>seen</u>....Establish the period you're writing about and maintain that—or explain any shifts. Are you writing about 'food in the South of my remembered childhood' or are you writing about food as cooked and et in Duval County in 1987? Both are interesting—but vastly different....Write the truth of your heart as your eyes see it."[70] Sadly, Ernie never finished writing the musical adaptation. It perhaps could have been a hit like the 1982 *Pump Boys and Dinettes*, but Ernie learned that he had contracted AIDS and threw all of his energy into completing his cookbook rather than the script.

Cal was having dinner with Eric and Vern when they learned that Charles Ludlam had died. They were devastated. Cal had seen him just a few weeks earlier when he was in New York at the opening performance of Jean Jesurun's production of *Black Maria* at La MaMa. Their eyes met, but Cal was so nervous and disoriented that he just walked on. He saw no visual hint that Ludlam was ill. It was a very rapid death; Ludlam had only known for about four months that he had AIDS. "What a loss!" Cal noted. "The already dim & flickering light of the American theatre has been considerably lessened by his death."[71]

Cal always felt he could trust his friends, especially the ones whom he had helped out financially. Michael Parker (Bag Boy) had been living in the Yeomans's house by the river for nearly eighteen months, rent free. In exchange, all Cal asked was that Michael take care of the grounds and maintain the house. When Cal knocked on the door one day, Michael opened it, wearing one of Cal's robes, the one that had been issued to him when he was a patient at Anclote Mental Hospital. Cal was taken aback, to say the least, since the robe had hung untouched for twenty years at the back of one of the closets. When Cal explained the robe's history, it was the first that Michael had ever known of Cal's breakdown. But what was much worse for Cal was seeing that general sloth had set in—clothes thrown about everywhere, dishes piled high in the sink, books and papers strewn about. It was particularly unsettling because Robert Chesley was visiting in about ten days, and Cal wanted to stay with him at the house. Cal felt he had no choice; he evicted Michael on the spot. When he discovered that Michael had left him with hundreds of dollars of unpaid utility bills, Cal concluded, "He turned out just like everyone told me he would."[72] With Vern's help, Cal worked furiously the next two weeks, cleaning up the house, mowing the lawn, restoring Vada's little goldfish pond, and generally making the place presentable again.

During Chesley's visit, Cal had arranged for him to give a reading at the Gay Talk group the evening he arrived. That went well. But the next few days were a nightmare, mainly because Chesley's boyfriend who accompanied him contradicted and ridiculed everything Cal said with phrases like "we saw better when we were in Greece last summer." Anything that smacked of "southern" was second rate. Cal took them to a restaurant and recommended the southern vegetables. The response: "That just means they're overcooked, doesn't it?" Cal's teeth were on edge. "City folks visits to the country don't always work out—and vice versa. Our ways are too different."[73]

When Cal received a letter from Michael Kearns inviting him to participate in an arts fair in Los Angeles in September, he was thrilled. He had enjoyed meeting Kearns a year earlier in Atlanta and hoped they could resume their conversation about Kearns directing a revival of *Sunsets*. Sponsored by Purple Stages and A Different Light Bookstore, the event lasted several days and occurred in several different venues. Cal described his participation as "POEMS, FRAGMENTS, PIECES, PICTURES, a sharing of my life as I've lived it 1985–'87. Southern gay neo-realism."[74] His photo exhibit of thirty-one photos opened on August 31, and ran the entire month of September. His reading was on September 6, and for the poster announcing the event, he used a hot, nude photo of one of his models.

It all went very well, especially the reading. The photos were considered so stunning that *Christopher Street* magazine published ten of them in its #114 issue with the caption, "Calvin Yeomans' plays, *Richmond Jim* and *Sunsets*, helped establish gay theater in New York City and San Francisco during the last decade."[75]

The editor of the magazine, Tom Steele, then commissioned Cal to provide photos for Andrew Holleran's (aka Eric Garber) regular column in the magazine. F. Glen Offield, art director for *Advocate Men*, wanted to publish some of them, but Cal had already signed an exclusive agreement with *Christopher Street*.[76]

Soon after Cal returned to Florida, he received news that an old building that he owned in downtown Crystal River finally had been sold. His father had purchased the property in the 1940s for $500, and Cal now got $50,000.[77] Unfortunately, their house by the river and the surrounding land of four acres where their fish house had stood was still on the market. Cal had put it up for sale in 1983, asking $1,350,000, but still there were no buyers in sight.

While he had been in California, Mark I. Chester had begged Cal to stay for a few more weeks so that Cal could see him perform in Cal's *Poiret in Exile* at San Francisco's very small and intimate Gregory Ghent Gallery. Uneasy about seeing the old play being done, Cal chose not to stay. Labeling the evening "Madness is my middle name," Chester

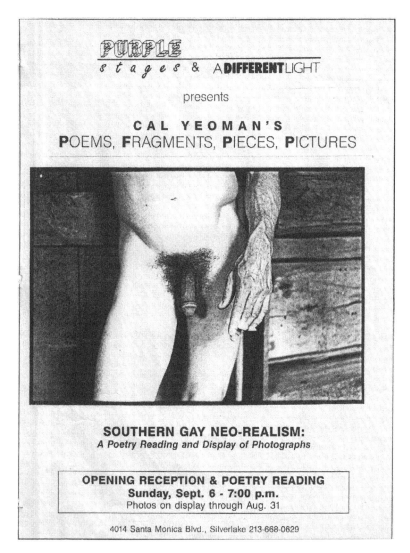

Figure 7.7   Cal used this photo on the flyer to promote his reading in Los Angeles.

Source: Courtesy Cal Yeomans Collection, Special Area Studies, George A. Smathers Libraries, University of Florida.

thought the monologue was more appropriate now than ever, since the AIDS epidemic seemed directly connected to the script. "It was filled," Chester explained, "with a sense of tragedy and loss, of a mind so shattered by the reality of death and loss and grief that it retreated into

Figure 7.8 This photo of Cal's appeared on the front cover of *Christopher Street*, issue #114.

Source: Courtesy Cal Yeomans Collection, Special Area Studies, George A. Smathers Libraries, University of Florida.

madness in order to survive."[78] Chester dyed his hair white and performed in the nude. The gallery was filled with the sculptures of an artist who did casts of full bodies and body parts that made the space moody and haunting, as if each sculpture was a memory of some person who had died. Large, xeroxed photographs of a young man that Chester had loved, who died from AIDS, were strewn throughout the space, many slashed with red paint like they were awash with blood. "We are living in such times of insanity," Chester wrote to Cal. "*Poiret* in some ways has helped ground me. Expressing the madness in my soul means that I don't have to hide it within." He ended his letter, "We need your heart and what you see."[79]

The day of Chester's performance, Cal leaned back and thought about his life, his career, and wondered what had happened. He flipped back through some old letters he had written to Johnny Ferdon and found the poem he was searching for. Though written two years earlier, it seemed so very appropriate.

> I long to turn away,
> begin again, but I go on being
> what I am and never what i
> intended.[80]

He had always intended on becoming a nationally successful playwright, but that no longer seemed a possibility. About the only nibble that had come his way for any professional production in recent years was from the lesbian actress Pat Bond, who told him she was very interested in playing the transvestite in Cal's, *Somebody's Angel Child*. They talked about it quite seriously when she was in Gainesville in 1987 with her one-woman show, *Eleanor Roosevelt: A Love Story*. The plans did not work out. AIDS was crippling his theatre and wasting so many of his friends. Who would be next?

CHAPTER 8

"I DO NOT DEATHFUCK"

The way 1988 began for Cal seemed to forecast much of his next couple of years. Michael Brennan (MAB) died on March 29, 1988. An alcoholic and a heavy drug user, he was suddenly attacked with pneumocystis pneumonia. Two of Cal's best friends in San Francisco—Tom Smith and Michael—now were gone, victims of the plague. Feeling alone and frightened, he tried to rally when he gave a reading at Gay Talk two days later, but he failed. The embarrassed, stunned silence of the audience was so total, he apologized and ran from the room in a panic.

In spite of their ongoing disagreements, Cal continued to promote Ellen Stewart and La MaMa and lobbied with the Atlantic Center for the Arts in Smyrna, Florida, to bring the La MaMa company for a residency, arguing that their presence would enrich the state immeasurably. He proceeded with great trepidation, constantly on the alert for Ellen to turn on him "with her annihilating cobra cunt" and claiming that he just wanted to have one of his plays done at La MaMa. "I feel a knowing [sic] fear in the back of my craw that I will somehow end up destroyed by daring to associate with monsters." After all, he wrote, Ellen's "ascent to stardom was not achieved without numerous human sacrifices."[1]

With Cal's efforts, the residency ran from April 17 to May 8, 1988, with Ellen Stewart, composer Elizabeth Swados, and set designer Jun Maeda as the master artists. All the company and workshop participants stayed in cabins, about six people in each. By the end of the first week, Cal felt reassured that the residency was going to be a great success and that his future with Ellen Stewart might be on the mend. By the middle of the second week, however, his hopes were shattered. He learned that James Murphy, director of programs, had invited Ellen to a dinner with board members of the Atlantic Center. Cal had arranged the residency, and yet he was not included in the invitation. He exploded. "Harvey Feierstein [sic] is the biggest Aunt Jemima since Hattie McDaniel. Edward

Albee died as a playwright when he forsook his gay roots. If you want to do the equivalent of minstrel shows, at La Mama [*sic*] that's your privilege. I don't care whether you put my plays on or not."[2] Clearly, another manic episode. Ellen heard him raving so hysterically in the cabin next to hers that she was fearful of opening her door. He apologized a few days later. Under the direction of Ellen Stewart, the twenty-five participants that included Cal as project consultant produced an adaptation of Ambrose Bierce's *The Monk and the Hangman's Daughter,* a medieval tale about a monk's falling in love with the daughter of the local hangman that ends in tragedy.

During the residency in Florida with Ellen, she had reluctantly agreed that Cal could return to La MaMa in the fall to exhibit his photographs and present another poetry reading. In preparation for the reading, Cal gave her a rough draft of a play he had been working on for over a year. Calling it *The 21st and 22nd Losses of Homer Lee Jackson,* Cal dramatized the account of the murder of two of his friends, George DuPont and his lover, Wesley Gordon, an African American. Their bodies were discovered by DuPont's mother on December 24, 1985, in a red jeep parked in the driveway of DuPont's country house near Alachua, Florida. Investigators determined they had been killed three days earlier. Eleven days after they were found, Homer Lee Jackson, also an African American, was charged with two counts of first-degree murder. According to the court records, the morning of December 21, Jackson, who had been working part-time for DuPont, went to DuPont's home, demanding money he said was owed to him. When DuPont refused, Jackson left, stole a gun, returned later that day, shot the two men in the back of their heads while they were in their car, and took the money that he felt was owed to him out of DuPont's wallet. Jackson ultimately confessed and was sentenced to life in prison, with a minimum mandatory term of twenty-five years for each murder.

What most of the news coverage neglected to reveal and what triggered Cal's interest in writing the play was the testimony of a psychologist who reported that Jackson claimed he had been "forced to engage in a sex act with the two men about a month before the murders." Jackson's lawyer tried a "gay panic" defense, claiming that Jackson had "acted out of frustration and anger resulting from the homosexual incident."[3] A month or so before the murder, DuPont had invited Cal to dinner with all three of them present. At that time, Cal had suspected tension among them. Jackson was surly and sat through the evening totally stone-faced and unresponsive. Cal described him later as "damned up ... a wired juggernaut," a "frustrated, rage-filled blackman." He sat unmoving and sulked and pouted as DuPont fawned, and bragged, and pampered him.[4]

Cal was cheered when he read portions of the script at his reading in Los Angeles just a month earlier. The audience was riveted. He maintained that his play was "wanted and needed.... I'll stand behind [it] 'til my last breath."[5] When he sent it to Ellen Stewart, he pointed out that he felt the play was "quite extraordinary.... I think Homer Lee's story deserves to be told—as does Henry's."[6] He hoped that some young director at La MaMa might choose to direct it.

What a shock he had in store. She raved on in a lengthy phone conversation, "I thought I'd made it clear to you that we don't do those kinds of cock plays at La Mama [sic]. We haven't done no cock plays in 15 years. The last cock we had at La Mama [sic] was when you gave your reading 2 years ago. I won't have no dialogue on the stage.... We won't put on that kind of play here *ever*. Why do you send that kind of stuff up here?" Silently, he let the phone fall from his hand into its cradle and broke down in tears, vowing "I'll never put my pearls before that old sow again!"[7] Once he recovered from her tirade, Cal swore that he would never change his work to suit her or anyone else. In a stinging letter to the director of the art gallery at La MaMa, Cal wrote, "Ms. Stewart made it completely and totally clear that me and my kind of truth/writing are under NO circumstances welcome or wanted at La Mama [sic]."[8] He learned a few weeks later that Ellen was telling everyone that Cal sent her the script because he was having a psychotic breakdown. What undoubtedly fueled her rage was that he had titled the program he planned to read "Poems For a Dead Theatre."

While having dinner with Vern one night, Cal got a call from Gary Jolley that Ernie Mickler was seriously ill. During the next few weeks, Cal recorded lengthy interviews with Ernie, hoping the activity would ease his suffering. In early November, Ernie was admitted to University Hospital in Jacksonville. Cal spent many hours with him during those last days, watching nurses as they injected morphine to help ease his breathing and changed the sheets on his urine-stained bed. Cal slathered Blistex on his parched lips and saw Ernie slipping deeper into sleep. As Cal sat there, he watched the IV drip, looked at the crisp, white sheet covering Ernie's bloated legs and his hugely swollen testicles. "God, take him soon," Cal prayed, "Gentle-like, without pain, without further disgrace and torture without further humiliation without further mutilation."[9] A nurse cleaned the room at one point when Cal had gone for a cup of coffee and threw out all the flowers. It was as if she was preparing the room for the next patient. As the end approached, Ernie was taken home the afternoon of November 15. His body had turned a brilliant, eerie bright yellow and was spotted with dozens of black-purple-brown lesions. His eyes were huge with terror, wildly searching, although he recognized

Cal and the flowers Cal brought. Cal's last words to him: "Don't talk, Ernie. You need to rest—just rest."[10] He died later that day, at the age of forty-eight. His second cookbook, *Sinkin Spells, Hot Flashes, Fits and Cravins*—the title was later changed to *White Trash Cooking II: Recipes for Gatherins*—came out just two weeks before his death. Cal's recipe for shrimp wiggle was included.

The day following Ernie's death, Cal closed on his purchase of forty-five acres along the Santa Fe River, outside the little, unincorporated village of Worthington Springs and twenty miles north of Gainesville. Surrounded by thick forests, fields of peas, and mustard greens, it was a spot of breathless quiet. It was an empty lot, no houses. In addition to building a new house for himself, his plan was to build a compound of three small houses to accommodate his overnight guests. He hired a local contractor to build what was an adaptation of a typical "cracker" house of the area. An enormous screen porch surrounded three-fourths of the house, and he had installed a luxurious fireplace, central heating, and air-conditioning.

Just a couple of weeks later, Cal's doctor discovered that he had a leaking valve in his heart, and he was admitted into the hospital for a heart catherization to determine the location and extent of the blockage. He was relieved to learn that the doctors had found something physically wrong with him for a change, not just mentally, and concluded that the malaise of recent years was not just caused by depression from his bipolar disorder. The year had been full of sorrow and disappointment. Two cherished friends had died—Michael Brennan and Ernie Mickler—and the news of others who were sick haunted him. "I think 1988 was the year I gave up on everything," he confessed, "every dream. Cooked down to nothing."[11]

Probably the most pleasant surprise of the year was his getting a letter from Carol MacCartree. She was interested in producing one of Cal's plays at the Red Barn Theatre in Key West, possibly putting it on a double bill with Sam Shepherd's *Savage Love*. It never materialized.

Lacking motivation to write another play, yet knowing he needed to write in order to live, he turned his attention to letter writing. He continued his frequent epistles to Robert Chesley, Johnny Ferdon, Joe Hendrix, and others but added two new authors to his roster. One was Boyd McDonald, known for his regular columns in *Blueboy* and *New York Native* magazines and for editing *Straight to Hell: The Manhattan Review of Unnatural Acts*, a collection of first-person descriptions of sexual encounters that were submitted to him by his readers and later called *The New York Review of Cocksucking*. Many of the accounts wound up in his books *Smut, Meat: True Homosexual Experiences from S.T.H*, and

Sex: True Homosexual Experiences from S.T.H. Writers. Cal pored over the Gainesville, Ocala, and St. Petersburg newspapers daily and sent McDonald clippings that he thought would be of interest—a man who procured teenage boys for a woman, a bachelor who was auctioned off for $1,000, a man in his thirties who blamed a six-year-old girl for seducing him, a university student who could not get an erection until he used a toothpaste tube as a dildo. McDonald incorporated some of Cal's clippings in his book, *Skin*.

McDonald was always very appreciative of what Cal sent and wrote to him that his "Key West *Citizen* indecent exposure items are probably the best I've ever had"[12] and used them in his column for *Advocate Men*. "I couldn't do all these columns without you," he explained. "You're my main contributor. Florida seems to be drenched with cum....It seems to lead the nation in precocious rapists and outdoor nudity."[13] Cal appreciated McDonald's rationale for his writing—"support therapy for about 50,000 homosexuals. I thus deal with more people than the busiest psychiatrist. My work seems to validate their desires and experiences and to attack the squares (straights)."[14] Cal told him that when he was composing *Sunsets*, he "wrote with the words you had liberated."[15]

Another regular correspondent was playwright Robert Patrick, a pioneer in Off-Off-Broadway and gay theatre, who had won critical acclaim in the 1970s for *Kennedy's Children* and for *T-Shirts*. Patrick told Cal that during an interview for cable television in late October, he had cited Cal as the master of S&M theatre. Ever since the show Patrick had done at La MaMa in 1972, he had felt unwelcome. Still steaming from Ellen Stewart's treatment of him, Cal agreed that La MaMa was Ellen's "sandbox" and that "she continues to shovel out the sand and replace it with kitty litter and dessicated [*sic*] cat turds....Everything is verboten these days as it was in Nazi Germany. But I just barely see, believe I see a new generation coming on that will take that 'next step' that we all had our legs raised to take before the plague stopped us frozen in our tracks."[16] Cal frequently sent Patrick photos of naked men covered with safety pins or clothespins all over them. They compared notes on the future of gay theatre, Cal's photography, and frustration that the officials at *Christopher Street* and *New York Native* refused to ship their magazines to the hinterlands, arguing that there were no gay people outside New York, L.A., and S.F. "Ha," Cal roared, "There's dicks everywhere." Those magazine executives, he wrote, "won't get off their asses and look beyond their nose boogers. It's a drag."[17]

With the beginning of 1989, Cal began to search more often for sex in Jacksonville. He attended meetings of Black and White Men Together and participated in private group orgies held at an EconoLodge. A favorite haunt was the Jacksonville baths. Some days he would stay half the night and not leave until three or four in the morning. As he joked with Eric, "There is a place for trolls at the baths."[18] Though he was very active, he always worried about the health risks he took and had to deal with the guilt of his indiscriminate behavior.

In March, he learned that his dear friend, Johnny Ferdon, was seriously ill with colon cancer. On April 8, he flew to New York to care for him. It seemed so odd to be back in the Orchard Street apartment that they had rented together in 1972. He turned the lease over to Johnny soon after he was institutionalized in 1975, but now he was back, helping Johnny die as peacefully as possible. As he wrote, "It was fucking INTENSE."[19] He cooked and cleaned and was Johnny's full-time caregiver. At one point, Johnny was in the bathroom and called out to Cal for help. When Cal entered, Johnny was sitting on the toilet, emptying his colonoscopy bag that was filled with watery, dark blood from a massive hemorrhage. "That's blood," Cal gasped, as he reeled back into the hallway and bounced off the door jam. "What does it mean?" he asked. It meant a dash to the emergency room at Beth-Israel Hospital where Cal stayed until three in the morning. Johnny never returned to Orchard Street. Cal visited him daily, bringing him fresh tulips, wiping the drool from his lips, rinsing out his vomit basin, waiting outside the room while his bed was freshened from the endless saturation of his body waste. He sat quietly by his side. Cal looked up one last time into Johnny's tortured face, felt his pain, and "turned away from another loved one knowing I'd never see him alive again—knowing we'd frolic and laugh no more. . . . I left him before he could leave me. ALONE."[20]

Cal was exhausted. He went back to the apartment, laid down for a long, three-hour nap, and then dragged himself to the Red Lantern, a Cajun restaurant on Avenue A, where he and Johnny had eaten so many nights when they were too devastated to cook and too broke to afford anything more than a $2.00 plate of spaghetti. Cal now had the sole responsibility of dealing with all of Johnny's possessions in the apartment. He stacked his books and journals on a large worktable and sorted through them. He kept most, and they eventually wound up as part of his own collection. Two years later, Johnny's sister managed to have the lease on the apartment transferred back to Cal.

From this point on, Cal's friends and family had great difficulty knowing where Cal was at any one time. It could be New York, Crystal River, Worthington Springs, or maybe even San Francisco. He owned twenty-five rental houses in Crystal River, so if he was staying there, he could be at any of the houses that might be vacant. Although he kept some people apprised of his whereabouts, most were kept in the dark.

Because he had agreed to a reading and exhibiting of his photography at Shades of Lavender, a new gay and lesbian bookstore in Jacksonville, he returned to Florida in June. It was another debacle. He had tried hard to select pleasing and palatable material, but the audience was very restless and embarrassed by the language in his poetry. For the first time, he felt his reading had been actually harmful, that the bookstore would never let anybody else read. "What am I going to do?" he asked himself. "I can't go on doing this to people."[21] As soon as he could, Cal fled back to New York.

His old friend from his La MaMa days, Jeff Weiss, was running a little theatre with his partner on 10th Street between First and A Avenues and invited Cal to a performance of a new script. It was a very intimate, salon-type theatre, as if you were sitting in someone's living room. Food and wine were served. Cal chuckled when he sat under a nude painting of Ellen Stewart, looking, as one person remarked, "Like the worst nigger prostitute you ever saw." It had hung at La MaMa at one time. During a pause in the performance, Jeff introduced Cal to the audience as "a great writer." Cal thanked Jeff for the praise before he left and said, "It really let me know I am back."

"You are back, aren't you. Johnny's gone and you are back."

"Yes. I'm back,"[22] Cal replied.

Perhaps colored by the horrific death of Johnny, Cal became extremely depressed as he once again walked the streets of New York. He was overwhelmed by the filth and violence and utter hopelessness of so many people, the endless lines of homeless black men who wandered the streets aimlessly. He saw all colors lying on benches along Houston Street. Like worn stumps, the men's feet stuck out from under their improvised tarps, some wrapped with rags and swollen with fungus and neglect. The air was rich and rotten from mounds of week-old garbage bags piled along the streets. Pigeons and ugly wrens foraged among the filth-strewn sidewalks, finding chunks of dropped Blimpies, and crusts of old pizza. Every night he saw the same woman curled up at the edge of an iron fence, lying on a nasty sheet of foam rubber, and wrapped in a filthy blanket of rags. It was her home; she was a fixture of the neighborhood.

Somehow Cal and Ellen Stewart managed to maintain a friendship of sorts. Shortly before her birthday, he sat on the toilet seat in her apartment and chatted while she knelt on the floor, washing her dog in the bathtub. As he got ready to leave, she gave him a lovely brass rubbing she had brought back from China, and he gave her a coffee mug with the words "One World" painted on it. He told her that she was the first person back in the 1970s he had ever heard say that phrase. It was a new concept for him back then. Leaning out the front door of La MaMa as he left, Ellen yelled out, "One world, honey, that's what I believe in. One world."[23]

In mid-November, he was surprised to get a phone call from London. A young, twenty-four-year-old German man he had met earlier, astonished him by announcing he was arriving in two days. Wildly punk, dressed in black leather, and with bleached blonde and spiked hair, Bernd Boetzher was a slender but still ravishing beauty. After their first night together again, Bernd confessed that he had AIDS. Shaken by the news, Cal found it difficult to have sex with him. Their previous sex together had always been unprotected. Was Bernd infected then, he wondered? Why hadn't he been told sooner? "I'm surrounded by LOSS.... I'm surrounded by the sick and dying. The boy I kiss every night, hold—has a T-cell count of 250. It's unfair, man, it's unfair."[24] They proceeded to have sex, but Cal feared that even though they used condoms, it often bordered on being unsafe.

In early December, Cal took Bernd with him to San Francisco where he gave another reading in conjunction with a month-long exhibition of his photography at Different Light bookstore. A special treat was that Bruce McCoy, whom Cal had known in Gainesville, was now living there and helped set up the photo exhibit and promote Cal's reading. The store manager, Richard Labonte, had unfortunately booked two events at the same time that caused problems. People arriving to attend the other event were extremely noisy as they drank wine and sampled the cheese and crackers. Cal knew he was going to be drowned out by the competing commotion. Once he started to read, Cal's "sole objective was to get it over with and out of there."[25] It was a nightmare. Like a weary, old dinosaur, Cal slumped out onto Castro Street and groaned to Bernd and Bruce, "Thank God it's over."

Since Robert Chesley knew he was going to be out of town, he told Cal that he and Bernd could stay in his San Francisco apartment. When they arrived, they found a note on the table from Chesley, telling them that they should try to meet porn star Scott O'Hara, who had read Cal's *The Daddy Poems* and was performing in town: "I think you'll like him— he's very bright & committed to erotic liberation." As a matter of fact, O'Hara, who held the title of "The Biggest Dick in San Francisco," was known for his rare ability of autofellatio. Apparently, he could cum on cue. Whether or not O'Hara demonstrated his talents for Cal is unknown, but Cal purchased one of his famous self-suck posters and hung it prominently in his New York apartment. Another highlight of the trip was posing for a photo shoot by Mark I. Chester—some of Cal alone and some with Bernd. Chester used one of the nude photos of Cal in his book, *Diary of a Thought Criminal*, self-published in 1996. It shows Cal standing in profile, his arms at the back of his head and looking down at the floor in deep contemplation with the caption, "Cal—in memory of dead friends."

Rather than return to New York, Cal and Bernd flew back to Florida, staying a week or so at Center. They spent New Year's Eve with Vern and his lover, Bobby Reed, at their home in Green Cove Springs. It was a pleasant evening until the end, when Bernd came on to Bobby. Embarrassed and ashamed, Cal pried him away and drove home in silence. What added to Cal's concern was that this had happened to his dear friend, Vern. Of all the young men Cal had taken a fancy to, Vern had always been the most loyal, kind, and attentive, and he feared this might hurt their close friendship. Soon after, Cal bought Bernd a train ticket for New York and sent him out the door.

In late March, Cal was back in San Francisco to attend Robert Chesley's forty-seventh birthday celebration at Mark I. Chester's apartment. Cal knew that Bobby had AIDS, but he was not prepared for what he saw. Bobby, whose body was covered with lesions, insisted on parading around the apartment wearing few clothes. It was part of his determination to confront the AIDS panic and homophobic hatred of gay sex. Hanging on the walls were portraits of Bobby taken by Chester, an exhibit that he later published under the title "Robert Chesley—ks portraits with harddick and superman spandex." There were photos of him bound and unbound. In one, Bobby wears a spandex Superman costume, half pulled down over his torso so as to reveal his kaposi sarcoma lesions. His erect penis sticks out of the spandex. Combined with the Superman costume, it was meant to show his strength and invincibility, despite a body that suggested future debilitation and death. Earlier in the year, when the New College of San Francisco censored these portraits, Chester argued, "These photos are simultaneously difficult and inspiring, witnessing in a very intense way the courage of a person with AIDS who refuses to give up his sexuality or prettify it for mass consumption."[26] Although Cal found the photos frightening, he somewhat agreed.

Cal suddenly had one of the strangest surprises of his career. He received notice that *Sunsets* was in rehearsals in Portland, Oregon, under the sponsorship of Spread Eagle Productions and was to be performed every Friday and Saturday from June 1, through July for a total of eighteen performances. Most unique was that it was being sponsored by the newly formed sex club, Oregon Activists in S&M (ORGASM), and would be performed in what was supposedly the largest sex dungeon in the country. Someone in the club had seen Cal's *Richmond Jim* in Portland a few years earlier and thought that a production of another of his plays would be a big draw for their membership. In advance publicity in their June newsletter, *Up and Cumming With ORGASM*, director Kevin Koesel "refused to give away the plot, saying only that the evening would end with a nude wrestling scene." The July newsletter announced, "Kevin Koesel has done a great job. The plays are excellent. If you haven't seen them yet, get with the program, get down to the space, and check it out."[27] When Cal learned of the plans, he wrote to Boyd McDonald, "My plays get done in the weirdest places."[28]

On December 5, Cal received a phone call from Mark I. Chester indicating that Chesley was actively dying. He lit a little votive candle, placed it beside the latest book of Chesley's plays that he had been given, and "recalled our friendship and all too few times together as the candle flickered and as I continued puttering about the house feeling his presence."[29] When Cal received the telephone call informing him of Chesley's death, he fell into uncontrollable tears. He had lost another friend, his closest ally in playwriting. He knew how supportive Chesley's mother had been of her son's work, and in a very emotional letter to her, Cal wrote, "One of the great sadnesses of my life is that I was unable to share my little successes in the theatre with my mother. . . . She could never bring herself to talk about any aspect of sexuality let alone the homosexuality that is rampant in my plays and in my life. Therefore, in a life that has been noteworthy mostly for its failures, I never could say 'Look! I did this in gay theatre. Now that's something, isn't it?' "[30] For the Chesley celebration at the WPA Theatre in New York the next spring, one of Cal's photos of Chesley was used for the program cover.

The last letter he received from Chesley included a copy of his essay, "Gay Theater for the 90's," which he hoped to get published in *The Advocate*. Intent on inspiring a new generation of writers, he urged them to "hold passionately to a vision of what gay theater can and should be; and have the guts to tell the truth." He continued, "We need plays that affirm that our sex is healthy and that explore the marvelous variety of human sexuality right out to its radical extremes." Undoubtedly, the reason the essay was not published was his vicious attack on Theatre Rhinoceros, which took up the last three pages of the typed essay. He complained of "chickenshit attitude of the leadership," their fear of offending their patrons, their lack of taste and knowledge of theatre, and the absence of professionalism. What was especially galling to Chesley was how they handled their production of his plays—his *Stray Dog Story* that included simulated acts of sex was relegated to the studio theatre, *Jerker* was on the main stage but not included as part of the regular season subscription, and any production of *Dog Plays* was simply rejected. Chesley ends his essay by threatening to set up a tomato stand outside the theatre when they open *The Boys in the Band*.[31] No wonder Cal was so distraught when Chesley died. They were so much alike.

And yet there was a major difference. Cal recognized that his friend kept speaking when he no longer could. "While no words came to me in any form acceptable to any theatre anywhere, after the 1982 advent of AIDS, Bob managed to continue and to be heard.... [He had] an eloquence and authority that I can only admire and, yes, envy.... Bob carried the torch for the rest of us who had been silenced by fear or rage or plain old-fashioned censorship."[32]

During the months that Cal was in Florida overseeing construction of his house in Worthington Springs, he resumed his friendship with Edward Balko, a thirty-year-old artist who already had a BFA and was working on an MFA in printmaking at the University of Florida. Cal was very fond of Edward—above and below the neck. Both he and Eric thought that Edward was much too talented and too handsome to remain in Gainesville and encouraged him to strike out for the Big Apple. By July, Cal agreed to let Edward stay in his Orchard Street apartment for free. Also, he convinced Ellen Stewart to give him a part-time job in the La MaMa box office. Soon, both Cal and Eric became concerned that Edward stopped communicating. No letters, no phone calls. In fact, when Eric went to New York on business and phoned Edward about getting together, he was brushed off. Edward did not want to leave the apartment, needed to devote all of his time to his art.

The reason soon became clear. Just before Christmas, Raymond Schanze, Cal's friend who had supervised the La MaMa box office for many years, called Cal and told him that Edward was sick all the time, was wasting away, and was not showing up for work. Cal drove immediately to New York and discovered that Edward was in total denial about his health. He clearly had AIDS and had lost a lot of weight. Cal bought a plane ticket for him and sent him home to Georgia where he soon was hospitalized with a blood disease and died the Saturday before Easter.

Cal was left to cleanup the apartment, the second time in two years. Among Balko's papers, Cal found this handwritten note: "The queer must be punished."[33] Naturally, Cal wondered if Edward knew he had AIDS when they were having unprotected sex. Was he himself infected now? Why had Edward been so secretive when Cal was being so generous? The experience with Edward was so typical for Cal. He was kind and generous, loved to rescue people in need, but when they did not reciprocate with any signs of appreciation, he could become very resentful. Could it be true, however, that none of these young men appreciated Cal? Or was it Cal's interpretation of their behavior—an interpretation fueled by his paranoia and his continual sense of worthlessness.

After a winter in Florida in his new home in Worthington Springs, Cal was back in New York, fluffing up the Orchard Street apartment in preparation for an extended stay. Even though Robert Patrick's *Haunted Host* was being revived, starring Harvey Fierstein, Cal apologized to Patrick that he couldn't "stomach 2 hours of Harvey, etc. Aunt Jemima trundles on.... He does so much good for the gay community, but isn't it sad that our oppression is at such a degree that only pushy, abrasive, sentimental crowd pleasers are able to survive as spokepersons." He continued, "Oh well.... They would lock us *all* up if I was telling it like it is."[34]

Nevertheless, Cal relented and eventually saw the production and wrote to Patrick that the play was a delight and sometimes Fierstein was as well. "He still can bedazzle and there is magic that come [*sic*] thru the mush-mush every once and a while and yes, darling I did HOWL.... He did serve your play much better than his own [*Torch Song Trilogy*] which was my dear nothing but a quagmire of sentimentality, an Okefenokee Swamp of the trite and sappy. Perhaps he should fade from the limelight for a time and reflect and then begin again to write."[35] There was probably a smidgeon of jealousy and resentment. Fierstein was a huge success; Cal was not. When approached to provide some of his recollections of having worked with Cal—even after several of his acquaintances approached him, including Robert Patrick, Doric Wilson, and Michael Kearns—Fierstein refused. Probably he was aware of Cal's criticism of his work.

In mid-July, Cal finally decided he had to be tested for AIDS. It was not an easy decision to make. He knew both sides of the issue. If he tested negative, he would certainly feel less anxious. If he tested positive, however, treatment could improve his long-term health. But he had seen so many friends suffer horrible months of pain and agony as they were dying. Would he be able to carry on knowing what was in store for him? Would a death sentence ruin his life? Hurt his chances of getting insurance? If positive results were not kept confidential, would he suffer from even more discrimination and rejection?

Like all active gay men at the time, he was terrified of the results. On the day of his appointment, Cal drove to Gainesville and parked his car in the lot directly across from Shands Hospital on the university campus. He trembled as he crossed the busy street and entered the coldly impersonal building. After he gave his name to the receptionist, he sat and shook, listening for his name to be called. And then, after the blood samples were taken, the long, horribly long, two-week wait to learn the results. He did not want to know. How could he possibly be negative? After all, he had certainly practiced unsafe sex with Bernd Boetzher, Edward Balko, and Vern Gransden—all three who had AIDS. In addition were his countless encounters at gay bathhouses, backrooms of bars, and at glory holes. Even if now he were to take a vow of total abstinence, he could not be sure if he were negative or not. All the reports were saying the incubation period could be several years. Friday, July 26—the day he returned to the hospital to get the results was even more terrifying. He had been advised to have a friend accompany him when he got the results, but he could not bring himself to ask anyone. As he approached the hospital entrance, he stopped and considered running back to his car. When the doctor entered the room where Cal was waiting, he could read the look on the doctor's face. He was shocked, but hardly surprised. He was positive. He had been given a death sentence.

Immediately, he called Grady and canceled a trip to see him. All he could think about was "How slowly will I die? How much time have I got left? Will I live 'til Xmas? Can I make it to 2001? . . . It was the loneliness ultimately that got me. I took chances because of it."[36] He thought about his past, reckless sexual activities, but could not bring himself to feel regretful: "I could not relinquish that freedom for which so much battle in my life had been waged with so much pain with so much hurt to so many. Even the fear of or the threat of death could not make me relinquish my right to love my fellow men."[37] He considered buying a gun or hitching a hose to his truck's exhaust and began compiling a new journal he called "Journal of My Death."

The first person he told was his longtime therapist, Dr. Phil Cushman, and he felt relieved afterwards for having shared the information. A few days later, he drove to Winter Park to see Grady. He had already told Vern and Eric. Telling Grady was very difficult, since he knew Grady was already so stressed out with caring for his mother. Grady reeled in confusion and shock at the news, "but thru it remained a staunch and strongly supporting friend."[38]

When Cal returned to Worthington Springs, he wondered if living alone in his new house was going to work. He had certainly enjoyed lazy afternoons, lying out on his hammock and watching the birds fly overhead and the land tortoises waddle past. He loved walking through the woods and along the riverbank. He and Eric had often hiked along the nearby, spring-fed, magical Ichetucknee River, looking for herons and egrets. As he contemplated doing that now, however, now that he was HIV+, Cal knew he would not venture into the water for fear of possible germs. He worried that his new home in the country without structure might not be compatible with his disease. Was it too isolated, too removed from society; would he have to move again?

He tried to keep busy, tried to keep his mind off his health issues. Because he had no health coverage, Cal convinced Ellen Stewart to let him work part-time in the La MaMa box office so that he might eventually qualify for insurance. He continued writing his journals, but no plays, no poetry, no photography. "The horrors of our days and nights go on: Life in the plague lane," he wrote. "It's like you've had electric shock—when you find out you're HIV+. It zaps you so strong: the knowledge you're going to die and also: I've failed."[39] On October 18, he attended a revival of *Futz* at La MaMa. Before he saw the show, he wrote that "the vibes are lethal." It had premiered there in 1968, and he thought it laughable that it now was being promoted as a "wild, barrier-breaking revival." According to Cal three members of the original cast were performing. They "have been propped up and have been released from geriatric confinement to recreate their original roles." None of them, he continued, required walkers.[40]

Though he tried and tried, he could never forget that he was positive and admitted in a journal entry that he was "massively depressed. Nothing to do. No future.... I'm just whipped and destroyed."[41] One evening, he walked to the nearest bookstore and bought *Final Exit*, hoping to find a graceful means of departure. As he later told Eric, "'I would like to bow-out before things get too grim. I have no fear of death. But I do fear the suffering.'"[42]

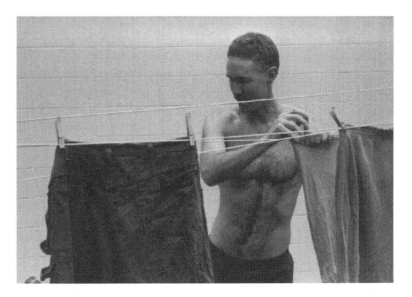

Figure 8.1   Cal often visited Eric Garber at his home in Keystone Heights.

Source: Courtesy Cal Yeomans Collection, Special Area Studies, George A. Smathers Libraries, University of Florida.

Somehow, he thought, he must end his own life. He saw no reason to endure what would surely lie ahead. One thought kept haunting him: "My play has ended without applause, without review."[43]

Undoubtedly, like most men who have been diagnosed as positive, Cal struggled to determine who had infected him. It was really pointless; there were so many. For some reason, he focused on a black man he called Joe A. and the night they met at a "parlor of necrophilia" called The Pyramid. "He deliberately, in the face of my resistance with rape-force relentlessness shot his poison cum down my fucked-raw throat—his dick like a knife—hard as steel—ripping delicate throat tissue preparing it to receive his Satanic host."[44] "Unwittingly," Cal wrote, "I found Death or it found me."[45]

And yet, Cal himself had regularly practiced unsafe sex, knowing there would be a chance of contracting AIDS. He had rationalized that having fought all his adult life for sexual liberation and struggled to overcome the shackles and oppression of homophobia, he had no choice but to adopt the safest sex practices he could tolerate, and proceed. He wore condoms to protect his sex partners, but he never required them to follow suit. He wanted everyone to know that he did not put other men's lives at risk, even when they wanted him to. He may choose to take cum, but he never gave it, declaring, "I do not DEATHFUCK."[46] He knew he was taking risks, but he also knew he could not turn back and accepted the fact that "accidents happen and warriors are wounded in battle."[47]

During one of his many periods of depression, now greatly intensified due to his health, Cal destroyed his friendship with Robert Patrick. Patrick had always shown great interest in Cal's writing and convinced a friend to look at Cal's plays with the prospect of publishing them. When he suggested to Cal that he send the plays to this publisher, Cal instead sent them to Patrick and demanded that Patrick submit them. In the accompanying letter, Cal noted that he was tired of Patrick's always asking to read his plays. "Many people have over the years," he explained. "The quickest way to get that to let-up is to give them something to read. Rarely do I ever hear anything about 'your writing' again. They just don't understand how I can be such a nice person and write such awful, heinous stuff." He acknowledged that though he had a fever near hundred degrees, he was "fully cognizant of [the letter's] raging anger, frustration, and perhaps misdirected venom."[48] Shocked by Cal's response, Patrick sent the plays back and severed all relations with him.

Cal's friends had become increasingly angry over his explosive and irrational behavior. Frank Regan was puzzled why Cal had been snubbing him when they were at The Ambush at the same time. He learned that Cal was angry that Frank had not shown enough enthusiasm over his new house and had decided not to talk to him again. They patched things up, but when Frank and Chuck Woods went to dinner with Cal one night at Steak and Ale, Cal took one bite of the hamburger he had ordered, stood up, and fumed out of the restaurant, complaining loudly that he could have gotten a better hamburger at Burger King!

Cal knew he was being obnoxious. "I've shut the door to other people. I have so little but anger to offer. Anger. And, of course, self-pity."[49] He was reminded of what Miss Vada had told him during her last years: "If you don't quit flying off the handle and talking mean to people, we won't have any friends left."[50] He even felt he was an outcast among his own family. "They do not understand or approve of the way I live my life. Just as they will not be sympathetic to the cause of my death."[51]

Sensing he needed to change his behavior, Cal decided, as he put it, to learn how to live with AIDS, rather than learn how to die with AIDS. He started attending occasional meetings of an HIV+ group sponsored by North Central Florida AIDS Network (NCFAN) in Gainesville. He was struck by those present, especially by the "local AIDS Diva" who had been exposed to HIV in 1980 when he was a senior in high school. Cal sat across from him and noticed a hearty bulge in his crotch. "He's very well hung," Cal thought. "The disease has not diminished his dick." Then the grim reality hit—the bulge was a diaper or absorbent napkin, or both. Diarrhea can be uncontrollable in the final stages of AIDS. Cal said very little during the meeting, but he was glad he went. Seeing the Diva rejoicing in his life even though he was near death was an inspiration.[52]

The ever-loyal Grady continued his friendship with Cal, even though they often sparred and sputtered. The day after one of his overnights with Cal in Worthington Springs, they drove down to Center for one last visit to Cal's little house that he had sold to old neighbors Martha and Tim Hoggard. It was a lovely and peaceful afternoon. The branches of the ancient, moss-draped oaks seemed to hide and protect them from the harsh realities of their new challenges. Grady was overcome with the rush of affectionate memories. Cal had bought the place about the time Grady was leaving New York, and the two of them had spent many weekends there, talking and trying to put together their shattered lives. After Grady drove away, Cal unchained the concrete eagle from the front gatepost that Zacq had given him as well as the few remaining pieces of Vada's driftwood, and drove away without looking back. His eyes were full of tears and his throat tight with suppressed cries. Somehow, he knew that Miss Vada was with him and saying, "Pshaw. We'll make us a new place that will be just as good."[53]

In June, Cal received an unexpected letter from Dennis Doph, who was interested in staging Cal's *Roadkill* at the Celebration Theatre in Los

Angeles. In a foreword to the play, Cal insisted that "the audience should not be able to escape the emotions of this play. They should be confined, forced...to confront the truths." And he pleaded, "Bear these pains with me." Much of the dialogue Cal lifted directly from his own journals. Full of images, dance, interpolated repetitions, and music, it begins with Cal's descriptions of how he was infected with the AIDS virus by the man he called Joe A. Halfway through the piece, a character recites the following poem.

> One of my fellow warriors
> turned traitor and fucked
> me in my mouth with
> his mighty weapon
> shot his poison cum
> into my torn throat
> tripping. Thought I
> was the Dad/enemy who abused
> him—paid me back
> for his own anger

An emaciated PWA crosses the stage in a dance of death, making no sound but contorted in fear. As he exits, he shrieks in silent laughter.

Doph's idea was to present the play almost as a confrontational event in some public space as opposed to a conventional theatre. He thought it would run about half an hour and urged Cal to extend the piece to a full hour. Unlike many producers Cal had dealt with, Doph told him not to worry about expressing anger, hurt, or disgust and reassured Cal that there would be no censorship. Cal replied about a month later that "*Roadkill* is of course high priority to get finished. But sad to say I'm not graced very much these days with the spirit to work on it."[54] There is no record indicating whether or not Cal expanded the script, but about another month later, Doph wrote that he could not get the play accepted by the board for a full production. He reassured Cal that he had a unique voice that deserved to be heard, but not, apparently, at his theatre.[55] After Cal got the news, he wrote, "I can't tell you how worthless I feel. I can't tell you how worthless I am."[56] Cal then drove to the Jacksonville gay baths where he stayed until late, checked into a room at EconoLodge overnight, and then went back to the baths for most of the next day.

In spite of his death sentence, Cal knew that he must start thinking more positively. He had reason to, after all he still had many close friends who were sticking by him in spite of his behavior. They had not turned their backs on him. Many other gay men were also learning how to cope with having AIDS, and many were living long lives. He must change his ways, change his life—what was left of it: "Realizing now—somehow—that it / my work, my career, my plays, my writings, my photographs [are] ALL over. He no longer felt the need to prove himself, and he was determined to celebrate a good New Year! I won't do any more of it—work on any of it any longer. December 31, 1992 and I am free at last."[57]

CHAPTER 9

"LIVING WITH A DEATH SENTENCE"

For one of his 1993 New Year's resolutions, Cal vowed he would not give in to despair. He would not isolate himself. He would not simply hide and die. Thinking he should have a more healthy diet, he even took a cooking class specializing in vegetarian recipes given by The Whole Foods Project at the Manhattan Center for Living. He gave up all thoughts of peddling his scripts, getting anything produced, entering play contests, or even exhibiting his photographs. He wanted to keep his life simple. He would continue to write, but never with any thought of a theatre production.

When he was in Florida he welcomed guests. When he was in New York, he frequently attended the meetings of Friends In Deed and Body Positive. He ventured to Broadway to see *Angels in America*. When he read of its overwhelmingly successful reception and of all the accolades that followed, he was stunned. He had found it to be "a mediocre and somewhat juvenile attempt at theatre that often was laughable.... What claptrap and hogwash and stereotypical Aunt Jemima patronization of the suffering of a people." "Not since *Torch Song Trilogy*," he continued, "has any play pandered to the hetero power structure with such fatuity and sure knowledge of what it takes to please a society eager to expiate their real human rights abuses with tokens of liberal acceptance and apology—but with no real effort to accept and understand our culture as it really is."[1] A few months later, after Dana Ivey sent him a copy of *Angels* to read, Cal wrote that he thought the play was "Tripe. One more rip-off scam night in the theatre. Hokum. Malarkey. Bat crap. Another coffin nail for a dying art."[2] He admitted that he had walked out before the play was finished. Such harsh reaction to the acclaimed play perhaps revealed Cal's jealousy and resentment that his plays had never been as successful.

In years past, Cal had often frequented gay bars, whether in New York, San Francisco, or Florida. He could almost always manage to trick.

His magnetic personality, breadth of knowledge, and wit could disarm the most guarded candidates. He could be dishy, wicked, and funny— all at the same time. Young men used to be charmed by his long hair, long legs, dark glasses, and engaging voice. Now that he had gained so much weight, however, and had AIDS, he felt out of sorts at his previous haunts. Instead, he became a regular at gay baths, and, when in Florida, went often to the infamous Parliament House, an ironic name because it had nothing to do with the making of laws, but rather the mocking of them. It was, and still is, a popular, gay, sex motel in Orlando, or as he called it "Whorelando." Cal's favorite room, #252, was on the second floor at the back of the complex, where he could lie on his bed and gaze through the huge window to a little lake edged with cabbage palms. The balconies of the motel were always crowded with men hanging over the railing to spot the treasures walking down below and with men peering into the rooms where the drapes were left boldly open.

Cal, like most of the men in the rooms, lay nude on his bed, pretending to watch CNN. If he saw some good meat stroll by or stop at his window, he signaled—with a nod by massaging his dick or by pinching his tits. He always put the chain on his door so that no one could enter uninvited. He needed to be ready. "Like an untouched asshole, I'm not [always] ready for penetration or the totality of anyone. But—like a glory hole, the 5 inch gap the chain allows the door suggests that appetizers are accepted."[3] There was always "the endless parade of the mutilated, the desperate, the confused."[4] He was there under no pretext of finding a lover; it was purely carnal. "Here amongst the soul-less mutilated and genitally deranged,...I am but one more tiny blip on the radar screen of low self-esteem and self-loathing night creatures who crawl these balconies like roaches in light or dark—brazen harlots, starving flesh urchins with nothing whatsoever to lose—or love."[5] On many occasions, Cal would check-in and stay for several days, sometimes accompanied by Eric Garber, who would get a separate room. One night as they were driving to the motel, Eric commented, "Oh, Calvin, I'd give anything to have your sex life!" "Well, I'll leave it to you when I die," Cal replied. "I'm sorry, Eric, I just couldn't resist."[6]

Cal certainly questioned the future of their friendship. He always hesitated to ask Eric anything about his writing projects, sensing that Eric really did not want to share. Cal felt that Eric was pulling away, not phoning or writing to him as he had. Cal took it personally. "Maybe I've come off the wall. It must be that he no longer finds me pleasant to be around....Is this the hell I have to look forward to as my illness escalates," he asked. "No one can stand to be around me because I'm so malignant...with anger—and pain?" Eric's reticence reinforced his anger, so he wrote to Eric, "We must answer all your questions when you vampire our lives for your so-called research....Can I not be forgiven excess and error in this struggle to remain functional?...Can I have no rage?"[7]

There is no record of Eric's response. The next time Eric is mentioned in a journal entry is when he called Cal to tell him that Boyd McDonald was found dead in the dingy, little room where Cal had once visited him. Cal could visualize his lying there amidst the empty Campbell's soup cans in this welfare hotel room with its single hot plate for cooking. "He sought, he listened, he cared, he shared," Cal wrote. "He shoved a giant shibboleth of an enema syringe into the shit-filled hypocritical asshole of a morally corrupt and spiritually bankrupt, bigoted hate-filled America, forced us to smell our rottenness and accept our foibles....He sent dishonesty straight to hell and increased the world's capacity for truth."[8]

In all likelihood, the last time anyone contacted Cal about producing one of his plays was in March 1993. Kelly Hill, who had tried unsuccessfully to drum up interest in *Sunsets* a few years earlier, wrote that he and his partner, Jim Ponder, were interested in reading the finished script of Cal's *Roadkill*. If Cal had been at all interested, Hill's relating the problems he had just encountered with producing James Carroll Pickett's *Queen of Angels* changed his mind. Hill and Ponder had approached Theatre Rhinoceros about including *Queen of Angels* in their season even though they feared it would be rejected due to the play's angry dialogue and chorus of naked queers. Eventually, they got the very clear message from Theatre Rhino that the play was too male in its content. As Hill explained to Cal, it seemed that men having sex just isn't done anymore.[9] As a result, he and Ponder were forced to produce it themselves. What they had faced reminded Cal so vividly of his struggles a decade earlier—censorship and ignorant theatre officials. There is little doubt that Cal never sent his script to Hill. As he explained to Joe Hendrix, "I do not think of [my writing] any further than the joy it gives me to get it out and down on paper. Sell anything? See anything published? I can't imagine I could survive the hassles involved if by chance the opportunity presented itself."[10]

Since Cal had great difficulty finding good tenants to rent the house by the river, he agreed to convert the residential part of the Miller's Point property where the house was located into commercial use and leased it out to Dwight Redmond for use as an antique mall and tearoom (The Manatea Room), with the understanding that Redmond would have to vacate in June 1995. The house was now open to the public with wheelchair ramp, parking lot, and fluorescent tube lighting in every room. "Fancy," Cal remarked. "Not worth talking about really. Just more of the same old shit. Progress marching on."[11] Never again would the house be used as a family home.

When he returned to his house in the woods near Worthington Springs after a month in New York, he discovered that it had been burglarized during his absence. Someone had entered the house repeatedly, and although they didn't take anything of very great value, they pretty much rummaged from top to bottom and took close to 200 CDs. A house isolated in deep woods may have had many virtues, but security and convenience were not among them, and Cal concluded that his country retreat was no place for someone with failing health to live alone. It was fifteen miles to the nearest grocery and restaurants, and medical care of any kind was at least thirty miles away. Anyway he looked at it, living so far away from everything and so alone just wasn't going to work in the years that lay ahead. So he used the burglary as a motivator to find another, more appropriate place to live. In just a couple of weeks, he put the house up for sale, asking $150,000, and decided that after he moved into a new home, he would rent it out until he found a buyer. It was a very difficult decision; he had to admit that his dream of living in the country—in the woods—was over.

By mid-November, he was back in New York. The night before Thanksgiving 1993, Grady took Cal to The Gaiety, a famous gay strip joint and male burlesque house on 46th Street near Broadway. It was a fun experience, watching the glorious bodies and lusting after all the dangling dicks. He was fascinated and envied the regular customers who seemed to know the routine near the backstage door where the young gods exited after performing. They would meet the boys and negotiate for whatever could be arranged.

On December 30, 1993, he took possession of a lovely, three-bedroom, two-bath condo of 3,500 square feet in the Cumberland Circle Community in Gainesville with a beautiful view of Hogtown Creek. A special feature was a secret room. When you entered the bathroom and slid open the shower door, the back wall of the shower was really another door. When slid open, it exposed a large Jacuzzi with an overhead sunlight and an elaborate sound system. Cal considered himself very lucky to have found such a perfect place and to have the money to buy it. He knew that most people living with HIV or AIDS were not nearly so fortunate. Not only did they have to cope with the disease, but also with severe financial helplessness as a result of ever increasing physical deterioration.

All the while Cal lived at Cumberland Circle, he placed personal ads in the Gainesville newspaper. A rough draft of one reads:

> If you're looking for an older guy who knows what he's doing and likes to do it, give me a call. Lay back, enjoy, leave the driving to Greyhound. No hassles, no complications, just good layed-back action, oral, massage, good feeling. Well-hung especially *welcomed*, but it's the person and the attitude, not the equipment. 30's to mid-fifties is a good age range. I'm in my late fifties, 6'2", grey beard, short grey hair, weigh about 195. Wide range of interests. Masculine, bi curious. I'm pretty versatile and do my best to please. Looking to meet guys for occasional action, one nighters, or quick.[12]

When he arranged to meet someone, he would drive to meet them in a strip mall parking lot. He would drive up close to the other car and look into the window to see if the person appealed to him. If not, he would drive away. Of course, sometimes the other car took off first.

Soon after porn star Scott O'Hara founded *Steam: A Quarterly Journal for Men*, he asked Cal to submit for an upcoming issue hundred words on what romance meant to him. Scott was thrilled with Cal's frighteningly candid statement.[13]

> Romance is what I used to hope sex would lead to. Cart before horse? No concept of recreational sex in first years of my fucking life. Hoped from every fuck a love would grow: fill the empties, solve the puzzle, complete. For 30 years I fuck. No real romance bloom. Don't misunderstand: rarely met a fuck I didn't enjoy. Finally became all big dicks, wet nasties, hot holes...: "A cup of coffee before you leave?" Now, with a T-cell count that is falling all too fast, AZT the only trick on my horizon...: Your place or mine?: 904-371-2049.

It must have flattered Cal when photographer Carolyn Jones contacted him about a book she was putting together, featuring people with AIDS. She asked if he would pose for a photo and submit a brief statement that would accompany the photo. When *Living Proof: Courage in the Face of AIDS* finally appeared in 1994 with a Foreword by British actor Ian McCellan, it included seventy-seven photos of men, women, and children along with a quotation from each. Cal provided the following:

> I knew when I chose to remain sexually active during a sexually transmittable plague that there was a chance I would be exposed to the virus that causes AIDS. But having fought all my adult life for sexual and human liberation, I had no choice but to adopt the safest sex practices I could and

proceed. Having glimpsed a world of unstinting love and joy, I could not turn back. Accidents happen and warriors are wounded in battle. In 1990 I became HIV positive. My first thought was of immediate death. Ha! Certainly it will claim me one day, as it will you. Meanwhile, I reach out for all the support that is available in my community for people living with HIV, and I find more love and joy, spiritual and physical, than ever before. Sex is good. It is not going away.[14]

When Cal received a copy of the book, he noted in his journal, "Unfortunately, AIDS has many faces, too many faces. Mine is only one of them."[15]

Although Cal had sworn off exhibiting any more of his photos, he agreed to take some of Eric for him to use in promoting his upcoming novel, *The Beauty of Men*. Eric could not handle the stark reality of how he looked in the photos and that he was aging. Cal was so fond of Eric and sincerely wanted to ease his sense of loss. "I wish Eric could get help for the neuroses that truly cause him *so much* suffering. But most probably that is where his writing comes from. If he began to enjoy life and its pleasures there probably would be no more great writing."[16]

Cal had his own challenges to deal with. He had explained to a friend that his goal was to become an "activist AIDS Diva....My objective is to change the world's attitude toward life challenging illness and the inevitable death and dying that all living things face sooner or later."[17] He became a member of GAAP (Gainesville Area Aids Project) and volunteered in their office, chatting with walk-ins, staffing the phone line. He quickly discovered that it was not going to be easy to achieve his goal. "AIDS discrimination is real," he wrote, "and people here not only have to cope with the horrors of the disease but with a stultifying degree of discrimination and ignorance." What was needed was education, he thought, since "everything is predicated on a subconscious and unadmitted deep-seated belief by all parties that anyone with HIV is somehow low-class, indigent, second rate and immoral."[18]

He contacted the local newspaper, the *Gainesville Sun*, about his writing a regular column titled something like "Living With HIV in Gainesville" that would "include vignettes and stories of who, how and why we are, tales of our sufferings and joys, our hurts and all the many and various violations of our civil liberties."[19] The newspaper showed no interest in his proposal. Thinking he needed to stay connected with the AIDS scene in New York, he returned there for three weeks in May, hoping to continue his education of living with HIV and then bring what he had learned back to Florida.

He was happy to get back to Florida in June. Although he knew he would miss the cultural offerings, the galleries, the shows, and the caliber of people, he wrote to Tom, "I am less and less able to find any *raison* to keep my ass stuck in muck and mud of the very chic lower east side of 'Manhattan'." He busied himself with GAAP and other AIDS organizations, trying to improve them and raise them from the dregs of ignorance and unknowing. He was so saddened to see "so many of our brothers and sisters here have lost the ability to say much of anything but Yessuh and Yessum and Thank you suh."[20] When he learned that the North Central Florida AIDS Network (NCFAN) was looking to add people to its board of directors, he submitted his name for consideration, arguing that the board should include people directly involved with the epidemic, since they "are the ones most capable of defining and articulating" what needs to be done.[21] He was not selected.

Cal was encouraged one night when he saw Larry Kramer interviewed on PBS. Three years earlier, and just shortly after he had learned that he was positive, Cal chatted with Eric about Larry Kramer and his ineffectiveness as a gay activist, having crossed some line of nuttiness that rendered him fatuous. Cal's opinion certainly changed now. When asked in the PBS piece what he wanted from his activism, Kramer said, "Civil rights. To be allowed to hold my lover's hand, kiss in public, have a legal marriage." Then, when Cal thought he might be wimping out, Kramer turned to the off-camera interviewer with lightening-bolt eyes and struck like a cobra: "I'd want the same things you've got, God Dammit. And I think I deserve them." Cal told Eric later that it was "A wonderful moment in the movement."[22]

By the end of the summer, disillusionment and depression had returned. He wrote to Don Tucker, Fred Chappell's former lover: "I was born in the wrong place at the wrong time in the wrong body to the wrong family....I still write when the spirit moves but mostly poetry: stuff that makes me feel better. I have no plans to share any of it."[23] Later in the month, he wrote, "I had hoped to dedicate the rest of my life to a great love. It appears I will devote it to a great illness."[24]

Fortunately, Frank Regan asked him to give a reading, which boosted his spirits temporarily. Sponsored by the Gainesville Community Alliance, on September 13, at the Santa Fe Community College downtown campus, he read excerpts from his journals and poems, telling his experiences of living with AIDS. He ended the reading with a selection from the play he had written about the murder of George DuPont. Frank remarked years later that he was very moved by the excerpt from the play and wondered why no one had ever produced it.

With very little advance preparation, Cal took off for Amsterdam in the late fall of 1994, beginning continuous flights between New York and Amsterdam for the next four years. He made dozens of trips, sometimes to check up on his real estate investments in Florida, but more often for health reasons—to refill prescriptions, to consult with his doctors, to search for ways to improve his strength—and sometimes remained at his destination for only a few days. Luckily, he had the funds to allow such frequent shuttles back and forth.

The main purpose of this trip was to explore the possibilities of future euthanasia. He was so ill most of the time, however, that he did not accomplish much. He began to run low-grade fevers that came quickly and disappeared just as mysteriously. During his flight back to New York, he ran a low fever the entire time and thought he was dying. He wrote to a friend in Amsterdam that "when I left wooden shoe land I thought I could never travel again: all the more case to acquire a doctor in Amsterdam and go on with my plans."[25] By the end of that year, his T cell count was down, below 500, which is quite low, even for someone with HIV. Although Cal was frightened with the news, he was not particularly surprised, since he seemed to be ill most of the time. He had already been taking several AIDS and depression drugs, including Celexa, Paxil, Sustiva, Epivir, Voltaren, Ziagen, Famvir, temazepam, and sometimes Prozac. And now he started with 600 mg of AZT every day, a relatively new drug used to delay the development of AIDS.

In spite of his health, important business transactions needed to be settled. In September, he finally completed the sale of his Key West house that he had been renting out since 1988, when he conceded that he could never become a part of the Key West culture. Also, he entered into serious negotiations for the sale of most of Miller's Point, the land his family had owned for nearly seventy-five years. In 1983, he put on the market the family house by the river with the surrounding land of four acres where the fish house had stood for $1,350,000. There had been no interested parties for years. Finally, in 1993, he had agreed to let a large part of the property be zoned as commercial and now was asking $700,000 for the commercial section. Cal felt ill at ease, however. Somehow putting it up for sale made him feel as if he were abdicating his responsibility, letting his father down after he had worked so hard to create the Yeomans dynasty.

January 10, 1995, the day that the sale was to be settled, the buyers were still haggling about the price. Cal had told his cousin, Sid Kennedy, that he would meet him for lunch and then meet his cousin, Sue Poling, for dessert later, since they could not arrange to meet all at the same time due to conflicting schedules. Cal sat quietly through most of the meeting as the potential buyers haggled away and claimed that Cal was asking way too much for the property. Cal, after holding his tongue for quite some time, fumed, "Because of all your dickering around, I have missed having lunch with my one cousin. I am now supposed to be having dessert with my other one. I will not miss that one." He then slammed down on the table a piece of paper that read "$700,000" and said, "Here is what I want. Sign it now because I am leaving." Startled, they quickly signed and the sale soon became the Sea Sweet Crab Company.[26]

Probably because he was feeling the effects of HIV and adjusting to the toxic invasion of the AZT, he became even more intent on his desire to become an AIDS activist. He attended a meeting in Gainesville of the administrators and representatives of all the AIDS service organizations in the community and was stunned to find himself one of only two gay males in the group of fifteen. What he found more astonishing, however, was that he was the only positive person in the room. Before he arrived at the meeting, he had vowed to be a silent observer. Toward the end of the gathering, however, someone brought up a recent controversy in the local AIDS community surrounding the choice of photographs used by the *Gainesville Sun* in an ad to cover an AIDS-awareness walk sponsored by NCFAN. The picture the *Sun* used was of two adult males, presumably gay, holding hands as they participated in the walk. Several people at the meeting said they were outraged that the *Sun* had chosen that picture to illustrate the article. Why didn't they pick the image of a child or of a woman or of a mother and child? Melanie Gasper, director of NCFAN, informed the group that she had called the paper to protest their using that photo.

At that point, Cal felt an old, all too familiar anger rising from some deep part of his being. Trying desperately to keep his mouth shut, he heard himself saying, "No! Don't ask them to take that one out! I think it's always good when images of same-sex couples touching appear in any mainstream media. Leave that one as it is, but add another." The only other gay male in the room objected, "But not when they connect us to disease." "But we are!" Cal insisted. He was surprised to hear himself say that.[27]

About a month after the meeting, Cal sent a letter to Judy Raymond, of GAAP. He described the meeting and enclosed an article that he asked her to publish in their next newsletter, admitting to her, however, the article "may be too hot (truthful) to handle." He suggested a title such as "HIV+ Man Speaks-Out!" or "A Positive Viewpoint." "The premise of my argument that remained unspoken," he wrote, is that

> I cannot let my "children" go back to suppressing accurate images of themselves no matter what they may be connected with and no matter

how uncomfortable these truths may make those who control mainstream American life.... To condemn a picture of two gay males of any ethnic background engaged in an innocent and certainly "safe" act of same-sex contact is to imply that some aspect of such an act is "wrong"—it is to go back to the old days when *any* image or mention of homosexuality in our daily newspapers was verboten.

The truth that HIV is indelibly a part of gay male life in the 1990's cannot be denied—just as it cannot be denied that HIV is indelibly a part of *all* life, worldwide, whatever the sexual preference. HIV affects all humanity and the sooner we admit this undeniable fact and stop trying to put the onus off onto weak, disenfranchised minorities that are perceived (consciously or unconsciously) as "inferior," the sooner peace and harmony will come to our planet and dread diseases such as HIV will be controlled. For middle America to continue enjoying the luxury of "AIDS IS NOT A PART OF *MY* LIFE" is to continue a dangerous form of deceit and denial—just as it is dangerous for gay men to deny that a disease called HIV is irrevocably connected to their culture.[28]

Regardless of his frustration, Cal continued to submit articles for the GAAP newsletter. Pat Swett, who had founded the organization in 1991 and a dozen years later was presented a leadership award by the National Episcopal AIDS Coalition, told Cal that his contribution to the newsletters was one of the best things that they had going for them.[29]

Not feeling at all well and not satisfied with his doctor in Gainesville, Cal went to New York for some new tests. He began seeing a new AIDS doctor, Dr. Paul Bellman, who recommended he see a cardiologist. To his surprise, Cal learned that he had significant heart malfunction. His having AIDS was not the only cause of his depression and lack of energy. About the same time, a strange itching developed above his left eye, became full-blown shingles by midsummer, and hospitalized him for seven days. Because of acute light sensitivity, the treatment, which involved lengthy dilation of the eye, kept him homebound for over two months, plunging him again into massive depression. The pills he was taking resulted in renal failure—loose, greasy stools with lots of gas and putrid odors.

He had finally been labeled a pain in the ass by almost everyone in the various AIDS groups he had volunteered with. His last serious involvement as an activist—trying to develop and implement a communal HIV home for people living with AIDS—had failed and had made him realize that emotionally he was not equipped to be a group leader or player. The stress of it had brought him down and had precipitated the serious attack of shingles. As he recuperated, he resumed his plan to explore the possibilities of euthanasia and informed friends in Amsterdam that he would be returning there in the fall, maybe accompanied by Eric, whom he described as "a pearl of very rare aspect and one of the best friends I've ever had." Cal explained, "He's always there for me richly and firmly when the chips are down, but in those silly in between times which don't really matter much in the great cosmic swirl of things, he can just about frazzle a saint to cuss."[30]

In October, accompanied by Jeff Wentzel rather than Eric, Cal again flew off to Amsterdam. Cal had met Jeff in 1992, just a few months after Cal had learned of his HIV status. He had attended a general community meeting of NCFAN and had complained how little the organization had to offer. Jeff, who was a student at the university, was the buddy coordinator at the time and decided he would sign him up as his buddy to make sure that Cal would get a more positive attitude about NCFAN. Even though Jeff self-identified as straight, he had been the "poster boy" for a newspaper advertisement, paid for by the alumni association, with the headline reading, "Your Gay & Lesbian Friends Welcome You Back to School." He was intrigued by Cal's pushing the limits of being openly gay. Cal was a survivor with a colorful persona. But to a naïve, young man with a conservative background such as Jeff, Cal was also a scary, older man who dressed in leather.

Encouraged by Cal, Jeff and his wife, Andrea Copland, moved to New York in August 1994 and lived in the Lower East Side, only a few blocks from "Uncle Cal." Although Jeff and Andrea were good friends, they had married shortly before they moved to New York for purely practical reasons. The job she had provided them both with health insurance and moving expenses. By 1995, however, Andrea wanted a place of her own, so Cal invited Jeff to move in with him in his Orchard Street apartment, with the understanding that Jeff would take care of the place during the months when Cal was either in Florida or Amsterdam. Jeff accepted the offer, but made it clear that having sex with Cal was not part of the arrangement.

Wanting a travel companion, Cal invited Jeff to join him in a trip to Amsterdam. For Jeff, it was to be a brief vacation. For Cal, it was to see if he could remain and make a new life for himself. "I must seek a 'new world' for myself," he felt, "or die a bitter, bored and unfulfilled old man."[31] Fed up with America and his perpetual feeling of being a misfit, he dreamed of becoming an expatriate. After Cal checked them into the small Armada Hotel, they went to dinner and then on to the night baths.

Cal worked at developing a social life and hoped to connect with new friends. Amsterdam had two gay saunas, one open during the day, another at night. Cal frequently went twice a day. He also attended the regular meetings of the English Speaking Group along with another American he had met, Brian Kirkpatrick. Brian wrote to Eric at one point that he noticed a serenity and energy in Cal that he had never seen before.[32] Cal had rented a small apartment in the attic of an old house at 1089 Prinsengracht for about $900 per month, calling it Mulberry View. On a long weekend, Cal joined Brian and his lover as they rented a car for a drive through the countryside to Arnhem on the Dutch eastern border. On their return to Amsterdam, they stopped at a British friend's minifarm for tea and a tour of her sculpture studio. Cal's spirits were so buoyed by the generosity of his new friends and by the openness and freedom he felt among the Dutch that he extended his stay by several weeks and decided he would return for a much longer period the following year.

In early December, Cal flew to New York for a few weeks prior to returning to Florida after the New Year. During the next three months, he prepared himself to leave for a new life in what he called the capital of the New World—Amsterdam. He considered becoming a legal citizen of the Netherlands, but after consulting with his lawyer, decided against it. Since federal taxes for Dutch citizens approached 70 percent, he felt it best to remain a visitor.

He landed at Schipol International Airport the morning of March 8, 1996, and told the customs officials that he planned to stay until June. He had all of his medications with him in a carry-on bag, but was not concerned about being rejected. After all, the Netherlands, unlike the United States, allowed PWAs to enter the country. Immediately, he was relieved to feel that he was welcomed. Exactly one week after he arrived and had settled into his Prinsengracht apartment, Cal met with Dr. J.M.V. Van de Meer and began the process of selecting a doctor. When Cal made it clear that he was interested in euthanasia, the doctor replied without hesitating or with any surprise. The Dutch medical system mandates that all illnesses must be approached first by a family doctor who is more-or-less assigned. Euthanasia, to be legal in Holland, requires the participating consent of two doctors. Cal was flabbergasted by a system "designed to cater to patients' needs rather than to give doctors plenty of time on the golf course." He was overwhelmed to find himself cast not as an "enemy/victim, but rather as wounded brother in need of care."[33]

The Dutch openness about sex and drugs was equally appealing. The culture seemed to encourage healthy and vibrant sexual activities for its citizens. Excellent cannabis products were readily available in coffeehouses, where you could not only buy clean, unadulterated hash and grass of the highest quality, but also use it while sipping your cup of coffee or tea, in civilized comfort. Their attitude of exceptional tolerance of most human needs and eccentricities fostered a society that was anything but hateful and angry, as in the United States. Since childhood, Cal had felt he was a total misfit everywhere in America except in the gay and Bohemian ghettos of large cities, but now was so relieved to be living where he was not judged by his sexual orientation or his illness.

He returned to New York on May 31. Although he loved being in Amsterdam because of his acceptance, he felt he had no purpose being there, but then, he realized he had no real purpose in the United States either. His attempt to become an AIDS activist ended badly, as he put it, "With the certain feeling I had done more harm than good.... So now I live with the frustrated impotence peculiar to outcasts."[34] While in New York, his doctor added Retrovir and atenolol to his regimen of antiviral pills. Cal knew his fight against the virus had reached a new plateau. "And I feel like shit. And why shouldn't I?"[35]

A few weeks later, Cal was back in Amsterdam. While walking to the tram after a dinner out, he noticed a marked blurring and floaters in his right eye. The next day, his eye doctor sent him to a specialist for further diagnosis and discovered a tiny hole where Cal had leaked blood inside his eye. Laser surgery was required to repair it and to prevent the danger of the retina detaching. Back and forth to the hospital three times the next week with his vision only slightly improved. The black floaters seemed like squirming scorpions inside his eye. Two months passed before he regained his eyesight. Another deep depression: "Now I know what Vada meant when she said, 'I can't do nothin' anymore.'"[36] In early August, doctors found malignant spots on his face and used liquid oxygen to freeze the tissue, leaving him with burned scars. "Look at this body. Look at it!" Cal cried. "I have to live in this ½ dead, mangled corpse. This mutilated, scarred, putrid carcass."[37]

The fall of 1996, Cal had several houseguests, probably too many. The first visitor was Mark Cowan, a young man from Gainesville whom Cal often had hired to clean his homes in Micanopy and Cumberland Circle when he was out of town. It did not go smoothly. Cal paid for his flight and invited him to stay in his apartment during his two weeks in Amsterdam. After the health issues he had undergone the past few months, Cal was not really prepared to be a good host, and once Mark arrived, he resented the infringement on his solitude. He was stressed out and gruff most of the time. Adding to the tension was Mark's being nearly penniless and smoking grass heavily. After a blow up, Mark was forced to transfer to a cheap hotel. He never talked to Cal again.

Cal was determined to be a better host with his New York roommate, Jeff Wentzel, who also had accompanied Cal to Amsterdam a year earlier.

Since he still lacked energy to entertain Jeff royally, he was delighted to see Jeff venturing out on his own. By this point, Jeff was finally admitting that he was gay and enjoyed exploring the bars and baths and cruising spots in Amsterdam. Jeff felt very close to Cal. For him, Cal "was a curmudgeonly, old gay-grandfather (or grandmother, as the case could sometimes be), who seemed to always be lecturing me in as loving a way as he could muster about the importance of getting over my sexual hang-ups, the evils of losing my soul and becoming 'a corporate whore' in NYC."[38] Cal's feelings toward Jeff were mutual. He wrote that it was hard not to fall in love with Jeff. "His energy and light are so bright and filled with good cheer. I long to hold him close....Like a son, I guess. We've formed a non-sexual bond that is deep and rich. I thought long and hard before I admitted to myself the above with all its complications and implicit reach-out dangers."[39]

A few weeks later, Cal found himself in a real muddle. Three old friends—Fred Chappell, Grady McClendon, and Eric Garber—had indicated in separate letters that they each wanted to visit Cal over Thanksgiving. "It's so funny," Cal wrote, "I who have no social life whatever (almost) must juggle and try to placate three divas."[40] Fred's request concerned Cal because Fred planned to have Diane Deckard accompany him. Cal had seen Diane occasionally after their aborted wedding plans in the 1960s, but the prospects of spending a week with her at this point he found "rather daunting....I find it difficult to reach back," he confessed to Fred.[41] He also explained to both Fred and Eric that since Grady had fallen on hard times, he already had promised to pay for Grady's flight. Fred understood and bowed out, but Eric felt there was some kind of plot or vendetta against him until Cal reassured him otherwise.

When Eric arrived in mid-November, before Grady, Cal was pleased to see him. His enthusiasm was brief. The shabby jacket Eric wore, combined with what Cal described as his unpleasant body odor, bad breath, and tattered appearance, annoyed Cal to no end. Even though he had warned Eric before he arrived that due to his health he had little energy and stamina and would be unable to accompany him in his tourist adventures, Eric seemed offended when Cal would not join in. One evening as Cal rolled a joint, Eric blurted out, "I just can't stand what drugs do to people." When Cal asked him to refrain from criticizing, Eric continued his diatribe. Cal proceeded to take his joint downstairs and felt he was "an unpleasant presence in my own 2 room home—paranoid or not." Another day, Cal was working at his desk while listening to a counter-culture radio station that was playing reggae. Eric walked into the room, immediately turned off the radio with no comment, and began eating the supper Cal had prepared. "The whole scene was so ugly and selfish; Eric at his worst," Cal wrote. "It's so sad we can't get along."[42]

What undoubtedly had set Eric off was reading Cal's journal entries while he was there. Cal left his journal open every night, in plain view, as if he wanted Eric to read it. He headlined the November 22 entry "Death in Amsterdam":

> Sad, very strange, and so unnecessary to feel our friendship dying within, but he's too isolated, unable to share and ultimately childishly selfish to be anyone's unstinting friend. His vanity is tiresome, his solitary ego-needs quite demented coupled as they are with agoraphobia and every other phobia known to man. . . . I feel I don't want to be around him a lot in the future. . . . Such a brilliant prose stylist, but unable to find or adhere to his own spine of truth.

Cal ended his criticism with a vow: "'Nothing but kind' should definitely be my motto. I must keep it simple and speak prudently until he leaves."

Eric was clearly shocked when he read Cal's remarks. There was no confrontation, and he left the next day. Cal admitted, "I'm *so* sorry to've FAILED again to revive a flagging friendship and Disappointed another house guest because of the sharpness of my truth and the boredom of my paranoia. . . . When something's over—it's over. The truth is I can't stand his ways no more. I'm moving on." He continued to examine Eric's visit for several days.

> Eric is constantly condescending and patronizing. It is one of his defense mechanisms born of total insecurity, but he's also selfish and vain and must always control the flow and direction of intellectual and social intercourse. . . . He will forever be the boarding school brat who was allowed his mommy only in the summer and on holidays and who is always grasping with knarled anorexic fingers for the love and attention his bored and rather alcoholic parents were too self-preoccupied to give. I could go on, suffice he is NUTS.[43]

If Cal ever had thoughts of trying to resume his friendship with Eric, they ended abruptly a few years later. In a collection of stories Eric published in 1999, Eric, using his customary pseudonym of Andrew Holleran, described his visit with Cal in Amsterdam. The two rooms in the canal house where Cal lived reminded Eric of Anne Frank's hiding place, and he wondered if Cal, like Anne, was hiding, "not from Nazis, but from people who had judged him." Although he does not acknowledge that it is a true story and changes the name of Cal to Roy, he quotes directly from Cal's journal.[44] Eric writes that he came to feel as if he were an enemy and that Cal, his friend of ten years, wished he was not there. Cal was enraged when he discovered that Eric had published this essay, especially since Eric quoted directly from his journals. He had been betrayed. They seldom spoke after that.

The first few months of 1997, Cal was back in the United States, splitting his time between New York and Florida. When in Florida, he frequently visited the Parliament House. On one occasion, he decided to take some photos, particularly one through a guest's window where he could see one of Eric's books lying on a table. He thought it would amuse Eric. The security people stopped him, however, thinking he was taking photos that he could use to blackmail the customers. While he was in New York, he was hospitalized for a few days in St. Vincent's. After extensive diagnostic procedures, they concluded that his cardiac problems were not due to a leaking heart valve, but by a hereditary, degenerative heart disease that produced a gradual thickening of heart muscle and caused, during physical stress, constriction and consequent reduction of blood flow. He was released in time to catch his Singapore Airlines flight to Amsterdam on April 16.

Back in Amsterdam, he began to suffer from extreme bouts of diarrhea and night sweats, waking up in the mornings with his pillow drenched with sweat and wondering how long his body could survive such torture. The end of May he was back in New York, since his medications had not made it through the customs inspections in Amsterdam. He had no choice but to return to New York and retrieve his meds. He had no time to appeal or to get a doctor to intervene.

He returned to Amsterdam in a matter of days and was encouraged by an offer he received from Ruth Drier, an American expatriate he had met in Amsterdam. She was a recording engineer for the Concertgebouw Orchestra and also a host of an unlicensed radio station. He agreed to read some poetry by Tennessee Williams for a program that would be broadcast over her station, Radio 100, the largest, noncommercial radio station in Amsterdam. The idea appealed to Cal, not only because he was such a fan of Tennessee Williams, but also because he had supported Radio 100 ever since arriving in the city.

Cal spent considerable time selecting material, rehearsing, and recording poems by Williams, including *Old Men Go Mad at Night*, *Winter Smoke Is Blue and Bitter*, *The Couple*, *You and I*, *Night Visit*, *The Lady with No One at All*, *Turning Out the Bedside Lamp*, and *Tangier: The Speechless Summer*. He relished the creative work, but was uncomfortable around Ruth. She always seemed so weary and shaky, especially when she was drinking and smoking pot, which she did almost nonstop. They continued to collaborate on these recordings for the next couple of years, hoping to introduce the Dutch to a new side of Tennessee Williams. Because of his deteriorating health, Cal flew back to New York on September 1, 1997, planning to stay for seven months. He had been feeling nauseous and dizzy so much of the time and could hardly move without becoming breathless. "Oh, mama," he wrote, "the pain just never stops."[45] By mid-October, his condition had worsened, and he was rushed to St. Vincent's Hospital where he stayed for six days, four of them in the cardiac intensive care unit. Even after he was released from the hospital, he was always tired. Feeling that death was near, he was desperate to return to Amsterdam where he knew he could request euthanasia. He booked a flight for December 2, not knowing for sure if he had the strength and energy to make it. Just two days after he was back in his old apartment on the Prinsengracht, he got up out of bed too quickly, got dizzy, tried to make it back to bed, but fell. When he awoke, there was blood on the floor and two nastily scraped fingers. He had blacked out for quite some time.

The first two weeks of February 1998, Cal was back in St. Vincent's hospital, this time with pneumonia. He wrote from his hospital bed, "My carousel ride is over. I just want it to slow enough to dismount. I hear the calliope no more nor am bedazzled by the lights. The smell of popcorn nauseates."[46] When he was finally dismissed, the doctors concluded that the pneumonia was due to fluid in his lungs that was caused by congestive heart failure. They labeled it idiopathic hypertrophic sub-aortic stenosis, or IHSS, and suggested that he consider a pacemaker, which he rejected.

By April, he was back in Amsterdam, this time staying at a larger apartment on the Herrengracht—with fewer stairs to climb. His dear, loyal friend, Bruce McCoy, visited him for a week. Bruce encouraged Cal to resume his interest in photography. Rather than focusing on nude men as he had, Cal became interested in architectural elements of buildings, fire hydrants, and open-air pissoirs common in Europe at the time. One night they had dinner at Ruth Drier's apartment on "slap alley," a very narrow passageway where the prostitutes would slap the butts of their potential clients as they walked by. From Ruth's apartment, you could hear them servicing their customers and spitting when they were done.

Feeling the need to see his doctor, Cal went back to New York in May. When he arrived at the apartment that he shared with Jeff, he learned that Jeff's lover, Sebastian Alvarez, had died two days earlier. Sebastian was an architect from Chile who was working on the new apartment of fashion model Stella Tennant's in the West Village. Jeff and Sebastian had planned to throw a "Welcome Home" party for Cal on her rooftop garden. In preparation, Sebastian pulled several huge potted plants to the edge of the roof in order to make room for the tables of food and drinks. As he leaned over and tugged on one, he slipped and fell overboard four stories to the street. He was rushed to the ER of the nearest hospital where he died two days later. It was left to Jeff to telephone Sebastian's parents in Chile and to make arrangements for the body to be returned to Chile. He was so distraught by the tragedy and all he had to do that he had not alerted Cal, who was in Amsterdam. The minute Cal opened the door to the apartment on his arrival, Jeff fell into his arms. Cal had sometimes been jealous of Sebastian and the attention Jeff showered on him, but now he could only hold his young friend and try in his embrace to comfort him.

As if that tragedy were not enough, Cal was told by his doctor that he needed to start taking protease inhibitors, the most toxic drug yet prescribed for him, eight times per day. Cal knew that potential side effects included diarrhea, nausea, loose stools, and abdominal discomfort. Furthermore, Dr. Bellman warned Cal that he could monitor his health if he were in the United States, but not if he returned to Amsterdam. The news triggered a further deep depression: "There is no place or function for me on this earth. My birth seems a mistake. My death will be a relief."[47]

Cal was now faced with a real dilemma. For the last few years, he had held on to the belief that he would end his days in Amsterdam where he felt more accepted and free. He had told Ruth Drier when he met her in 1996 that he had come there to die. Yet during the past two to three years, the drugs for PWAs had advanced dramatically so that life expectancy was extended, even improved. It gave him a shred of hope. It was a mixed blessing for Cal, however; he now had to contemplate living longer with the disease rather than a quick death. If he accepted his doctor's prescriptions and heeded his advice, he could perhaps live several more years. Would he rather do that, or would he rather end his own life sooner? Having made all the required arrangements for euthanasia, Cal was relieved. He knew that he would not have to bear the ghastly suffering he had seen other gay men endure as they died from this horrid plague. The choice was his to make. His trip back to Amsterdam, in the fall of 1998, must have been made with great hesitation. When and how should he make a decision on his future path?

Walking home one night after working on the radio recordings at Ruth Drier's apartment, he stopped several times on bridges and against buildings to gather strength and to catch his breath. He doubted if he could make it up the few stairs to his apartment. Indeed, he doubted if he could make it back to New York to die. "I think I can and I feel that is what I must do," he wrote. "The time has come."[48] At this point, he decided finally against euthanasia. Instead, he would return to New York and hope the new plan of his doctor might solve some of his medical issues, improve his spirits, and maybe even provide him with a few more good years.

CHAPTER 10

"THE RAP OF IGNORANCE"

In preparation for his return to New York, Cal wrote to Jeff that he was returning, perhaps permanently, and that he preferred not to have a roommate in his Orchard Street apartment. He asked Jeff to vacate by January 9, 1999—the date he planned to be back. After Cal arrived in New York in late 1998, however, he stayed only a few days in order to see his doctor and then flew to Gainesville where he remained for several months. Staying at Cal's Cumberland Circle condo in Gainesville off and on, through 1998 and into 1999, was his longtime, straight friend, Joe Hendrix. Because he had always loved Joe and had fantasized about an alliance with him, their living together when Cal was there was a sort of substitute for a normal relationship.

Concluding that he would be in Gainesville for some time, Cal subscribed to a matchmaker service where he could make contacts, have phone sex, or arrange to meet tricks at the local McDonald's. As before, he often visited Whorelando's Parliament House. Due to his failing health, he would typically sweat all night and wake up with his sheets drenched. Regardless, he boasted three or four sexual encounters each day.

Sensing that there may be a time approaching when he might not be able to live so independently in his Cumberland Circle condo, Cal purchased for $40,000 a one-bedroom condo in the Seagle Building on West University Avenue, near downtown Gainesville. Begun in 1926 as a luxury resort hotel, it remained unfinished until the mid-1930s when the University of Florida started using it for their museum. In the 1980s it was totally renovated, remodeled, and placed on the National Register of Historic Places. The first six floors were converted into commercial space, and the remaining five floors became residential units, with four units per floor. Cal's was on the eighth floor. He was particularly attracted by the panoramic views of the city, as well as the Heritage Club, a private, dining club on the second floor where he could choose to take his meals. He furnished it but then sublet, never living there himself.

A more enterprising venture was Cal's purchase of a large piece of property near downtown Crystal River that contained eight run-down town houses. Naming the property "The Anhinga," after the Florida waterbird, he set out to remodel all the units, planning on turning them into individually designed residences and catering to a gay clientele. He was even attempting to come up with names of famous visitors to Crystal River, so he could design the units thematically around each person. In one of his last journals, Cal composed a description he planned to use in advertising: "This is a good place to spend a month junking & antiquing. Glorious thrift antique malls shops. The Anhinga's homelike ambience is created from the detritus of these broken homes. Each unit unique but furnished comfortably. All new queen size mattresses."[1] Soon after the purchase, Cal hired his cousin, Sid Kennedy, to oversee the remodeling, and he returned to New York.

For most of 2000, Cal lived alone in New York. One of his neighbors who had lived in the building for many years was shocked to see him having to walk with a cane. She noticed that he often seemed out of breath as she watched him walking down the streets, always dressed in jeans and flannel shirts. And yet, he was always so kind and generous with her, helping her haul up groceries and her children to the second floor. Much of his energy was devoted to dolling up the apartment. Fresh paint, some new furniture, and hanging on prominent walls some of his favorite purchases—a floral painting by his former lover Jon Porch, a poster of porn star Scott O'Hara sucking his own dick, a picture of a distinguished and elderly man on which Cal had drawn an erection dripping with cum. Cal spent many hours sitting leisurely under the picture, reading and listening to music. He did not mind if straight friends were stunned when they entered the room. In fact, it pleased him. Although he was no longer writing poetry or plays, he still maintained and argued for sexual freedom. He still liked to shock.

Although Jeff no longer lived with Cal, he often visited him in the apartment and introduced Cal to www.gay.com on the internet. Using the same screen name as his Crystal River property, Anhinga, Cal, who was thinking of moving back permanently to Gainesville, was eager to find a way of staying connected with gay men both online and in the sheets.

He was not at all interested in the porn sites, but rather in being able to chat online. His last journals are filled with dozens of telephone numbers and email addresses. By November 2000, perhaps because of his deteriorating health, Cal invited Jeff to move back into the apartment with him.

Figure 10.1   Cal made cards with his email address at the top. In the background hangs a poster of porn star, Scott O'Hara.

Source: Courtesy Cal Yeomans Collection, Special Area Studies, George A. Smathers Libraries, University of Florida.

He returned to Florida frequently in order to check up on the progress of his real-estate ventures. During one of his visits, he was approached by Roger Goettelmann, the Community Redevelopment Director, about selling the property that included his house by the river. The city was interested in converting the land into a park with "a visitor's center and museum featuring exhibits related to the history of fishing, crabbing, and cedar mill industries which once provided the primary economic impetus of the town."[2] Cal did not trust the city officials and quizzed Goettelmann. Would they pave the land and turn it into a parking lot? Would they maintain the natural quality of the land? Goettelmann guaranteed him that it would be a lovely park and offered Cal lifetime occupancy in the house. It was Goettelmann's intent to attract more gays to the area with Cal as the catalyst, believing it would benefit the city. For several months, the two of them chatted often over the telephone about the project, leading Goettelmann to believe that Cal might even donate the land to the city.

But his visits back to Crystal River were not always pleasant. It ate away at him when he was always reminded that his family "never could beat the rap of ignorance."[3] When he was in Crystal River on Mother's Day 2001, he wrote,

> I am the troubled
> son of a troubled
> mother…
> we have the same
> genes—the same
> scars

A week later, he bumped into high school friend, Roger Carol, and her mother, Mrs. Daniels, at the Crystal Paradise Café. "You sure don't look like Calvin Yeomans," Mrs. Daniels said.

Diplomatically, Cal responded in his best politician's-son voice, "Well you know I'm sixty-two now."

Roger Carol said with a puzzled look, "Sixty-two? I thought I was a year older than you." "I'd hate to ruin your day, R.C., but I think you are," he replied. It cracked them both up and the years rolled away.

"My lord, I just told the doctor today I was sixty-one," she laughed.

Mrs. Daniels never showed a smile. "You sure don't look like Calvin Yeomans," shaking her head.

"Space aliens invaded my body," he thought of saying. "The forces of evil took me over long ago. They got me." Out of respect for her ninety-three plus years, he held his tongue, smiled sweetly, laughed, cried a pair of tears, and tried to forget it.[4]

In mid-August, Jeff flew with his mother down to visit Cal in Florida, saw his weakened condition, and took him immediately to the ER of a hospital in Orlando. He was kept there for two weeks, then released as cured. Cal knew he had to get back to New York to be treated by Dr. Bellman, so he booked a flight for September 13. But the terrorist tragedy of 9/11 intervened; no planes flew in the entire country that week. He rebooked for the next week, but before the date arrived, he suffered a relapse—fevers, and extreme shortness of breath. He had no choice except to go quickly to the ER of the Crystal River hospital, where he stayed for a week, until they acknowledged their treatments were not working. It was then decided that he should make a last-ditch dash for New York where they had greater experience with HIV-related pneumonia. One of his last telephone calls before he left was to tell Roger Goettelmann that he was still interested in the city's proposal, but that he had to return temporarily to New York. He left the hospital at 8 A.M., and was driven to Tampa to catch an 11:30 A.M. flight. He was wheelchaired to the plane and then to a taxi in New York, which took him straight to his doctor's office. He arrived there about 3 P.M.. They checked his vital signs and found his temperature was 102 degrees, his blood pressure and heartbeat, almost undetectable. He was then rushed to St. Vincent's for another eight days.

"I hope they get it cleared up for if they don't I may return to Holland for what I went there in the first place for: EUTHANASIA," he wrote.[5] He was released September 21. "I'm out now but my lungs have still not cleared completely....Meanwhile, I'm something of a shut-in on Orchard St. Very low energy and a great fatigue. The onslaught has quite depleted me. Everything languishes in Florida. The Anhinga stopped in its tracks."[6]

By October, Cal's health was failing dramatically. One night, two of his friends, Peter Ware and John McGorty, planned to accompany Cal to a meeting of their AIDS support group. When they arrived at Cal's apartment, they found him gasping for breath and called 911. He was rushed back to St. Vincent's Hospital and remained there for another week. "1/2-realized lives litter my highway, unrealized loves, my heart," he complained. A week later, he wrote, "Would you like to make love to a dying man with AIDS?"[7] Even though the infection in his lungs was still present, he left the hospital and was out of touch with almost everyone.

With thoughts of his own impending death, he remembered the last days he had spent in the hospital with dear friend Ernie Mickler. "Morphine, Mr. Mickler? Take it. It will help you do what you gotta do, Mr. Mickler," the nurse had said.[8] On October 17, Cal was informed that cancer, not AIDS, was causing his pneumonia. Doctors decided they would remove part of his lung, use chemo, and examine him with a flexible bronchoscope—a needle through the chest cavity into the infiltrated lung to check for bleeding, tumors, or any foreign bodies. What the doctors discovered must not have been good. On October 29, Cal wrote, "Satan is all up in you. Tell Satan to kiss your ass and leave." It was the last thing he ever wrote. He died two days later, on October 31, 2001, at the age of sixty-three.

Since Cal had been in and out of the hospital so many times in recent months, Jeff did not realize that Cal's death was imminent and took off to visit friends for a few days in Geneva, Switzerland. He arrived back home on Monday, October 29. Although he found several phone messages from Cal's doctor, alerting him that Cal was in the hospital, Jeff knew from past experience that Cal disliked having visitors and could become very cranky if they showed up. During Cal's previous hospitalizations, Jeff would regularly take him the *New York Times* and flowers. He had never told people when Cal was hospitalized. Cal did not want people to know because then he would feel rejected if they did not show up. The third night he was back from Geneva, Jeff got home from work and listened to a devastating phone message. Cal had died and had personally made all the advance decisions about having his body returned to Florida for burial. When Jeff went to the hospital to collect Cal's belongings, he learned that Cal had actually died of a heart attack. The morning of his death, the doctors had performed the biopsy that confirmed the extremely advanced stage of Cal's lung cancer. Since all the AIDS medications that he was on at the time would have complicated any potential treatment options, his doctor reassured Jeff that the heart attack was a blessing. Cal would not have to endure endless months of more suffering.

His funeral was held on Friday, November 9. Although Cal had signed a prearranged funeral agreement in 1994 with the Charles E. Davis Funeral Home in Inverness, Florida, the service actually took place at the Strickland Funeral Home in Crystal River with the Rev. Lloyd Bertine of Gulf to Lake Baptist Church officiating. There was no announcement of his death or funeral in the local newspaper. Cal was dressed in his typical jeans and flannel shirt. Among those in attendance were old friends—Joe Hendrix and his son Jonah, Zacq Reid, Michael Parker, Tim Hoggard, Jeff Wentzel and his mother—the few family members still living, and a few officials, including the mayor.

Michael Parker was shaken when he saw a man he recognized from an encounter several years earlier. The man was a city official at this point and was probably required to attend. Michael and Cal had been walking down the street in Crystal River when a truck drove by and this same man had yelled at them, "You fucking faggots." At the conclusion of the funeral service, Michael was at the coffin, holding on to the handle, when the man approached him. Michael glared at him, "What are you doing here? I remember what you said."[9] Following the burial next to Cal's parents, Parker hosted a reception for several people at his home. A few weeks later, Jeff Wentzel invited Cal's friends in New York to an intimate memorial celebration.

After his death, people were amazed not only at the extent of Cal's wealth, but also with how he chose to distribute it. In a trust fund, he left $1,000 each to dozens of people who had been important to him at different times of his life. Some, he had lost touch with years earlier; others, he had befriended in recent years. It was clearly Cal's way of saying, "Please remember me." The long list included Donald Arrington, Raymond Schanze, Grady McClendon, Mary Will Burton, Marc Cowan, Michael Parker, Diane Deckard, Fred Chappell, Zacq Reid, Joe Hendrix, Eric Garber, Tim and Martha Hoggard. Signed in 1995, his will, along with the trust fund, designated the University of Florida Foundation as the beneficiary of all his written work, photographs, negatives, correspondence, and autographed books for use by the Department of Special Collections. All of the real estate he still owned, including his home in Worthington Springs, his two condos in Gainesville, The Anhinga property, and his family's little house by the river in Crystal River, was also awarded to the University of Florida Foundation.

By the time all the property was sold, the total amounted to over $1,000,000 with $800,000 coming just from the city's buying the property by the river.[10] Cal made clear decisions on how he wanted the money used. With at least $300,000, he established the Vada Allen Yeomans Term Professorship in the Women's Studies Department of the university. Holders of the professorship are required to demonstrate expertise in feminist theory, with a preference given to scholars with research interest in Africa, Asia, or Latin America. The description notes that Vada Yeomans "was a teacher, mother and foster parent. She is remembered as a contributor to her community and a great businesswoman in a time when women were not seen in the business world."[11] In 2005, Dr. Florence Babb became the first recipient.

His interest in the University of Florida began as early as 1978, soon after he had returned to Florida following his several months in San Francisco. He was interested even then, even before he had become known for his gay plays, in establishing, with his personal papers, a gay archives at the university library. After years of discussion, in 1986 the Department of Special Collections representative, Marcia Brookbank, accepted the first twelve boxes as a donation to be added to the Belknap Collection for the Performing Arts. Through the years, he continued to add forty more boxes to the collection and spent many hours in the reading room, attempting to organize the contents.

Recurring themes in his forty years of journal writing were his obsession with escaping from what he considered the ignorance and poverty of Crystal River as well as his deeply rooted feeling that he was a disappointment to his parents—that he had let them down. He often reminded people of what his father had told him when he was a young boy, "I

worked so that none of us, none of my people would ever suffer ignorance again."[12] The generous gifts he made to the University of Florida
were clearly his attempt to help the next generation "beat the rap of ignorance." The Yeomans name would now be forever linked to the pursuit
of higher education. Cal must have known that his parents would have
been proud of him, perhaps for the first time.

When he was alive, Cal lacked the funds to be very generous until
he was in his forties. But when he assumed more control of the family
wealth upon his return to Crystal River in 1978, and especially after
his mother's death in 1985, which left him with real estate valued at
nearly a half million dollars, he was now in a position to assume the role
of patron. He had always complained bitterly about Crystal River, the
ignorance of the people and their insular, conservative values. During
his last several years, he clearly had a change of heart. It wasn't that he
had softened or had grown fond of the city. Rather, he became interested in creating a local, permanent legacy, and one that would have
pleased his parents.

Actually, fifteen years before he died, Cal had begun to honor the
memories of L.C. and Miss Vada. In June 1986, the Citrus County
Historical Society opened the Coastal Heritage Museum in Crystal
River. That November, Cal completed cleaning out the house where his
mother had spent her last years and donated to the museum an endless
offering of family items that reflected the life and times of the early pio-
neers of Citrus County, including quilts, dishes, handmade braided rugs,
framed photographs, Christmas ornaments, rings, lapel pins, furniture,
a cookbook and cooking utensils, eyeglasses, and clothes. In 1998, the
same year the building was placed on the National Register of Historic
Places, the director of the museum, Molly Johnston, wrote to Cal that
they planned to honor the Yeomans family with a Christmas exhibit and
thanked him for the many donations that enabled the museum to open in
Crystal River. They led the way for others to donate so they could preserve and present the history of the town.[13] He continued donating to the
collection at the historical society until shortly before he died.

In 1993, he gave forty acres of land to the city that had been homesteaded originally by Vada's grandfather in the 1850s. Telling a reporter
that he remembered Crystal River when it was a Garden of Eden with
lush wetlands shaded by palms and pines and an abundance of wildlife,
Cal pointed out that he wanted the current children of the city to have
"equally fond memories of their hometown."[14] At the time, City Manager
Merv Waldrop announced that it was the first step toward establishing
a conservation park in the city. Cal's main stipulation was for the park
to remain a back-to-nature preserve. When it was finally dedicated four

years later and they opened the first six acres to the public, Cal's cousin, Sid Kennedy, who oversaw Cal's real estate in town, remarked, "A pair of pruning shears and a machete is all I want to see in there. If they go in with a bulldozer, I'll be there to take the property back."[15]

Cal had insisted on a unique contract with the city that allowed him to reclaim the property if the city did not use it solely as a nature park. About a month prior to the dedication, Cal made a surprise visit to the park. When he saw four pieces of fitness equipment had been installed, he marched immediately to city hall and insisted they be removed. They were not in keeping with his vision for the land. Open from dawn to dusk daily, the park offered canoe and hiking trails through the brush and moss-hung oaks, an elevated boardwalk over native vegetation, picnic tables, a covered pavilion, public restrooms, and a parking lot.[16]

About the same time, with $350,000, Cal endowed a fellowship in his father's name, the Lee C. Yeomans Fisheries and Aquatic Sciences Fellowship. A percentage of the endowment fund balance is made available for spending each year, making an annual award available to a student of approximately $18,000. Eligible to apply are graduate students and students in any industrial internship who are studying any aspect of rearing, transporting, processing, and distributing aquatic food products. With an undisclosed amount, he also established The Calvin Yeomans Special Collections Enrichment Fund, an annual endowment for the George A. Smathers Libraries at the university. It is used to support the acquisition of materials for the Department of Special Collections. As of April 2007, the balance of the fund was $604,000.[17]

Cal was also able to assist certain gay causes. When Pat Swett of the Gainesville Area AIDS Project told him that the organization needed money to purchase a stove so they could prepare hot food for their clients, Cal bought it for them. In 1986, lesbian actress Pat Bond was about to reject an offer to perform at the Gay Sweatshop in London because she did not have the money for the flight. Cal bought her ticket.

For many years, he supported various people with whom he had enjoyed longtime friendships. Raiford Ragsdale had taught him playwriting in the 1960s when he was in Atlanta. Every Christmas he sent her a large check and renewed her subscriptions to several magazines. When she was especially hurting financially, he bought her a car. He had known Joe Hendrix before Joe moved with his family to Tennessee in the late 1970s. Cal commissioned several paintings from this struggling, rebellious artist, and gave one of them to Ellen Stewart. He helped Joe with mortgage payments, sent money for his children, and allowed Joe to live in his Cumberland Circle condo in Gainesville for months at a time, rent free.

Cal had known Michael Brennan (MAB) from his days in Atlanta and later when he lived in San Francisco. Beginning in 1980, MAB began asking Cal frequently to help him financially. At first, it was a suggestion that he move to Florida and that he and Cal open up a restaurant together. Cal made it clear at the time that he was not interested. A year later, MAB asked to borrow $300 so he could pay his monthly credit card bill, plus another $2,000 to help build up his credit. Cal sent the $300 and warned MAB against "getting back on the great charge card spiral."[18] Then, in 1984, Michael, who was unemployed, begged Cal for a loan of approximately $4,000 to pay his bills and a mortgage payment on his cabin at Cobb Mountain in northern California. After several emotionally charged letters between them wherein Cal expressed anger at Michael's refusal to curb his alcoholism, Cal finally agreed on a loan of $2,200.[19] Cal knew that it would never be repaid.

Cal developed an interest in contemporary American paintings and purchased works by such young, aspiring artists as Gary Bukovnik and Michael Haykin. In 1983, Cal walked into Harold's frame shop in Micanopy to have some work done on one of his pieces and found "some powerful, devastatingly beautiful paintings." He was overwhelmed by the extraordinary deep, deep beauty of the work. Cal bought two pieces and wanted more. "I've never seen paintings that affected me so deeply," he remarked, "strong, gutsy—yet intricately intellectual and richly allegorical; touches of abstracted surrealism."[20] Cal and the artist, Peter Zettler, soon became good friends. Cal bought a dozen of his paintings and commissioned others. When Cal organized Ellen Stewart's Café La MaMa for the residency at the Atlantic Center for the Arts in 1988, he arranged to have Peter hired to help construct the scenery. Four years later, he sponsored an art show at the La MaMa Galleria that featured the works of Peter as well as that of Eglé Gatins Wieland, who had been a student of Jim Sitton's, Cal's friend in Atlanta who had been murdered in 1975. Cal made the arrangements for the exhibit and paid all the shipping costs. He had asked Jon Wesley Porch, Cal's lover in the late 1970s, to exhibit with them, but, in the end, Jon felt unprepared and withdrew. When Lois Goettelmann, nee Williams, was searching for an apartment in Crystal River where she could set up a studio for her stained glass art work, she became Cal's charity project. He installed new carpets in one of his rentals, repainted all the rooms, and offered it to her for a very reduced rent.

Although Cal resisted feeling financially responsible for his relatives, since most of them had pretty much rejected him, he looked differently on his gay cousin, Rayford Meeks. Cal understood him; they were kindred spirits. Like him, Rayford was an only child, who had grown up in a conservative and homophobic Florida town. His parents had divorced when he was a little boy. The two gay cousins did not know each other as they were growing up, since Rayford was seventeen years older than Cal and moved to New York at an early age where he reportedly lived quite an active, gay social life, but earned very little money. He moved back to Florida in the mid-1970s to care for his aging mother and opened up a combination florist and boutique shop in downtown Inverness. On the ground floor of the two-storey, run-down house where he lived, he ran a little antique shop. Nothing seemed to work for him, however.

By the time Cal got to know him in the late 1970s, Rayford was an aging, gay man, living alone in a small town where he was not accepted and often ridiculed. To make it even worse, Rayford was a poor business-man and always living on a shoestring. Cal and his friend Grady occa-sionally drove to Inverness and made purchases at Rayford's businesses, mainly for the purpose of trying to help him financially. For many years, Cal paid all of his medical expenses, real-estate taxes, utility bills, and periodically sent him checks for groceries. He was very tactful about it, however, since Rayford was very sensitive to his sad situation. "Cal was lovely to him," Grady recalled, "never fussed at him as he could have."[21] In the end, Rayford became an alcoholic. When he died in his home in 1999, his body was not discovered for several days. The funeral home did not want to embalm him, but Cal strongly insisted and paid for a regular funeral service. Only a handful of relatives attended. Cal, who was the executor of Rayford's estate, gave them Rayford's house keys and turned all of his affairs over to them.

Cal adored Jeff Wentzel. Even though he was critical of Jeff's mar-riage to Andrea, when she wanted to find a place of her own, Cal lent her $20,000 for a down payment on a one-bedroom apartment in Brooklyn. According to his journal entry in early 2001, the loan had not been paid off. And shortly before he died, Cal opened up a bank account for Jeff with $5,000. Again, his way of saying, "Please remember me." Cal's money allowed him to be in control of so many relationships, but if he felt he was losing control and was no longer needed or appreciated, his patronage was withdrawn. Vern Gransden remembered Cal remarking, "If you don't want to sit at Buddha's feet and take this from him, Buddha doesn't want anything to do with you."[22]

In spite of their love-hate, volatile friendship, Cal had indicated to Ellen Stewart that he planned to leave Café La MaMa a generous con-tribution. As early as 1991, she had phoned him from her theatre cen-ter in Spoleto, Italy, to tell him, "The money's run out. There won't be any more MacArthur Grant money."[23] She had received one of the foundation's huge "genius grants" in 1985 and was looking to Cal as her next "angel." But Cal, annoyed by her obvious, direct request, wrote a very blunt rejection. "Please take my name off your 'patron' program as soon as you can. I appreciate the gesture but find it pretentious.... I would also ask you to stay away from me and not try to communicate with me in any way at any time in the future."[24] There must have been some kind of reconciliation, however, for in early May 2001, Cal had ordered a group of reserved seats for himself and several friends to see Ellen's production of *Seven Against Thebes*. When he entered the theatre and saw that his name was not on the reserved signs placed on the seats for his group, he was furious and charged out of the theatre, screaming that he was taking her out of his will.[25] She was not mentioned in his will, nor was she one of the persons noted in his trust to receive a $1,000 remembrance gift. Apparently, she had not sat at the foot of Buddha. His reaction was classic Cal.

Although he was not diagnosed with a bipolar disorder until he was in his mid-thirties, he had suffered from the illness his entire life. Even as a youth, he walked the streets of Crystal River as if he were a prince one day and hung his head in shame the next, convinced that his classmates and people in town were laughing at him. His forty years of journal writing reveal dramatic rushes to the peaks of ecstasy and then quickly dropping into depths of despair. Unrealistic overconfidence and grandiosity would suddenly turn to thoughts of suicide. During periods of hypomania, he could be productive and prolific, entertaining, and fun to be with. But times of deep depression brought intense pessimism, irritability, and hopelessness. Nothing made sense.

For his entire life, he tried to find recognition and acceptance. From an early age, he believed his birth was a mistake and that his parents preferred Van, his more "normal" cousin. Neither his father nor his mother could provide the love and warmth he needed. Rather than remain home and assume the family real-estate business when he could have, he fled from Crystal River and embarked on a life in the theatre—certainly disappointing his widowed mother, who was sixty-five at the time and needing help in running the business. She never showed interest or pride in his successes, and even though she undoubtedly knew he was gay and enjoyed socializing with many of his gay friends, she would not allow intimate discussions about his personal life.

His obsession for acceptance complicated Cal's life. He never stopped yearning for love and a meaningful relationship with another man. But he had endured so much rejection by his parents and ridicule in the repressed and alien society where he lived that he came to expect disapproval and criticism. He learned to cope by trying to control all his personal friendships. From the time of his first, meaningful sexual connection as an adult, Cal assumed the role of mentor and advisor. As his love interest matured and became more independent, however, Cal felt he was no longer in control of the relationship, dreaded the possible rejection, and would end it. Yet his intense desire for love fueled his sexual appetite, which became still another obsession. Toward the end of his life, he lamented with a strange mixture of despair, self-deprecation, and humor, "I wasted my life chasing dick. My life seems to be in the toilet."[26] Although Cal reveled in his sexual adventures, Eric Garber felt that his obsession to talk and write about sex, "betrayed something. It betrayed, I suspect, the very thing he was protesting—the guilt brought on by a small town Southern upbringing."[27]

He died with many unfulfilled dreams. He had battled and labored to reach them—recognition as a successful gay playwright, poet, and photographer; security with the love of a man; acceptance and gratitude as a friend and patron; and fame as a champion of sexual freedom. After years of struggle, he finally found his voice, but only because he wrote about the life he personally knew, the challenges and turmoil he had suffered while trying to accept his own sexuality. His vision was unique, to have a new genre of gay theatre—gay men writing plays about the lives of gay men and intended solely for a gay audience. In explaining the plays being written during the height of the AIDS crisis, Michael Feingold declared, "Plays are ... models of behavior, imitations of life which reflect back onto it. They give us patterns to follow or reject, motives and meanings of action, consequences to hope for or avoid; in their ambiguities they offer alternatives."[28] That was precisely Cal's point of view. He yearned for a theatre of, for, and by gays that would imitate their life, look back on it, and provide them with patterns to follow or reject.

What he explored in his writing and what he accomplished was remarkable. He was an award-winning trailblazer in the advance of post-Stonewall gay theatre. He completed over twenty plays—mostly one-acts, dozens of scene sketches, hundreds of poems and photographs, and nearly fifty years of journals. Of his nine plays that were produced, four were chosen to play at National Gay Arts Festivals. His plays were seen in San Francisco, New York, Chicago, and Portland, Oregon. But he burst the boundaries of what was considered acceptable in legitimate theatre—and, perhaps for this reason, his work was not celebrated, not lasting, not considered legitimate.

Besides his work in the theatre, Cal presented poetry/play readings in San Francisco, Los Angeles, New York, Key West, Atlanta, and both Gainesville and Jacksonville, Florida. His photography was exhibited in San Francisco, Los Angeles, and Gainesville, as well as in *Christopher Street* magazine.

In all of his creative work, Cal Yeomans traveled a lifelong journey. It was a bumpy road. He was terrified that he would wake up one day "writing like a gay Johnboy of *The Waltons*." His quest was "to speak the most complete truth I can *in my own voice*."[29] He understood that few people would think that he wanted to make the world a better place to live in. But he did. "I am a sexual revolutionary," he proclaimed, "and want to...demystify sex into freedom. I want to help stop sexual malignancy and dysfunction and therefore diminish human suffering."[30] When questioned why he stopped submitting his plays for production, he sneered, "Honey, when I went out there and put that stuff on the stage, it rocked them right off the peter meter, and they never were right again and they never have written anything like it since and they aren't gonna ever do it again because gay people are afraid of who they are."[31]

Curbing his career, however, was not just the growing criticism that arose from the AIDS epidemic, though that was certainly instrumental. Cal's fear of rejection meant that he could not relinquish control of his plays and hand them over to directors and actors to interpret, explore, and adapt. Unlike most gay playwrights at the time whose characters spoke in a kind of code or avoided gay subjects altogether, Cal's gay men spoke directly and openly to gay audiences. Their lives were portrayed honestly and vividly on stage as never before. Collaborating in a workshop setting or compromising his style was not in his cards. If he had needed money like so many struggling artists, perhaps he would have buckled under, held his tongue, and forced himself to submit his plays to theatre companies. That was not the case. Particularly after his mother died in 1985, he had sufficient income so that he never had to work, never had to make money from his writing—possibly a luxury that ultimately worked against him.

Whenever Ruth Drier tried to describe Cal's contributions to her friends in Amsterdam, she remarked that he was a diva in gay theater before gay theater even knew it existed.[32] Playwright, screenwriter, and director Victor Bumbalo, who established the Robert Chesley Foundation, called Chesley and Cal "two revolutionary playwrights."

> Revolutionary in the truest sense of the word. They brought radical change to gay theatre as it was evolving. Onto their stage some of our most secret thoughts were given breath. Some kinky, some funny, often bathed in beauty, some frightening, many pornographic...all in the spirit of exploring freedom. They examined honestly and without fear their own psyches. Never did they generalize and claim that all gay men were

alike. They were charting new territories in order to celebrate, and now and then have great fun with, the human sexual psyche. Sometimes they were sensational, but they always were theatrical. They are so missed and needed today in this puritanical world in which we now live.[33]

What prominence Cal Yeomans might have realized if only circumstances had not silenced him.

NOTES

Preface

1. Cal Yeomans Journal, December 17, 1977, Cal Yeomans Collection, Special and Area Studies Collections, George A. Smathers Libraries, University of Florida, Gainesville, Florida. Hereafter cited UFL.
2. Cal Yeomans Journal titled Final Island Journal, (Part II), November 25, 1979, UFL.
3. Letter from Cal Yeomans to Johnny Ferdon, July 28, 1987, UFL.
4. Last Will and Testament of Lee Calvin Yeomans, November 28, 1995.
5. Email from Carl Van Ness, August 7, 2008.
6. Georges Gusdorf, (1980) "Conditions and Limits of Autobiography," in James Olney (ed.), *Autobiography: Essays Theoretical and Critical* (Princeton, NJ: Princeton University Press), p. 35.
7. Email from Mark Thompson, November 4, 2009.

Chapter 1

1. Cal Yeomans Journal, 1992, UFL. In this journal account, Cal writes the story of the fire as if it were his mother writing. Several family members have verified its accuracy.
2. Cal Yeomans Journal, 1992, UFL.
3. Interview with John Grannan, May 6, 2008.
4. Unmarked draft of a short story by Cal Yeomans, dated March 1993, UFL.
5. Ibid., p. 47.
6. The receipt for the bill of sale was dated April 3, 1925, Yeomans Collection, Citrus County Historical Society. Hereafter cited CCHS.
7. Unmarked clipping, CCHS.
8. Unmarked clipping, CCHS.
9. Letter from Cal Yeomans to Ellen Stewart, February 1, 1990, La MaMa Archives.
10. Interview with John Grannan, May 6, 2008. L.C.'s cousin rented a building in downtown Crystal River where he ran a large hardware store. Every time he asked to buy the property from L.C. so he would not have

to pay monthly rent, L.C. would refuse. He wanted the monthly check more than he wanted to help a relative.

11. Vada Yeomans Diaries, CCHS.
12. Cal Yeomans Journal, October 11, 1985, UFL.
13. Ibid.; Interview with Frank Regan, May 5, 2008.
14. Cal Yeomans Journal, January 26, 1972, UFL.
15. Vada Yeomans Diaries, CCHS.
16. Cal Yeomans, "Description of my mother," an essay written for an English class dated June 29, 1970, UFL.
17. Cal Yeomans Journal, May 9, 1995, UFL.
18. Email from Grady McClendon, June 25, 2007.
19. Interview with Grady McClendon, April 28, 2008.
20. Cal Yeomans Journal, February 4, 1993, UFL.
21. Letter from L.C. Yeomans to Vada Yeomans, September 14, 1951, UFL.
22. Interview with Byron Nichols, May 9, 2008.
23. Writings of Cal Yeomans, CCHS.
24. Ibid.
25. Interview with Dr. Phillip Cushman, May 1, 2008.
26. Interview with Byron Nichols, May 9, 2008.
27. Interview with Roger Carol Dumas, nee Daniels, May 7, 2008.
28. Evelyn C. Bash and Marge K. Pritchett (2006), *A History of Crystal River, Florida* (Crystal River, Florida: Crystal River Heritage Council), p. 65.
29. Interview with Byron Nichols, May 9, 2008.
30. Ibid.
31. Cal Yeomans Journal, November 11, 1967, UFL.
32. Cal Yeomans interview with Ernie Mickler, October 7–8, 1988, Mickler Collection, UFL.
33. Letter from Cal Yeomans to Johnny Ferdon, December 5, 1988, UFL.
34. Letter from Cal Yeomans to Tom Smith, August 18, 1981, UFL.
35. Cal Yeomans Journal, July 23, 1998, UFL.
36. Regent Theatre folder, UFL.
37. Cal Yeomans Journal, July 21, 1994, UFL.
38. *Citrus County Chronicle*, March 22, 1956; May 31, 1956; June 7, 1956.
39. Cal Yeomans Journal titled Final Island Journal, September 3, 1979, UFL.
40. Interview with Bobby Wilder, October 19, 2008.
41. Interview with John Grannan, May 6, 2008.
42. Writings of Cal Yeomans, CCHS.
43. Interview with Bobby Wilder, October 19, 2008.
44. Cal Yeomans Journal, February 7, 1994, UFL.
45. Cal Yeomans Journal, January 2, 1979, UFL.
46. Cal Yeomans Journal, August 16, 1977, UFL.
47. Cal Yeomans Journal, November 4, 1978, UFL.
48. Interview with Vern Gransden, July 28, 2007.
49. "1956 Senior Class Prophecy," *Tesora Arca*, published by Student Council of Crystal River High School.

Chapter 2

1. Writings by Cal Yeomans, UFL.
2. Writings by Cal Yeomans, UFL.
3. http://www.religioustolerance.org/hom_sbc.htm, accessed September 18, 2007.
4. Interview with Chuck Woods, May 8, 2008.
5. On August 9, 1945, Governor Johns invited Cal's father to "come and see me.... Friends that are made in the Legislature are lasting friendships and are never forgotten," CCHS.
6. Cal Yeomans, speech given as part of the University of Florida Lesbian and Gay Society Speakers Series, August 25, 1983, UFL.
7. Cal Yeomans Journal, May 9, 1995, UFL.
8. Cal Yeomans interview with Ernie Mickler, October 7–8, 1988, Ernie Mickler Collection, UFL.
9. Letter from Cal Yeomans to Vern Gransden, April 9, 1994, located in file "VERN4994," on disk titled "Letters 5–93," UFL.
10. Letter from Cal Yeomans to Tom Smith, March 13, 1980, UFL.
11. Cal Yeomans Journal, June 18, 1994, UFL.
12. Cal Yeomans Journal, 1984, UFL.
13. Interview with Fergus (Tad) Currie, July 31, 2008.
14. Ibid.
15. Interview with Bobby Wilder, October 19, 2008.
16. Interview with Fergus (Tad) Currie, July 13, 2008.
17. Ren, "A Play for the Young in Heart," unmarked clipping, Fergus Currie Private Collection.
18. Ren, "A Madcap Fleet Is in at Wingspread," unmarked clipping, Fergus Currie Private Collection.
19. Ibid.
20. Ren, "'Salad Days' Playing to Wingspread Capacity Audience," unmarked clipping, Fergus Currie Private Collection.
21. Cal Yeomans Journal, October 19, 1967, UFL.
22. Interview with Fergus (Tad) Currie, July 31, 2008.
23. Cal Yeomans Journal, November 4, 1978, UFL.
24. Letter from Cal Yeomans to "Victor," March 4, 1975, UFL.
25. Hal Gulliver (September 27, 1963), "Earnest Is Still a Witty Show," *Atlanta Constitution*, p. 27.
26. Writings of Cal Yeomans, UFL.
27. Cal Yeomans Journal, Spring 1967, UFL.
28. Cal Yeomans Journal, March 11, 1967, UFL.
29. Cal Yeomans Journal, 1967, UFL.
30. Ibid.
31. Cal Yeomans Journal, Fall 1967, UFL.
32. Cal Yeomans Journal, December 26, 1967, UFL.
33. Interview with Mary Will Burton, nee Woodard, June 1, 2007.
34. Ibid.

35. Cal Yeomans Journal, April 21, 1969, UFL.
36. Interview with Troy Sanders, October 25, 2007.
37. Cal Yeomans Journal, July 29, 1991, UFL.

Chapter 3

1. Cal Yeomans Journal, 1980, UFL.
2. Comments of Yeomans's acting students.
3. Ibid.
4. Interview with Patrika Darbo, December 12, 2008.
5. Interview with Grainger Hines, October 1, 2008.
6. Interview with Fergus (Tad) Currie, July 31, 2008.
7. Interview with Grainger Hines, October 1, 2008.
8. Cal Yeomans Journal, January 19, 1983, UFL.
9. Cal Yeomans, "Self-Description," written for English 315 at Georgia Tech University, June 17, 1970, UFL.
10. Cal Yeomans, "Description of my Mother," written for English 315 at Georgia Tech University, June 29, 1970, UFL.
11. Cal Yeomans, *In a Garden of Cucumbers*, UFL.
12. Cal Yeomans Journal, June 8, 1970, UFL.
13. Interview with Grainger Hines, October 1, 2008.
14. Cal Yeomans Journal, 1971, UFL.
15. Cal Yeomans Journal titled The Island, 1970, UFL.
16. Ibid.
17. Cal Yeomans Journal titled The Island, Fall 1970, UFL.
18. Ibid.
19. Cal Yeomans Journal titled The Island, January 6, 1971, UFL.
20. Cal Yeomans Journal, June 13, 1971, UFL.
21. Cal Yeomans Journal, Spring 1971, UFL.
22. Terry Kay (July 22, 1971), "*The Immoralist* Opens," The *Atlanta Journal*.
23. Interview with Grainger Hines, October 1, 2008.
24. Interview with Fergus (Tad) Currie, July 31, 2008.
25. Cal Yeomans Journal, 1970, UFL.
26. Letter from Cal Yeomans to Ellen Stewart, June 24, 1971, La MaMa Archives.
27. Cal Yeomans Journal, 1970, UFL.
28. Cal Yeomans Journal, July 4, 1971, UFL.
29. Cal Yeomans Journal, November 31, 1967, UFL.
30. Letter from Cal Yeomans to Michael Brennan, January 29, 1981, UFL.
31. Letter from Cal Yeomans to Tom Smith, December 21, 1979, UFL.
32. Ellen Stewart explains her motivation for selecting and producing *Medea* on http://www.youtube.com/watch?v=OyjiKHtJrrM. Margaret Croyden's can be found at http://www.catarchive.com/detailPages/741124.html. Both web sites accessed January 5, 2009.
33. Cal Yeomans Journal, August 4, 1974, UFL.

34. Cal Yeomans Journal, November 16, 1971, UFL.

35. Cal Yeomans Journal, December 13 and 22, 1971, UFL.

36. Cal Yeomans Journal, 1975, UFL.

37. Cal Yeomans Journal, April 3, 1972 and August 4, 1974, UFL.

38. The manuscript for the play is in the Cal Yeomans Collection, UFL.

39. Cal Yeomans, *Swamp Play #2: Earthly Chariot of Jesus Man, Inc.,* UFL.

40. Letter from Cal Yeomans to Ellen Stewart, July 11, 1972, UFL.

41. Cal Yeomans Journal, June 24, 1972, UFL.

42. Cal Yeomans Journal, August 8, 1972, and December 15, 1977, UFL.

43. Postcard from Cal Yeomans to Ellen Stewart, no date, La MaMa Archives.

44. Cal Yeomans Journal, August 4, 1974, UFL.

45. Cal Yeomans Journal, January 24, 1975, UFL.

46. Tom Smith, "Psychiatric Evaluation," February 8, 1978, UFL.

47. Cal Yeomans Journal, December 15, 1977, UFL.

48. Letter from Cal Yeomans to Eastern Airlines, no date, UFL.

49. Cal Yeomans Journal, December 24, 1972 and January 4, 1973, UFL.

50. Cal Yeomans Journal, January 31, 1973, UFL.

51. Cal Yeomans Journal, January 31, February 28, and March 5, 1973, UFL.

52. Cal Yeomans Journal, dated NYC/1973, UFL.

53. Cal Yeomans Journal, August 4, 1974, UFL.

54. Cal Yeomans Journal, 25 September 1973, UFL.

55. Cal Yeomans Journal, 1973, UFL.

56. Cal Yeomans Journal, September 14, 1974, UFL.

57. Cal Yeomans Journal, February 6, 1974, UFL.

58. Letter from Jeff Weiss to Cal Yeomans, dated 1974, UFL.

59. Cal Yeomans Journal, entry titled "The Meeting with Ellen," February 1974, UFL.

60. Cal Yeomans Journal, September 19, 1992, UFL.

61. Cal Yeomans Journal, April 4, 1973, UFL.

62. Cal Yeomans Journal, July 16, 1974, UFL.

63. Letter from Cal Yeomans to Ellen Stewart, 1974, UFL.

64. Letter from Cal Yeomans to Fred Chappell, January 8, 1981, UFL.

65. Cal Yeomans, typescript of *One Two Boy Man*, p. 31, UFL.

66. Cal Yeomans Journal, December 1, 1974, UFL.

67. Cal Yeomans Journal, March 6, 1975, UFL.

68. Cal Yeomans Journal, December 11, 1974, UFL.

69. Cal Yeomans Journal, February 1975, UFL.

Chatper 4

1. Cal Yeomans Journal, February 1975, UFL.

2. Cal Yeomans Journal, January 25, 1975, UFL.

3. Ibid.

4. Cal Yeomans Journal, 1975, UFL.
5. Cal Yeomans Journal, September 17, 1975, UFL.
6. Letter from Cal Yeomans to Eglé Gatins Wieland, no date, UFL.
7. Unless otherwise noted, all quotations concerning Cal's breakdown and his relationship with Jacques are found in a journal titled "Breakdown" and dated September 24, 1977, UFL.
8. Ibid.
9. Ibid.
10. Ibid.
11. Ibid.
12. James Purdy in an Associated Press interview, *Canadian Broadcasting Centre News*, March 13, 2009.
13. (March 13, 2009), "James Purdy, Darkly Comic Writer, Dies at 94," *The New York Times.*
14. Cal Yeomans Journal, December 15, 1977, UFL.
15. Cal Yeomans Journal, Summer 1975, UFL.
16. Cal Yeomans Journal, September 20, 1975, UFL.
17. Cal Yeomans Journal, no date but probably September 26, 1975, UFL.
18. Letter from Cal Yeomans to Michael Brennan, March 24, 1980, UFL.
19. Letter from Cal Yeomans to Tom Smith, May 9, 1984, UFL.
20. Scrap of paper found in Cal Yeomans Collection, UFL.
21. Cal Yeomans Journal, January 28, 1975, UFL.
22. Interview with Jacques-Pierre Caussin, May 7, 2007.
23. Florida case #263 So. 2d 256 (Fla. Dist.Ct. App.1972).
24. Cal Yeomans Journal, December 14, 1977, UFL.
25. Cal Yeomans Journal, February 10, 1976, UFL.
26. Cal Yeomans Journal, February 12, 1976, UFL.
27. Cal Yeomans Journal, August 16, 1976, UFL.
28. Letter from Cal Yeomans to Jacques-Pierre Caussin, UFL. The letter was handwritten on Anclote Manor stationery. Since Cal writes in the letter that his evaluation "comes up in about a month," the letter was undoubtedly written before he was released on April 14.
29. Cal Yeomans Journal, July 27, 1976, UFL.
30. Cal Yeomans Journal, April 18, 1976, UFL.
31. Cal Yeomans Journal, April 15, 1976, UFL.
32. Cal Yeomans Journal, July 27, 1976, UFL.
33. Cal Yeomans Journal, July 6, 1977, UFL.
34. Cal Yeomans Journal, December 31, 1976, UFL.
35. Cal Yeomans Journal, June 26, 1977, UFL.
36. Cal Yeomans Journal, July 18, 1977, UFL.
37. Cal Yeomans Journal, July 31, 1977, UFL.
38. Cal Yeomans Journal, August 3, 1977, UFL.
39. Ibid.
40. Cal Yeomans Journal, June 25, 1977, UFL.
41. Cal Yeomans Journal, October 2, 1977, UFL.

42. Cal Yeomans Journal, November 14, 1977, and mailed to Tom Smith, November 29, 1980, UFL.
43. Cal Yeomans Journal, October 16, 1977, UFL.
44. Cal Yeomans Journal, November 3, 1977, UFL.
45. Cal Yeomans Journal, November 15, 1977, UFL.
46. Tom Smith, "Psychiatric Evaluation," February 8, 1978, UFL.
47. Cal Yeomans Journal, July 1978, UFL.
48. Cal Yeomans Journal, December 18, 1977, UFL.
49. Cal Yeomans Journal, May 4, 1978, UFL.
50. Cal Yeomans Journal, July 24, 1978, UFL.
51. Cal Yeomans Journal, July 22, 1978, UFL.
52. Letter from Cal Yeomans to Grady McClendon, July 31, 1978, UFL.
53. Cal Yeomans Journal titled Final Island Journal, September 3, 1979, UFL.
54. Letter from Cal Yeomans to Tom Smith, 1978, UFL.
55. Letter from Cal Yeomans to Tom Smith, September 10, 1979, UFL.
56. Cal Yeomans Journal titled Final Island Journal, (Part II), November 11, 1979, UFL.

Chapter 5

1. Cal Yeomans Journal titled Final Island Journal, (Part II), November 10, 1978, UFL.
2. Cal Yeomans Journal titled Final Island Journal, (Part II), August 11, 1978, UFL.
3. Unmarked newspaper clipping, CCHS.
4. Cal Yeomans Journal titled Final Island Journal, (Part II), December 15, 1978, UFL.
5. Cal Yeomans Journal titled Final Island Journal, (Part II), November 28, 1978, UFL.
6. Cal Yeomans Journal, November 7, 1978, UFL.
7. Interview with Michael Parker, October 11, 2007.
8. Cal Yeomans Journal titled Final Island Journal, (Part II), November 24, 1978, UFL.
9. Letter from Raiford Ragsdale to Cal Yeomans, April 7, 1983, UFL.
10. Letter from Cal Yeomans to Tom Smith, September 21, 1978, UFL.
11. Letter from Cal Yeomans to Tom Smith, November 7, 1978, UFL.
12. Dick Hasbany (June 24, 1982) "Revelations: Wanted or Not," *The Advocate*, p. 51.
13. Cal Yeomans, speech given as part of the University of Florida Lesbian and Gay Society Speakers Series, August 25, 1983, UFL.
14. Cal Yeomans Journal, July 21, 1977, UFL.
15. Letter from Cal Yeomans to Hugh Mercer, January 30, 1978, UFL.
16. Cal Yeomans Journal, August 5, 1978, UFL.
17. Program notes for *The Tenderloin Suite*, June 1979, UFL.

18. Cal Yeomans, introduction to *Poiret in Exile*, UFL.
19. Email from Mark I. Chester, March 27, 2007.
20. Letter from Tom Smith to Cal Yeomans, October 1978, UFL.
21. Letter from Cal Yeomans to Tom Smith, 1978, UFL.
22. Letters from Tom Smith to Cal Yeomans, November 20 and December 4, 1978, UFL.
23. Letter from Cal Yeomans to Tom Smith, December 6, 1978, UFL.
24. Cal Yeomans Journal titled Final Island Journal, (Part II), November 4 and 7, 1978, UFL.
25. The letters from Jon Porch to Cal Yeomans are all in the Yeomans Collection, UFL.
26. Email from Jon Porch, May 30, 2007.
27. Letter from Cal Yeomans to Tom Smith, October 8, 1978, UFL.
28. Cal Yeomans, "Richmond Jim," *Folsom Magazine*, (1981), number 4.
29. Cal Yeomans, *Richmond Jim*, UFL.
30. Letter from Vance (Joe) Hendrix to Cal Yeomans, May 25, 1979, UFL.
31. (May 25, 1979), "Male Rites," *Bay Area Reporter*.
32. Hasbany, *The Advocate*, p. 51.
33. William Albright (June 3, 1980), "Minority Theater Thriving by the Bay," *Houston Post*, p. 6B.
34. Neal Obstat, Jr. (May 16, 1980), "One Win, Two Losses at Theater Rhinoceros," *The Sentinel*.
35. Letter from Cal Yeomans to Tom Smith, December 21, 1979, UFL.
36. Letter from Cal Yeomans to Tom Smith, June 7, 1980, UFL.
37. Letter from Cal Yeomans to Tom Smith, April 3, 1980, UFL.
38. Carl Driver (no date), "Carl's Followspot," *San Francisco Crusader*.
39. Robert Chesley (June 28, 1979), "Who Took Richmond," *The Advocate*, p. 39.
40. Hasbany, *The Advocate*, p. 51.
41. Letter from Vance (Joe) Hendrix to Cal Yeomans, March 8, 1980, UFL.
42. Cal Yeomans Journal, June 4, 1979, UFL.
43. Hasbany, *The Advocate*, p. 54.
44. Cal Yeomans Journal, 1979, UFL.
45. Email from Jon Porch, June 16, 2007.
46. Cal Yeomans Journal titled Final Island Journal, (Part II), October 5, 1979, UFL.
47. Hasbany, *The Advocate*, p. 51. Letters from Guy Bishop to Cal, April 18 and 29, 1980, UFL.
48. Liam Martin, no title, *About Town*, no date.
49. Letter from Fred Chappell to Cal Yeomans, April 9, 1980, UFL.
50. Letter from Guy Bishop to Cal, April 18, 1980, UFL.
51. Letter from Cal Yeomans to Robert Chesley, August 7, 1984, UFL.
52. Email from Jon Porch, September 2, 2009.
53. Cal Yeomans Journal, January 1, 2, and 10, 1980, UFL.
54. Cal Yeomans Journal, January 13, 1980, UFL.

55. Cal Yeomans Journal, January 27, 1980, UFL.
56. Cal Yeomans Journal, February 20, 1980, UFL.
57. Letter from Cal Yeomans to Michael Brennan, March 24, 1980, UFL.
58. Letter from Cal Yeomans to Tom Smith, March 19, 1980, UFL.
59. Letter from Cal Yeomans to Tom Smith, December 21, 1979, UFL.
60. Letter from Cal Yeomans to Fred Chappell, January 8, 1981, UFL.
61. Les Attitude (November 1980), "Theatre Rhinoceros Scores Again," unmarked clipping; and Mark Topkin, "a Giddy Matinee from Theatre Rhinoceros," *Bay Area Reporter*, Cal Yeomans Collection, UFL.
62. Letter from Lanny Baugniet to Cal Yeomans, November 4, 1980, UFL.
63. Letter from Vance (Joe) Hendrix to Cal Yeomans, January 5, 1981, UFL.
64. Letter from Cal Yeomans to Fred Chappell, January 8, 1981, UFL.
65. Letter from Vance (Joe) Hendrix to Cal Yeomans, February 2, 1981, UFL.
66. Cal Yeomans Journal, February 15, 1981, UFL.
67. Letter from Tom Smith to Cal Yeomans, February 14, 1981, UFL.
68. Letters from Cal Yeomans to Dana Ivey, January 16, 1981, UFL.
69. Letter from Cal Yeomans to Tom Smith, December 21, 1979, UFL.
70. Letter from Cal Yeomans to Johnny Ferdon, March 23, 1981, UFL.
71. Cal Yeomans Journal, December 13, 1979, UFL.
72. Cal Yeomans Journal, August 6, 1978, UFL.
73. Letter from Cal Yeomans to Tom Smith, December 21, 1979, UFL.
74. Cal Yeomans, "From the Daddy Poems," *Gay Sunshine: A Journal of Gay Liberation*, (Winter 1981–1982), numbers 46, 13.
75. Cal Yeomans Journal, January 18, 1981, UFL.

Chapter 6

1. Cal Yeomans Journal, February 8, 1981, UFL.
2. Note in the *Sunsets* folder, UFL.
3. Letter from Cal Yeomans to Tom Smith, December 2, 1980, UFL.
4. Cal Yeomans Journal, January 19, 1982, UFL.
5. Cal Yeomans, "Confessions of a Librarian," 1982, UFL.
6. Letter from Cal Yeomans to Tom Smith, May 29, 1981, UFL.
7. Letter from Cal Yeomans to Evan Senreich, April 18, 1981, UFL.
8. Interview with Billy Cunningham, May 9, 2007.
9. Ibid.
10. Interview with Evan Senreich, May 10, 2007.
11. Ibid.
12. Interview with Larry Hough, May 14, 2007.
13. Letter from Cal Yeomans to Dana Ivey, August 8, 1981, UFL.
14. Cal Yeomans Journal, April 14, 1981, UFL.
15. James M. Saslow (November 26, 1981), "Reviews: 'Sunsets: Three Acts on a Beach,'" *The Advocate*, p. 46.

16. Email from James M. Saslow, February 16, 2008.
17. Robert Chesley (October 19–November 1, 1981), "Theater: Taxi Zum Closet," *New York Native*, p. 31.
18. Robert Massa (October 21–27, 1981), "Bits," *The Village Voice*, p. 79.
19. Letter from Cal Yeomans to Raiford Ragsdale, October 28, 1982, UFL.
20. Letter from Cal Yeomans to Tom Smith, June 21, 1981, UFL.
21. Letter from Cal Yeomans to Johnny Ferdon, January 19, 1982, UFL.
22. Letter from Cal Yeomans to Tom Smith, June 13, 1982, UFL.
23. Cal Yeomans Journal, October 1981, UFL.
24. Letter from Mark I. Chester to Cal Yeomans, December 14, 1982, UFL.
25. Letter from Cal Yeomans to Mark I. Chester, February 6, 1983, UFL.
26. Cal Yeomans Journal, July 8, 1984, UFL.
27. Letter from Cal Yeomans to Tom Smith, July 8, 1984, UFL.
28. Cal Yeomans Journal, January 25, 1980, UFL.
29. Cal Yeomans Journal, March 24, 1981, UFL.
30. Cal Yeomans Journal, January 28, 1982, UFL.
31. Cal Yeomans Journal, July 8, 1984, UFL.
32. Letter from Cal Yeomans to Tom Smith, June 30, 1981, UFL.
33. Cal Yeomans Journal, February 9, 1983, UFL.
34. Cal Yeomans Journal, June 7, 1986, UFL.
35. Letter from Cal Yeomans to Tom Smith, August 14, 1981, UFL.
36. Howard Casner (October 7, 1982), "'Sunsets' to Busch: a Look at Part of the Gay Arts Festival in Retrospect," *Gay Life*, n.p.
37. Cal Yeomans Journal, January 25, 1981, UFL.
38. Cal Yeomans Journal, January 31, 1981, UFL.
39. Letter from Cal Yeomans to Tom Smith, May 2, 1982, UFL.
40. Letter from Cal Yeomans to Tom Smith, November 9, 1982, UFL.
41. Email from Mark Thompson, November 5, 2009.
42. Hasbany, *The Advocate*, pp. 51–55, 63.
43. Cal Yeomans, speech given as part of the University of Florida Lesbian and Gay Society Speakers Series, August 25, 1983, UFL.
44. Letter from Peter Hartman to Cal Yeomans, June 9, 1982, UFL.
45. Cal Yeomans, speech given as part of the University of Florida Lesbian and Gay Society Speakers Series, August 25, 1983, UFL.
46. Letter from Peter Hartman to Cal Yeomans, October 30, 1982, UFL.
47. Cal Yeomans Journal, 1981, UFL.
48. Email from Mark I. Chester, August 18, 2007.
49. Mark Tomkin (September 16, 1982), "The Urge from Suggestive to Bold," *Bay Area Reporter*, p. 22.
50. Charles Faber (October 28, 1982), "Theater," *The Advocate*, n.p.
51. Letter from Robert Chesley to Cal Yeomans, September 15, 1982, UFL.
52. Cal Yeomans Journal, 1982, UFL.
53. The description of Yount and his performance is in a letter or journal entry written by Cal Yeomans, dated April 17, 1984, UFL.
54. Cal Yeomans Journal, October 5, 1982, UFL.

55. Letter from John Ponyman to Cal Yeomans, June 27, 1983, UFL.
56. Letter from Cal Yeomans to Johnny Ferdon, March 5, 1983, UFL.
57. Letter from Cal Yeomans to Tom Smith, August 28, 1983, UFL.
58. Ibid.
59. Letter from Cal Yeomans to Tom Smith, August 29, 1983, UFL.
60. Letter from Cal Yeomans to Michael Brennan, October 2, 1983, UFL.
61. Letter from Cal Yeomans to Tom Smith, October 1, 1983, UFL.
62. Cal Yeomans, copy of a speech presented August 25, 1983, at the University of Florida, UFL.
63. Letter from Cal Yeomans to Raiford Ragsdale, September 21, 1982, UFL.

Chapter 7

1. John Glines, speech at the annual convention of the Association for Theatre in Higher Education in New York City, August 9, 2009.
2. Michael Kearns (2009), *The Drama of* aids: *My Lasting Connections with Two Plays That Survived the Plague,* (Portsmouth, NH: Heinemann), p. 14.
3. Letter from Cal Yeomans to Tom Smith, May 12, 1984, UFL.
4. Kearns, *Drama of AIDS,* p. 18.
5. Doric Wilson web site, www.doricwilson.com/perfect.asp, accessed October 14, 2009.
6. John Clum, "Contemporary Drama," *GLBTQ Encyclopedia of Gay, Lesbian, Bisexual, Transgender & Queer Literature,* p. 5. Accessed October 27, 2009.
7. Kearns, *Drama of AIDS,* p. 42.
8. Email from Doric Wilson, October 26, 2009.
9. Letter from Robert Chesley to Cal Yeomans, November 20, 1983, UFL.
10. Letter from Robert Chesley to Cal Yeomans, December 31, 1984, UFL.
11. Letter from Cal Yeomans to Jerry West, August 30, 1983, UFL.
12. Email from Doric Wilson, May 30, 2007.
13. Cal Yeomans Journal, February 1, 1984, UFL.
14. Cal Yeomans, "For John Ponyman: Who Lies Dying," mailed to Tom Smith, February 5, 1984, UFL.
15. Letter from Cal Yeomans to Tom Smith, March 5, 1984, UFL.
16. Cal Yeomans Journal, August 7, 1983, UFL.
17. Letter from Cal Yeomans to Johnny Ferdon, Spring 1981, UFL.
18. Email from Mark I. Chester, March 27, 2007.
19. Letter from Cal Yeomans to Tom Smith, February 24, 1984, UFL.
20. Cal Yeomans (Spring 1987), "The Daddy Poems (Excerpts)," *Amethyst: A Journal for Lesbians and Gay Men,* p. 30.
21. Letter from Cal Yeomans to Tom Smith, March 4, 1984, UFL.
22. Letter from Cal Yeomans to Johnny Ferdon, May 1985, UFL.
23. Letter from Cal Yeomans to Tom Smith, March 5, 1984, UFL.
24. Cal Yeomans, "Application to study with Allen Ginsberg at Atlantic Center for the Arts," UFL.

25. Letter from Cal Yeomans to Tom Smith, May 31, 1984, UFL.
26. Letter from Cal Yeomans to Johnny Ferdon, July 28, 1987, UFL.
27. Cal Yeomans Journal, July 17, 1985, UFL.
28. Interview with Michael Parker, April 29, 2008.
29. Poem written by Calvin Yeomans for his mother, UFL.
30. Cal Yeomans Journal, January 23, 1994, UFL.
31. Cal Yeomans Journal, May or June 1985, UFL.
32. Cal Yeomans Journal, July 17, 1985, UFL.
33. Letter from Cal Yeomans to Johnny Ferdon, August 30, 1987, UFL.
34. Letter from Dana Ivey to Cal Yeomans, March 14, 1994, UFL.
35. Letter from Cal Yeomans to Johnny Ferdon, June 1985, UFL.
36. Letter from Cal Yeomans to Tom Smith, February 6, 1985, UFL.
37. Letter from Cal Yeomans to Robert Chesley, August 21, 1986, UFL.
38. Letter from Cal Yeomans to Tom Smith, August 5, 1985, UFL.
39. Cal Yeomans, *Hibiscus*, UFL.
40. Letter from Cal Yeomans to Tom Smith, September 5, 1985, UFL.
41. Cal Yeomans Journal, February 3, 1986, UFL.
42. Cal Yeomans Journal, February 6, 1986, UFL.
43. Letter from Cal Yeomans to Michael Haykin, January 25, 1986, UFL.
44. Letter from Cal Yeomans to Johnny Ferdon, May 13, 1986, UFL.
45. Cal Yeomans Journal, January 2, 1986, UFL.
46. Email from Michael Haykin, April 15, 2007.
47. Letter from Cal Yeomans to "J", November 25, 1988, UFL.
48. Cal Yeomans Journal, April 8, 1986, UFL.
49. Cal Yeomans Journal, June 1986, UFL.
50. Cal Yeomans Journal, April 28, 1986, UFL.
51. Letter from Robert Chesley to Cal Yeomans, May 2, 1986, UFL.
52. Letter from Robert Chesley to Cal Yeomans, June 10, 1986, UFL.
53. Letter from Cal Yeomans to Robert Chesley, June 14, 1986, UFL.
54. Cal Yeomans Journal, November 4, 1986, UFL.
55. Letter from Cal Yeomans to Robert Massa, c/o *The Village Voice*, July 23, 1986, UFL.
56. Letter from Cal Yeomans to Robert Chesley, October 30, 1986, UFL.
57. Ibid.
58. Letter from Cal Yeomans to Ellen Stewart, October 24, 1986, UFL.
59. Don Shewey (June 21, 1987), "AIDS on Stage: Comfort, Sorrow, Anger," *The New York Times*.
60. Lynn Witt, Sherry Thomas and Eric Marcus (eds.) (1995), *Out in All Directions:The Almanac of Gay and Lesbian America* (New York: Warner Books), p. 126.
61. Email from Kelly Hill, November 30, 2009.
62. Letter from Cal Yeomans to Ellen Stewart, September 1, 1986, Café La MaMa Archives.
63. Calvin Yeomans (1987), "CS Portfolio," *Christopher Street* (issue 114, volume 10, no. 6), p. 40.

64. Letter from Cal Yeomans to Raiford Ragsdale, March 5, 1987, UFL.

65. Cal Yeomans Journal, January 16, 1987, UFL.

66. Cal Yeomans Journal, January 29, 1987, UFL.

67. Letter from Cal Yeomans to Vance (Joe) Hendrix, March 26, 1987, UFL.

68. Letter from Vance (Joe) Hendrix to Cal Yeomans, March 1987, UFL.

69. Cal Yeomans Journal, April 5, 1987, UFL.

70. Letter from Cal Yeomans to Ernie Mickler, November 10, 1987, Ernie Mickler Collection, UFL.

71. Cal Yeomans Journal, May 30, 1987, UFL.

72. Cal Yeomans Journal, August 24, 1987, UFL.

73. Letter from Cal Yeomans to Johnny Ferdon, July 19, 1987, UFL.

74. A handwritten note by Cal Yeomans on the flyer for his reading and photo exhibit (seen in Figure 7.7), UFL.

75. Yeomans, *Christopher Street*, p. 40.

76. Letter from F. Glen Offield to Cal Yeomans, January 1986, UFL.

77. Cal Yeomans Journal, October 2, 1987, UFL.

78. Email from Mark I. Chester, March 27, 2007.

79. Letter from Mark I. Chester to Cal Yeomans, October 10, 1987, UFL.

80. Letter from Cal Yeomans to Johnny Ferdon, January 20, 1986, UFL.

Chapter 8

1. Letter from Cal Yeomans to Johnny Ferdon, February 20, 1987, UFL.

2. Letter from Cal Yeomans to Eric Garber, April 27, 1988, UFL.

3. Al Hall (July 22, 1986), "Boxer is sentenced to 2 life terms," *Gainesville Sun*.

4. Cal Yeomans, "The 21st and 22nd Losses of Homer Lee Jackson," 1987, p. 3, UFL.

5. Letter from Cal Yeomans to Johnny Ferdon, December 5, 1988, UFL.

6. Letter from Cal Yeomans to Ellen Stewart, 1988, UFL.

7. Cal Yeomans Journal, October 29, 1988, UFL.

8. Letter from Cal Yeomans to Lawry Smith, November 2, 1988, La MaMa Archives.

9. Cal Yeomans Journal, November 12, 1988, UFL.

10. Cal Yeomans Journal, December 27, 1988, UFL.

11. Ibid.

12. Letter from Boyd McDonald to Cal Yeomans, August 21, 1989, UFL.

13. Letter from Boyd McDonald to Cal Yeomans, October 28, 1988, UFL.

14. Letter from Boyd McDonald to Cal Yeomans, May 21, 1990, UFL.

15. Letter from Cal Yeomans to Boyd McDonald, April 1, 1990, UFL.

16. Letter from Cal Yeomans to Robert Patrick, December 26, 1988, UFL.

17. Letter from Cal Yeomans to Robert Patrick, March 11, 1989, UFL.

18. Cal Yeomans Journal, December 2, 1990, UFL.

19. Cal Yeomans Journal, April 8, 1989, UFL.

20. Cal Yeomans Journal, April 25, 1989, UFL.
21. Letter from Cal Yeomans to Eric Garber, June 1989, UFL.
22. Ibid.
23. Cal Yeomans Journal, November 8, 1989, UFL.
24. Cal Yeomans Journal, 1989, UFL.
25. Letter from Cal Yeomans to Robert Patrick, August 6, 1991, UFL.
26. Quoted in Susan Wright, "Suppression of Sexual Diversity in Art," National Coalition for Sexual Freedom, February 7, 1998, accessed on December 4, 2009 at http://www.ncsfreedom.org/index.php?option=com _keyword&id=210.
27. *Up and Cumming with ORGASM*, June 1990, p. 2 and July 1990, p. 3.
28. Letter from Cal Yeomans to Boyd McDonald, April 1, 1990, UFL.
29. Letter from Cal Yeomans to Mrs. Rottger (Robert Chesley's mother), December 12, 1990, UFL.
30. Ibid.
31. Robert Chesley, "Gay Theater for the 90's," Earnest Mickler Collection, UFL.
32. Cal Yeomans Journal, December 1990, UFL.
33. Quoted in Cal Yeomans *Roadkill*, p. 9, UFL.
34. Letter from Cal Yeomans to Robert Patrick, May 21, 1991, UFL.
35. Letter from Cal Yeomans to Robert Patrick, July 11, 1991, UFL.
36. Cal Yeomans, July 30 and August 4, 1991, located in files 2 and 4, on disk titled "Journal of My Death I," UFL.
37. Cal Yeomans Journal, July 29, 1991, UFL.
38. Cal Yeomans Journal, no date, 1991, UFL.
39. Cal Yeomans Journal, November 14, 1991, UFL.
40. Cal Yeomans Journal, October 16, 1991, UFL.
41. Cal Yeomans Journal, October 25, 1991, UFL.
42. Cal Yeomans Journal, August 30, 1992, UFL.
43. Cal Yeomans Journal, January 21, 1993, UFL.
44. Cal Yeomans Journal, October 1991, UFL.
45. Cal Yeomans Journal, February 27, 1993, UFL.
46. Cal Yeomans Journal, February 8, 1992, UFL.
47. Letter from Cal Yeomans to an anonymous person, no date, Smith-Corona disk.
48. Letter from Cal Yeomans to Robert Patrick, August 26, 1991, UFL.
49. Cal Yeomans Journal, May 22, 1992, UFL.
50. Cal Yeomans Journal, January 23, 1992, UFL.
51. Cal Yeomans Journal, December 1991, UFL.
52. Cal Yeomans Journal, January 23, 1992, UFL.
53. Cal Yeomans Journal, February 7, 1992, UFL.
54. Letter from Cal Yeomans to Dennis Doph, July 15, 1992, UFL.
55. Letter from Dennis Doph to Cal Yeomans, August 19, 1992, UFL.
56. Cal Yeomans Journal, October 3, 1992, UFL.
57. Cal Yeomans Journal, December 31, 1992, UFL.

Chapter 9

1. Letter from Cal Yeomans to Kelly Hill, July 19, 1993, located in file "KELLY2" on disk titled "Letters 5–93," UFL.
2. Letter from Cal Yeomans to Dana Ivey, May 17, 1993, located in file "Dana" on disk titled "Letters 5–93," UFL.
3. Cal Yeomans Journal, early January 1993, UFL.
4. Letter from Cal Yeomans to Ruth Drier, mid-January 1998, UFL.
5. Letter from Cal Yeomans to Jeff Wentzel, June 8, 1995, UFL.
6. Cal Yeomans Journal, May 21, 1993, UFL.
7. Cal Yeomans Journal, no date, Fall 1993, UFL.
8. Cal Yeomans Journal, October 18, 1993, UFL.
9. Letter from Kelly Hill to Cal Yeomans, March 23, 1993, UFL.
10. Letter from Cal Yeomans to Joe Hendrix, October 20, 1993, UFL.
11. Letter from Cal Yeomans to Joe Hendrix, October 20, 1993, UFL.
12. The ad is dated May 1999.
13. Letter from Scott O'Hara to Cal Yeomans, January 14, 1995, UFL.
14. Carolyn Jones (1994), *Living Proof: Courage in the Face of AIDS* (New York: Abbeville Press Publishers), pp. 16–17.
15. Cal Yeomans Journal, no date, 1994, UFL.
16. Cal Yeomans Journal, February 20, 1994, UFL.
17. Letter from Cal Yeomans to Kelly Hill, July 19, 1993, UFL.
18. Letter from Cal Yeomans to Tom Wilson, April 8, 1994, UFL.
19. Ibid.
20. Letter from Cal Yeomans to Tom Wilson, June 1994, UFL.
21. Letter from Cal Yeomans to North Central Florida AIDS Network, June 19, 1994, located in file "NCFANLTR" on disk titled "Letters 5–93," UFL.
22. Cal Yeomans Journal, June 28, 1994, UFL.
23. Letter from Cal Yeomans to Don Tucker, August 1, 1994, UFL.
24. Cal Yeomans Journal, late August 1994, UFL.
25. Letter from Cal Yeomans to Brian Kirkpatrick, June 4, 1995, UFL.
26. Interview with Sid Kennedy, May 7, 2008.
27. Cal Yeomans Journal, April 1995, UFL.
28. Letter from Cal Yeomans to Judy Raymond, April 14, 1995, UFL.
29. Letter from Pat Swett to Cal Yeomans, April 12, 1996, UFL.
30. Letter from Cal Yeomans to Brian Kirkpatrick, June 4, 1995, UFL.
31. Cal Yeomans Journal, October 1995, UFL.
32. Letter from Brian Kirkpatrick to Eric Garber, October 31, 1995, UFL.
33. Cal Yeomans Journal, March 18, 1996, UFL.
34. Cal Yeomans Journal, May 1996, UFL.
35. Cal Yeomans Journal, May 1996, UFL.
36. Cal Yeomans Journal, July 1996, UFL.
37. Cal Yeomans Journal, August 9, 1996, UFL.
38. Email from Jeff Wentzel, August 16, 2007.

39. Cal Yeomans Journal, October 27, 1996, UFL.
40. Letter from Cal Yeomans to Fred Chappell, November 1996, UFL.
41. Letter from Cal Yeomans to Fred Chappell, November 1996, UFL.
42. Cal Yeomans Journal, November 1996, UFL.
43. Cal Yeomans Journal, November 24 and 26, 1996, UFL.
44. Andrew Holleran (2000), *In September, the Light Changes* (New York: Plume), pp. 265–294.
45. Cal Yeomans Journal, 1997, UFL.
46. Cal Yeomans Journal, February 8, 1998, UFL.
47. Cal Yeomans Journal, May 10, 1998, UFL.
48. Cal Yeomans Journal, November 4, 1998, UFL.

Chapter 10

1. Cal Yeomans Journal, no date, early 2001, UFL.
2. R. Goettelmann (2002), *Management Plan for the City of Crystal River: King's Bay Park* (Crystal River: Community Redevelopment Agency), p. 1.
3. Cal Yeomans Journal, April 6, 2001, UFL.
4. Cal Yeomans Journal, May 17, 2001, UFL.
5. Cal Yeomans Journal, September 2001, UFL.
6. Letter from Cal Yeomans to F.M., October 13, 2001, UFL.
7. Cal Yeomans Journal, October 3 and 10, 2001, UFL.
8. Cal Yeomans Journal, October 15, 2001, UFL.
9. Interview with Michael Parker, October 11, 2007.
10. The property was purchased by the city through a grant acquired through the Florida Forever Program and named King's Bay Park.
11. http://www.uff.ufl.edu/FacultyEndowments/ProfessorshipInfo.asp ?ProfessorshipFund=011735, accessed November 29, 2010.
12. Letter from Cal Yeomans to Tom Smith, January 17, 1980, UFL.
13. Letter from Molly Johnston to Cal Yeomans, September 8, 1998, UFL.
14. Carolyn Russo (no date, 1993), "A Man Donates His Memories," *Citrus Times.*
15. Amylia Wimmer (May 16, 1997), "Pioneer Homestead Blooms into Preserve," *St. Petersburg Times.*
16. Ironically, the only time the park was ever shut down was one month after Cal's death. Citing public safety issues, city officials closed the park temporarily after receiving reports that some people were engaging in sexual activity. Although there had been no arrests in two years and only a dozen reports of suspicious activity, the city wanted to make its position clear. There was to be no gay cruising in Yeomans Park.
17. Email from James Liversidge, March 29, 2007.
18. Letter from Cal Yeomans to Michael Brennan, October 28, 1981, UFL.
19. Letter from Michael Brennan to Cal Yeomans, August 13, 1984; and Cal Yeomans's reply, August 18, 1984, UFL.

20. Cal Yeomans Journal, May 19, 1983, UFL.
21. Email from Grady McClendon, February 26, 2010.
22. Interview with Vern Gransden, July 28, 2007.
23. Cal Yeomans Journal, October 9, 1991, UFL.
24. Letter from Cal Yeomans to Ellen Stewart, May 3, 1992, La MaMa Archives.
25. Interview with Ellen Stewart by the author, October 24, 2007.
26. Cal Yeomans Journal, September 2001, UFL.
27. Interview with Eric Garber, April 18, 2008.
28. Michael Feingold (1990), *The Way We Live Now: American Plays & the AIDS Crisis* (New York: Theatre Communications Group), p. xv.
29. Letter from Cal Yeomans to Raiford Ragsdale, August 4, 1986, UFL.
30. Letter from Cal Yeomans to Raiford Ragsdale, March 5, 1987, UFL.
31. Interview with Vern Gransden, July 28, 2007.
32. Email from Ruth Drier, May 11, 2007.
33. Email from Victor Bumbalo, January 8, 2010.

INDEX